Francis Barton Gummere

A Handbook of Poetics

For Students of English Verse

Francis Barton Gummere

A Handbook of Poetics
For Students of English Verse

ISBN/EAN: 9783337778385

Printed in Europe, USA, Canada, Australia, Japan

Cover: Foto ©Thomas Meinert / pixelio.de

More available books at **www.hansebooks.com**

A

HANDBOOK OF POETICS

FOR

Students of English Verse.

BY

FRANCIS B. GUMMERE, Ph.D.,

HEAD MASTER OF THE SWAIN FREE SCHOOL, NEW BEDFORD, AND FORMERLY
INSTRUCTOR IN ENGLISH IN HARVARD COLLEGE.

BOSTON:
GINN & COMPANY.
1888.

PREFACE.

This book is published in the belief that many teachers have felt the lack of a concise and systematic statement of the principles of poetry. Such text-books are taught with good result in German schools, and are intended to simplify, not to complicate, the study of literature. The greater part of the literature taught in our schools and colleges is in verse; but, in too many cases, the scholar studies poems without having acquired any definite and compact knowledge of the science of poetry. This "Handbook of Poetics" is meant to aid the teacher in laying so necessary a foundation.

The author has tried to take a judicious position between exploded systems on one hand, and, on the other, those promising but not yet established theories of the latest writers on Poetics — especially in the matter of Versification — which, brilliant and often enticing, have nevertheless failed so far to win general assent. Effort has been made to be accurate without being pedantic, and to avoid the bareness of the primer as well as the too abundant detail of the treatise.

Whether this effort has been successful or not, must be tried by a practical test, — by the judgment, not — as King James puts it — of "ignorants obdurde," nor of "curious folks," nor even of "learned men, quha thinks thame onelie wyis," but rather of "the docile bairns of knowledge."

The *examples* are by no means intended to be exhaustive. Many obvious ones, as the Olney Hymns or the Dunciad or the Epitaph on the Countess of Pembroke, are omitted for the same reason which Cato gave for the absence of his statue from the forum. The pupil should collect his own examples as far as he can; and every scrap of verse which he reads should be subjected to a close analysis as regards its meaning, its style, its rhythm. This study of the science of poetry is altogether distinct from the art of rhetoric: the two should be carefully held apart.

Of the many books consulted, Wackernagel's Lectures on *Poetik*, and the works on Metre by Child, Schipper, Ellis, and Ten Brink, may be named as especially helpful. The article on "Poetry" in the last volume of the *Encyclopædia Britannica* did not come to hand in time to be of use even in the revision of the proof-sheets.

F. B. G.

NEW BEDFORD, 7 September, 1885.

PREFACE TO SECOND EDITION.

THE belief that this little manual would be of use in the study of English poetry has been strengthened by the welcome it has received from many of our best scholars. In this second edition only such corrections are made in the text as seem needed for the clear statement of facts. Attention must here be called, however, to a slight inaccuracy in the first paragraph on p. 11 : the myths about Beowa arose, it is true, before the fifth century; but the legendary and historical basis of the epic of *Beowulf* belongs to the end of the sixth century (*cf.* Wülker, *Grundriss zur Gesch. der Ags. Litt.* p. 306). As the paragraph is worded it does not seem to agree with what is said on p. 13. — Again, in speaking of *The Owl and the Nightingale* (p. 32), I have unaccountably forgotten to mention that sort of poem known as *Flyting*, of which the piece in question is the first specimen found in English verse, though it is not strictly identical with later *Flytings*, — such as that between Dunbar and Kennedy. Both forms, however, are undoubtedly borrowed from the old French *jeu-parti* (*cf.* Bartsch, *Chrestom.* 343 f.) in which two poets take opposite sides of a question; and which, in its turn, Wackernagel refers to the influence of the Vergilian eclogue. This pastoral flavor, however, hardly justifies Mr. Stopford Brooke in calling the delightful but noisy dialogue an Idyll.

In Paul and Braune's *Beiträge*, Vol. IX, Professor Kluge has recently treated the history of rime in Germanic verse, and has sought to establish certain rules and tests important for the study of Anglo-Saxon metres. His general results still further strengthen the assertion, made on p. 145 of this book, that rime is a natural product of the accentual system; that beginning-rime is for a while sole factor in binding together the halves of a verse; but that end-rime is necessarily developed from the same impulse, increasing with the distance from such early works as *Beowulf*. Kluge thus adds end-rime to the tests of later composition. In regard to beginning-rime itself (151 ff.), it is perhaps well to add a caution about its use in modern verse. Beginning-rime, or alliteration, *is detected by the ear, not by the eye* (*cf. Eng. Stud.* VIII, 390), as is evident if we compare '*king : knave*' with '*right : wrong*'; and further, *it counts chiefly in accented syllables*, though (*cf.* p. 153) there is a sort of subordinate alliteration. In Swinburne's lines—

> A delight that rebels, a desire that reposes:
> I shall hate sweet music my whole life long,

we see the force of the second rule. No real beginning-rime exists in the first verse; it does in the second (*hate: whole*). Of course, the first has subordinate beginning-rimes as well as assonance; but the fact that it contains no real alliteration needs to be insisted on, were it only to counteract the influence of such thoughtless assertions as are found in some of our standard histories of English Literature, — *e.g.* that alliteration consists in "words beginning with the same letter." — The controversy in regard to Middle-English word-accent is still very active, but the whole subject is here practically untouched, as it seemed out of place in a book of this kind. The description of the *King Horn* metre is, therefore, meant merely as the most general information possible, and will not bear a critical analysis. Meanwhile, Schipper's recent remarks in the current volume of *Englische Studien*, 184 ff., seem very sensible. His views were set forth in his *Englische Metrik:* an attack upon them by Wissmann will be found in the *Anglia*, V, 466 ff.; and there are many other voices which have been raised in this dispute. A brief statement of the question will be found in *The Nation*, 1882, Oct. 12th. But these special matters of controversy belong outside the proper limits of a text-book.

Lastly, teachers will permit the suggestion that where a class has some knowledge of French, it would be profitable to bring out the excellence of our own rhythm by comparing it with the metres of French verse. Rules and examples helpful for this exercise will be found in T. de Banville's *Petit Traité de Poésie Française*, Paris, 1881.

F. B. G.

NEW BEDFORD, 21 January, 1886.

TABLE OF CONTENTS.

                                                              PAGE

INTRODUCTION 1

PART I: SUBJECT-MATTER.

CHAPTER I.—The Epic. Epic Poetry. Written Epic. Later Forms: Legends, Allegory, Reflective, Descriptive, Pastoral, Satiric, Ballads 7

CHAPTER II.—Lyric Poetry. Sacred Lyric. Patriotic Lyric. Lyric of Love. Of Nature. Of Grief. Reflective Lyric. *Vers de Société*. Other Forms. Lyrical Ballads . . 40

CHAPTER III.—Dramatic Poetry. Beginnings. Miracle Plays. Moralities. Foreign Models. Interlude. Different Kinds of Drama. Tragedy. Comedy. Reconciling Drama. Other Forms. Outward Form of Drama 58

PART II: STYLE.

CHAPTER IV.—Poetic Style. Historical Sketch. Tropes. Metaphor. Personification. Allegory. Simile. Tropes of Connexion. Of Contrast 83

CHAPTER V.—Figures. Repetition. Contrast. Combination 118

PART III: METRE.

CHAPTER VI. — Rhythm. Quantity. Accent. Pauses. Rime. Blank Verse. Qualities and Combinations of Sound. Slurring and Eliding 133

CHAPTER VII. — Metres of English Verse. General Principles. Anglo-Saxon Metres. Transition Period. Chaucer's Metres. Modern Metres. Verse of One Stress; of Two Stresses; of Three; of Four; of Five; Shakspere and Milton; Verse of Six Stresses; of Seven; Miscellaneous 166

CHAPTER VIII. — The Stanza or Strophe. The Sonnet. French Forms 234

INTRODUCTION.

POETRY belongs with music and dancing, and is opposed to the arts of painting, sculpture, and architecture. The latter class is concerned with relations of *space;* we see and touch and measure its products. But the former class has for main principle the idea of motion, of succession, and therefore deals with relations of *time*. In fact, the three arts—poetry, music, dancing—were once united as a single art. Little by little, their paths diverged; but for the oldest times they were inseparable. The principle governing this single early art was *harmony*. Harmony consists really in a certain repetition. Thus two parallel lines agree or harmonize because one repeats the conditions of the other. So in poetry, or music, or dancing, a certain succession of accents, or notes, or steps is repeated, thus establishing the relation of harmony. To be sure, this harmony of recurrence is found to some extent in all speech; in poetry, however, it is carried to a system, and under the name *rhythm* or *metre* is the distinguishing and necessary mark of poetry. Aristotle and his school maintained that "invention" was the soul of poetry. The substance, say they, is the main thing. But later criticism asserts that in poetry the form (metre) is the principal requisite. A late writer has declared that "metre is the first and only condition absolutely demanded by poetry."

Not only, however, was harmony carried further in poetry than in common speech (prose); the element of *Adornment*, the so-called *figurative* tendency of language, grew into a system, and became a secondary mark of poetry. Hence Poetics must treat not only Metre, but also *Style*.

Further, it is hardly necessary to add, the metre and the style must be used in setting forth some worthy *Subject*. Hence the three divisions of Poetics: Subject-Matter, Style, Metre.

The *origin* and the *nature* of poetry are subjects on which it is easy to say a great deal, but hard to say anything definite or satisfactory. Poetry had its beginning in religious rites; it was a ceremony in which voice and foot kept time,— a wild sort of hymn. This rude germ grew, became an art, and went through the process of "differentiation"; till, with maturing time, Epic was developed and yielded certain territory to Lyric; both, finally, ceded ground to Drama; and from these three as centres went out a variety of minor divisions.

We may be quite sure of the early origin of poetry. It is about as old as language itself; and it invariably precedes prose. The domain of prose includes the relations of things in themselves and among themselves. Poetry submits all objects to an imaginative process, and asks how they concern not real, but ideal, interests. The popular use of the words "poetic" and "prosaic" — as applied to a landscape, or the like — shows this difference. Perception, imagination, are found in vigorous development among primitive races; whereas the reasoning powers, the faculty of abstraction, are at their feeblest. Hence we can easily understand that a splendid poem could arise among a people utterly unable to follow the simplest processes in algebra or geometry, — sciences which deal with the relations of things among themselves. Undeveloped races, like the North American Indians, in common with ordinary children, speak a "poetic" language, — *i.e.*, one based on fancy and not on reason. Every known literature asserts this precedence of verse. Homer came before Herodotus, — and turn to what language we will, its oldest monuments are song. Fables and traditions all point to the great age of poetry. The Greeks said that poetry was invented by the gods. In the Norse myth, Sagâ was Odin's daughter : " like the Muse, Zeus' daughter, she instructs men in the art of song." "The old poetry," says J. Grimm, " was a sacred matter, immediately related to the gods, and bound up with prophecy and magic." The Gallic druids taught their sacred lore in verse ; and many ancient laws (*e.g.*, of the Cretans) were in poetic form. Indeed, Macaulay went so far (*Essay on Milton*) as to assume that the older poetry is, the better, — that it degenerates as civilization advances.

The nature of poetry, — what is poetry? No comprehensive, positive answer can be given. Many have essayed a definition of poetry. "It is a criticism of life," says one. "It is the beautiful representation of the beautiful, given in words," says another. "It is imitation by words," says Aristotle. "Poetry," defines Carriere, " speaks out the thought that lies in things." Ruskin (in his *Modern Painters*, corrected in his *English Prosody*) calls poetry " the presentment, in musical form, to the imagination, of noble grounds for the noble emotions." For a longer and spirited definition, *cf.* Carlyle, *On Heroes*, Chap. III. It is easy to see that no one of these definitions is scientific; they are all æsthetic and vague. Or else they simply predicate certain qualities of poetry, — as that it is "simple, sensuous, and impassioned." Only a negative definition of poetry can be given in precise terms; so all agree in calling many characteristics of language unpoetical. But there is really no established standard by which we can try true poetry, as a chemist tries gold. Practical tests fail. Thus, Mr. Swinburne (with other critics) condemns Byron and lauds Coleridge; Mr. Matthew Arnold praises Byron, and so does the best German criticism; while Mr. Ruskin lays violent hands on *Christabel* (*Eng. Prosody*, pp. 31, 32). Again, as we have seen, modern criticism is inclined to test poetry by its *form;* but so sound a critic as Dryden declared *invention* to be the true criterion of the "maker's" work.[1]

The reason of this is plain. Poetry, so far as the higher criticism goes, cannot be an exact science; for we saw that it differs radically from prose in that it deals with fancy, and is foreign to abstractions and the rational consideration of objects in themselves. The qualities of a triangle appeal to the rational judgment, and admit of absolute precision in the verdict passed upon them by the mind. Poetry makes no such appeal; we look upon poetry in the shifting lights of the imagination. In order to be precise, therefore, we must abandon the higher criticism, — give up all inquiry as

---

[1] Sidney, too, regarded verse as "an ornament [but] no cause to Poetry," and says: "One may bee a poet without versing, and a versifier without poetry."

to the inmost nature of poetry, and the tests by which we try the highest forms of poetic expression, — and, accepting poetry as an element of human life, simply regard those facts in the different phases of poetry about which most men agree. Ben Jonson distinguishes "the thing fain'd, the faining, and the fainer: so the *Poeme*, the *Poesy*, and the *Poet*." All study of the first and last of these, the poem and the poet, whether it is in the domain of criticism, or in the school-room, should be based on a knowledge of "the faining," of Poetry itself, its principles and divisions. It is the object of this little treatise to lay down those principles in as simple a way as possible. Great care should be taken to distinguish this science of poetry from the art of verse-making. Thus, there were Old-Norse schools of poetry; and the same sort of instruction was given among the "Meistersänger" of Germany. The science, on the other hand, aims to formulate, as far as it can, the principles of poetic expression. It has received special attention in modern times from the Germans; but it is as old as Plato and Aristotle. Among the modern writers who have brought to its discussion a wealth of critical insight are Lessing (especially in his *Laocoon*, 1766), Kant, Goethe, the brothers Schlegel, Schiller, Hegel, and Vischer.

Part I.

SUBJECT-MATTER.

CHAPTER I. — THE EPIC.

EVERYONE knows that two of the most important factors in human affairs are Church and State. Again, every student of history is aware that the further back we go, the more intimate are the relations between these two great powers. Looking towards the beginnings of civilization, we see the lines of statecraft and priestcraft steadily converging. Where a Gladstone stands to-day, stood, some three centuries ago, a Cardinal Wolsey. In the remote past, in the dawn of history (a relative term, differing with different nations), we find law and religion to be convertible terms. Even in highly-civilized Greece, the Laws — *cf.* Sophocles, *Oed. Tyr.* 864 *sqq.* — were sacred. So it was with our own ancestors, the Germanic tribes, whose nature and customs fell under the keen eyes of Tacitus, and are noted down in his *Germania*. Let us take his description of the Germanic custom of casting lots, — a ceremony at once legal and religious. He says (c. 10) that "a branch is cut from a fruit-bearing tree and divided into little blocks, which are distinguished by certain marks, and scattered at random over a white cloth. Then the state-priest if it is a public occasion, the father of the family if it is domestic, after a prayer to the gods, looking toward heaven, thrice picks up a block. These he now interprets according to the marks previously made."

What renders the ceremony of importance to us is the fact that the "interpretation" Tacitus mentions was *poetical*, and that the "marks" were *runes, i.e.,* the rude alphabet employed by the Germanic tribes. According as these mystic symbols fell, the priest made *alliterating verses* declaring the result of the ceremony. The letters gave the key to the rimes. Since the beech-tree (Anglo-Sax. *bôc*, "book," but also "beech," like German *Buch* and *Buche*) was a favorite wood for the purpose, and the signs were cut in (A.-S. *wrítan*, "cut into," then "write"), we win a new meaning for the phrase "to write a book." Further, *to read*, really means to *interpret,* — as in the common "rede the riddle." So in the original, literal sense, the priest *read the writing of the book.* Since he read it poetically, and as a decree of the gods, and as something legally binding on the people, we may assume (bearing in mind the antiquity of priestcraft) that *poetry, the earliest form of literature, begins among the priesthood in the service of law and religion.* [*Cf.* p. 3 of the Introduction.]

But this unit of sacred law had two sides. On the one hand were such ceremonies as the above, — a practical use, which concerned the people. Late "survivals" of these rites may still be found in the peasant's hut and in the modern nursery, *e.g.,* the time-honored custom of saying a rime to see who shall be "*it*" for a game. But on the other hand was formal worship, — the purely religious side. The tribe boasted its origin from a god, and at stated seasons joined in solemn worship of its divine ruler and progenitor. To this god the assembled multitude sang a hymn, — at first merely chorus, exclamation and incoherent chant, full of repetitions. As they sang, they kept time with the foot in a solemn dance, which was inseparable from the chant itself and governed the words (*cf.* our metrical term "foot"). As order and matter penetrated this wild ceremony, there resulted a rude *hymn*, with intelligible words and a connecting idea. Naturally this connecting idea would concern the *deeds* of the god, — his birth and bringing up and his mighty acts. Thus a thread of *legend* would be woven into the hymn, — a thread fastened at one end to the human associations of the tribe, but losing itself in the uncertainty of a miraculous and superhuman past.

But a third element comes in. Besides the legendary thread, we have the *mythological*. In order to explain the natural processes about him, early man peopled the universe with a multitude of gods. Or, to speak more clearly, he attributed will and passion to the acts of nature. Something dimly personal stood behind the flash of lightning, the roaring of the wind. The ways and doings of these nature-gods were set in order, and, of course, were in many cases brought in direct connection with the tribal or legendary god. Hence a second sort of thread woven into the hymn, — *mythology*. But both legend and mythology are *narrative*. The hymn thus treated ceased to be a mere hymn. The chorus and the strophe were dropped; instead of sets of verses (strophe) the verses ran on in unbroken row. Single persons (minstrels) took the place of the dancing multitude, and chanted in a sort of "recitative," some song full of myth and legend, but centred in the person of the tribal god. Now what is such a song? It is *The Epic*. [Epic, from Greek *Epos*, a "word," then a "narration": *cf.* Sagâ = something *said*.]

It is important to remember that the Epic was not the result of that individual effort to which we now give the name of poetical composition.

To use Mr. Tylor's words (*Primitive Culture*, 1. 273), epic poetry goes back " to that actual experience of nature and life which is the ultimate source of human fancy." Perhaps "source" is not quite accurate; we should prefer to say that it is experience of nature and experience of life (*i.e.*, mythology and legend), which awaken and stimulate the inborn human fancy, that is, the creative power of poetry. This creative power, in early times, when the great epics were forming, when their materials were gradually drawing together, lay rather in the national life itself than in any individual. There were no poets, only singers. The race or nation was the poet. For the *final shape* in which these epics come down to us, we must assume the genius of a singer-poet.

We note further that the personages of the Epic must be humanized, — *i.e.*, partake of our passions and other characteristics. Otherwise they could not awaken human interest. But the background across which these huge beings move must be the twilight of legend and myth. — Instead of taking the Homeric poems as illustration, we prefer to give a brief outline of our own national epic, — *Beowulf*.

[*Beowulf*, the only complete epic preserved from Anglo-Saxon heathen poetry, is based on legends and myths that arose among the northern Germanic tribes before the conquest of Britain in the Fifth Century. The poem in its present shape was probably composed at one of the Northumbrian courts before the Eighth Century. The Ms. is a West Saxon copy of the Tenth Century. There are besides a few fragments preserved. Probably many other Anglo-Saxon epics were lost in the wholesale and wanton destruction of Mss. when the monasteries were broken up under Henry VIII.]

The story of *Beowulf* is now becoming familiar to all readers; we give a bare outline. A powerful king of the Danes (Hrôthgâr) builds a banquet-hall. But he does not enjoy it long. A dreaded monster (Grendel) lives in the neighboring fen, and hears with envious heart the sounds of revelry. So he comes at dead of night, enters the hall, seizes thirty of the sleeping vassals, and bears them off to be devoured in his home. Nothing can withstand him. The banquet-hall lies empty and useless. Over the sea lives a hero who is moved to help Hrôthgâr. The hero's name is Beowulf. He bids his men make ready a boat, and with fourteen vassals puts to sea. He arrives at Hrôthgâr's court, and a grand banquet is held in the hall; but at night the Danes retire, leaving Beowulf and his warriors to guard the post of danger. Grendel comes, and a terrific combat follows between him and Beowulf, which ends in victory for the latter. He tears out Grendel's giant arm from its socket; with "shrill death-song" the monster reels away to die amid his fen. That day the Danes and their deliverers rejoice, and there is another feast. The Danes now remain in the hall; Beowulf goes elsewhere. With night comes the mother of Grendel, a huge and terrible monster, to avenge her son's death, and kills one of the dearest vassals of the king. The next morning Beowulf goes on a quest of vengeance. He comes to the dismal home of the monster, plunges into the dreary waters, and far below the surface meets and conquers the hideous being. The foes of Hrôthgâr are now put to death, and Beowulf, laden with gifts and honor, returns home.

Fifty years pass. Beowulf is an old king who has ruled with strong hand and gentle heart over his people. But now a dragon comes to waste the land. The old hero girds on his armor for a final struggle. He goes down to the dragon's cave; but at sight of the monster, belching flame, the vassals of Beowulf ignominiously fly, and the king fights single-handed and weary against the fire and poison of the dragon. At last, one young warrior, ashamed of his flight, returns; and together, king and vassal slay the monster. But Beowulf is mortally wounded. After a few strong words, exulting that he has fought the good fight of life, he dies. They build a great mound for him by the sea, and bury him with honors of flame and song.

This is the epic of *Beowulf.* Now let us try to trace those threads of myth and legend mentioned above. We should guard against a too implicit trust in apparently conclusive parallels between mythology and epic; but still, in taking the following analysis (mainly that of Müllenhoff and Ten Brink), we shall not be far out of the way. The principle is sound.

The northwest coast of Europe, where our epic had its origin, is exposed to the ravages of ocean storms. Over the low lands, along the borders of the Cimbrian peninsula, swept in fury the tempests of spring and fall.

The sea broke its bounds and raged over the flat country, sweeping away houses and men. Against these wild storms came the gentle spring-god, the god of warmth and calm. This god men called *Beowa*. The god conquers the monsters of the stormy sea, follows them even into their ocean home and puts them to death. Grendel and his mother may fairly be taken as types of these storms. In autumn they burst forth afresh. The waning power of summer closes with them in fiercest struggle. After long combat both the year and the storms sink into the frost-bound sleep of winter.

So much for "the experience of nature,"— *i.e.*, mythology. Now for the "experience of life,"— legend. History tells us that early in the Sixth Century, one Hygelac, king of the Getæ, came down from the north and went plundering along the Rhine. The Frankish king, Theudebert, met and fought Hygelac, and the latter fell. His follower and nephew, however, Beowulf, son of Ecgtheow, did great deeds. Fighting until all others had fallen, he escaped by a masterful piece of swimming, and went back to his island home. His fame spread far and wide. He grew to be a national hero. Songs were sung about him. Wandering minstrels chanted his praise from tribe to tribe. What these wandering minstrels were, and how important was their profession, may be gathered from an Anglo-Saxon poem, which is probably "the oldest monument of English poetry,"— *Widsîth*, "the far-wanderer." In the one hundred and forty-three verses preserved to us, the minstrel tells of his travels, of the costly gifts he has received, of maxims of government he has heard, of famous heroes, kings and queens whom he has visited (a wild confusion of half historical, half mythical names from different lands and times), and of the countries he has seen. He refers to some evidently well-known legends. Widsîth is the ideal minstrel; and this strange poem gives us ample hints as to the spread of legends by men of his craft. Then, too, Tacitus tells us of this custom (*Ann.* 2, 88); Arminius, liberator of Germany, "*caniturque adhuc barbaras apud gentes.*"[1] In all this singing, there was small risk that Beowulf's deeds would lose any of their greatness. In fact, they acquired at length certain touches of the supernatural.

Thus, then, we have hymns in honor of Beowa, the liberating and national god; songs in honor of Beowulf, the national hero. Little by little, the two became one person; and myth and legend, hymns and songs, crystallized about the common centre, until some gifted minstrel gave them form and unity in the epic of Beowulf. Unfortunately the form halts behind the matter: owing to the rapid christianizing of England, the epic, says Ten Brink, was "frozen in the midst of its development." Such as it is, however, it is a noble herald of the long line of English poetry. — We now abandon the historic method, and look at the epic as it lies before us as well in the *Iliad* and the *Odyssey*, as in *Beowulf*.

---

[1] Jornandes, writing about 552 A.D., mentions the legendary songs of the Goths. Thus, in regard to their migration toward the Black Sea: "quemadmodum in priscis eorum carminibus, pæne historico ritu, in commune recolitur." *Cf.* W. Grimm, *Heldensage*, I.

§ 1. GENERAL CHARACTERISTICS OF THE EPIC.

1. The epic must rely solely on Imagination and Memory. It deals with the past, while lyric poetry deals with the present. The *individual author* has little to do with the epic. The singer is a part of what he sings, whereas in lyric poetry the lyric is a part of the singer, is subjective. We may call most modern poetry a manufacture, something *made;* the epic is a *growth.* It is based on what has happened (history), or what men think has happened (legend and myth). An epic nearly always begins by telling *what* it is going to sing: it is the wrath of Achilles, the wanderings of Ulysses, the woes of the Nibelungen. Very striking is the form of the Germanic epic, "We have heard," or "I (the singer) have heard." There is no invention. Indeed, the fate and story of his hero were generally well known to the minstrel's audience. His skill lay in presenting the legend with freshness and force.

2. The epic is simple in construction. It must flow on with smooth current, bearing the hearer to a definite goal. The metre must be uniform.

3. The epic enforces no moral. It tells a story, and the moral is in solution with the story. As Aristotle says, the epic "represents only a single action, entire and complete." There is no comment on that action.

4. The epic concentrates its action in a short time. In the *Iliad* the important events happen in a few days, though the war lasts ten years. In the *Odyssey* the time is six weeks. In *Beowulf* we have two main situations, in the first part taking up little time, and in the second part one brief scene.

5. Among the minor characteristics of the epic may be mentioned its love for *Episodes*. An episode is a story apparently not needed for the main plot of the poem, but really necessarily connected with some part of the action. In the *Aeneid*, the story of the destruction of Troy is a good example of the episode.

6. The singer's memory in those days of no written records was prodigiously strong. Often, too, he improvised passages. Hence he needed rests in his song. These were supplied by the repetition of certain sentences, often of whole speeches — as frequently in the *Odyssey*. So there were many phrases and epithets which were common property and became epic formulas: "the wine-dark sea" was such an epithet; "now when they had put away the wish for meat and drink" was such a sentence. Epithets were particularly characteristic of our own epic. Thus for "sea" we have "the whale's path," — a trope known to the Norse epic as a *Kenning*. (*Cf.* Part II.)

7. The epic loves *dialogues*. This dramatic element makes the story livelier, and gives the singer opportunity to do a little acting as he chants his verses.

8. Finally, we must remember, that in general it is the action of the whole, rather than the character of the particular, that is of chief importance in the epic. In the drama, on the contrary, the action depends on the characters; they shape it, determine it: in any mind the character of Hamlet outweighs, in importance, his story.

These are the more prominent traits of the epic. In its purity such a form of poetic composition is national, *i.e.*, it is the spontaneous growth of a whole people.

It belongs to the first vigorous manhood of a race, just as the race is becoming conscious of itself and its importance, and mostly it springs from some victorious contact with neighboring tribes. Thus the Greek epic points to the struggle between Hellenic tribes of the western and eastern shores of the Aegean.

[For a fair summary of the rise of an epic, see the brief Introduction to Butcher and Lang's translation of the *Odyssey*.]

§ 2. THE WRITTEN EPIC.

Fancy and memory, the factors of the national epic, soon have a rival. As in individual life, so in the life of the race, close upon imagination and memory follows *reason*. As reason waxes, fancy wanes. Reason induces man to search after causes, not to trust the mere impression of the senses. But belief in the impressions of sense is the foundation of the early epic. To illustrate: a child, and the world in its youth, are alike satisfied, if told that the fire is *eating* the wood. That is an impression of sense; that 'tongues' of flame 'devour' the wood is still a poetic figure. But reason begins to ask what fire really is, — to seek the cause, to exercise the judgment instead of the fancy.

Henceforth reason and fancy are at strife; *poetry* and *science* separate. This means, too, that *poetry becomes conscious of itself.* Conscious poetry cannot be spontaneous, like the old national poetry. Hence, further, the poet becomes a distinct personage; there is a "maker" as well as a singer. The word "maker," which is exactly equivalent to the Greek word "poet," is used by our earlier writers: *cf.* Dunbar's *Lament for the Makaris.* Now it is on the threshold of this new age that the great epics are written,—such as the *Odyssey* or the *Iliad*, and our own *Beowulf.* The singer is still lost in his song; no personality peeps out of his work; but it is his genius which binds together the scattered songs and hymns, and breathes into this mass the creative breath of a rich imagination. While the result is still national and spontaneous in origin, while the poet has simply given an artistic unity to his materials, we must not lose sight of this unifying process and its importance. The *Odyssey*, for example, with its consummate art of construction, is no mere collection of ballads jostled into unity.

But in the next epoch, the period of the written epic, when the "maker" claims the material as well as the form to be his own work, there is a great change. It is not the epic; it is epic poetry. Men ask, "Who wrote this?"

Thus, our *Beowulf* is impersonal — a true epic. The epic poems of Cynewulf (Eighth Century), though like *Beowulf* in style, are very different in other respects. First, the poet weaves his own name (in Acrostics) into his verse, thus claiming ownership; secondly, *he uses a written account as the basis of his narrative.* He reads (not "hears" as the older minstrel did) a story, and puts it into verse. But this implies another characteristic of the new age,—literature. Further, this literature is not only *national;* — the spread of Latin and sacred lore makes it *international.* Poetry can now deliberately choose its subject; it has different roads before it. The epic process still goes on, but new customs disturb it and break up the grand march into petty detachments.

§ 3. LATER FORMS OF EPIC POETRY.

(1) LEGENDS ACCEPTED AS TRUE.

The tendency to sing about national heroes, and the battles which they fight, continues in force. Thus in the Anglo-Saxon Chronicle, scattered songs flash out from the monotony of prose; *e.g.*, *The Battle of Brunnanburh* (937). Another such battle-ballad (not in the Chronicle) is *Byrhtnoth's Fall* (sometimes called *The Battle of Maldon*), a spirited song, composed, says Rieger, so soon after the fight that the poet is ignorant of the hostile leader's name. All the fire and the impetuosity of the old epic style live again in this 'ballad' (993). Under the Norman yoke, our forefathers still sung their favorite heroes; though not preserved to us, these songs were used by the later prose chroniclers of England. Then there were legendary characters of a less definite kind: *cf.* the Lay of *Horn* and of *Havelok*. In another similar story, Ten Brink sees a late form of the Beowulf myth.

The most important of these legendary poems is the famous *Brut* of Layamon (about the beginning of the Thirteenth Century). It is simply the mythical history of Britain. In tone and manner the *Brut* approaches the old national epic; it is partly based on tradition by word of mouth, though Wace's *Geste des Bretons* was Layamon's chief authority. Compared, however, with modern ventures in the same field — say, with Tennyson's *Idylls of the King* — the *Brut* has much of the real epic flavor. From Layamon down, these national legends have been extensively drawn upon by our poets. A catalogue of such poems belongs to the history of our literature. — The above concerns (*a*) *National* legends. We now glance at (*b*) *Legends of the Church.*

In the first place, many paraphrases were made of the Bible. The Old Testament was partly done into English verse. Thus, that Ms. which Franciscus Junius took to be the work of Beda's hero, Cædmon, but which is really a collection of poems by several authors and from different times, contains, among other poetical versions of the books of the Bible, a splendid paraphrase of *Exodus*. Later, there were other versions of Genesis and Exodus. There is also preserved the conclusion of a noble Anglo-Saxon epic poem, — *Judith*. Cynewulf turned for material to the numerous sacred legends: *cf.* his *Elene, or the Finding of the Cross*. Later poets treated the lives of the saints. Hovering between national and sacred legend are such cycles of poetry as that which treats the legend of the Holy Grail, — *e.g.*, the story of "Joseph of Arimathie." These all have a strongly marked moral purpose, — something foreign to early epic. But in the way of pure narrative for the narrative's sake, nothing can be better than those of Chaucer's *Canterbury Tales* which treat sacred legend: *e.g.*, the exquisite *Prioresses Tale*.

We have, further, international literature as source for poetry, — *Legends based on General History* (*c*). Latin once made possible the ideal for which Goethe sighed, — a world-literature. In the mediæval Latin there was already collected a rude history of the world. In distorted shape, the heroes of old time passed through the Latin into the various literatures of Europe, which all began with and in the Latin itself. Each great hero formed a centre for certain 'cycles' of stories and legends: prominent were the Alexander Legends, the Æneas Legends;— later, the Legends of Charlemagne, though these are more *national.* A branch of the Æneas or Troy legend was that of *Troilus,* which afterwards busied the pens of Chaucer and Shakspere, and was immensely popular in the middle ages. A great aid to these legends was the mass of stories which had their origin in the East, — in India and elsewhere, — and came in the wake of the returning crusades, gradually drifting into every literature in Europe. Such is the famous story of the *three caskets,* brought in with so much effect in *The Merchant of Venice.* [*Cf.* the story itself in the E. E. T. Soc.'s ed. of the *Gesta Romanorum.*] Stimulated by these stories, and fed by them in great measure, arose a vast array of *Romances,* all of a historical coloring. Their name is derived from the Romance or corrupted and popular Latin, in which many of these tales appeared. Romances were greatly beloved in the middle ages, and made an important part of the first books printed by Caxton, — "joyous and pleasant histories of chivalry." Finally, they were killed by their folly and extravagance. *Cf.* Chaucer's *Tale of Sir Thopas;* for the prose romances, *Don Quixote* was at once judge and executioner. — More serious work — not strictly romances — may be seen in Chaucer's *Legende of Goode Women,* and above all in the great *Canterbury Tales.* As writer of tales, as "narrative poet," Chaucer is without a peer in English Literature. His reticence, in that garrulous age, is sublime. He omits trifling details, not caring "who bloweth in a trump or in a horn." — We must here note a strange use of the word "tragedy." It meant for Chaucer's time the story of those who had fallen from high to low estate. It had nothing dramatic:—

> " Tregedis is to sayn a certeyn storie,
> As olde bokes maken us memorie,
> Of hem that stood in greet prosperité
> And is y-fallen out of heigh degré
> Into miserie and endith wrecchedly."

A "comedy" was a narrative that did not end tragically: *cf.* Dante's great work.

With far wider sweep of history, modern poets have greatly increased the variety of romances and legendary poems. Think of *Evangeline* or *Hiawatha* on one hand, and on the other, of the Norse legends or the classic stories of William Morris. No classic themes have ever been revived with such power as in Marlowe's (and Chapman's) *Hero and Leander*, and in Keat's *Hyperion*. The field is practically boundless. There is great license of treatment. The poet can adhere closely to his original, or he can invent and change at will. Such cases may be cited as the romances of Scott and Byron.

Under this head belong the *Riming Chronicle* and the *Narrative Didactic* poem. The first is a history in rime. In the Thirteenth Century Robert of Gloucester wrote such a chronicle of England; later (end of Fifteenth Century) we have *Harding's Chronicle*. As poetry they are of no value whatever. — The second class we may illustrate best by describing its best example. In 1559 appeared a book called "*A Myrroure for Magistrates*, wherein may be seen by example of other, with how grevous plages vices are punished, and howe frayle, unstable worldly prosperitie is founde, even of those whom fortune seemeth most highly to favour. *Felix quem faciunt aliena pericula cautum*, Londini, &c." This work, begun by Sackville on the model of Boccaccio's *De casibus virorum illustrium*, resembles in plan the "Tregedis," described above, which make up the *Monk's Tale* in Chaucer's *Canterbury Tales*, except that in the former the characters are all English.

(*d*) Lastly, we note *the revival of the supernatural* in modern tales. This sort assumes a belief on the part of its readers that the supernatural is possible. The greatest example is Coleridge's *Christabel: cf.* the same poet's *Ancient Mariner*, and Scott's less successful *Lay of the Last Minstrel*.

(2) ALLEGORY.

Here we still have narrative, but it is no longer based on history, on actual events. *Invention* begins to play a leading part. A certain series of events is *supposed* to have taken place, and these events generally point out some moral, or else tell one story in terms of another. Allegory was the favorite form of the sacred Latin poetry of the early church. The last poets of profane Latin literature had a strong leaning toward allegory; and it was taken up with ardor by the Christians as particularly suited to their purposes. *Prudentius* (born in Saragossa, 348 A.D.) was the first Christian poet who regularly used pure allegory, and he employed it first in his *Psychomachia*, which is therefore important as the herald of a long line of allegorical poems. Its example and its effect upon mediæval literature can hardly be overestimated. It belonged, says Ebert, to the "standard works," was recommended for study, and was copied by many of the church poets. This, as we must remember, is *the first purely allegorical poem, but not the first use of allegory in poetry*. The latter is a point of *style*. In profane poetry, allegory soon became very popular, notably among the French poets, whom Chaucer copied. It was used quite apart from any moral purposes, and is often the vehicle of pure amusement. Such in part is the *Romaunt of the Rose*, — though there are many satirical touches in it, — a French poem of which we have a translation attributed to Chaucer. But we must regard first the

(*a*) Didactic Allegory.

The supreme allegory of the world is the *Divina Commedia* of Dante. It is at the same time a noble epic, of which, as has been said, Dante himself is the hero. Exactly what it is intended to teach is a question on which commentators still differ. In general, however, we may call it an allegory partly of political events, but chiefly of Dante's own life and religious belief. The poem is of the greatest importance aside from its splendid composition; it sums up the highest results of the middle ages and is filled with their loftiest and purest spirit. It is often imitated by Chaucer — as in his *House of Fame*. Further, the Scotch school of poets who followed Chaucer — Dunbar especially — showed great fondness for this sort of allegory, as well as for *Visions*. Visions belong with allegory, and were beloved by the middle ages. Gregory the Great, St. Boniface (Winfried), and many other famous writers, have left "Visions" among their works, — wonderful dreams, full of help or warning from the other world. Among the prettiest specimens of this sort of literature is a poem called *The Pearl* (North of England, about 1370). A father has lost his dear and only daughter, but in a dream he sees her in heaven and is comforted. Probably by the same author is a poem founded on the Arthurian legend and called *Sir Gawayne and the Green Knight*. This teaches in allegorical wise the lesson that manhood must be purified by doubt, temptation, and sorrow successfully combated; the poem may be compared with the great German poem of Wolfram von Eschenbach, — the *Parzival*. The finest allegorical poem in our own literature is, of course, *The Faery Queene*. Other famous poems of the kind are, on one hand, the *social allegory*, mourning the wrongs of certain classes in society: example, *The Vision concerning Piers the Ploughman* (Fourteenth Century); or, on the other, the *political allegory*, aiming at abuses in government or factious opposition: example, Dryden's *Absalom and Achitophel*, where English contemporary characters are introduced under the veil of a story from the Bible. Saul is Oliver Cromwell, David is King Charles II., Absalom is the Duke of Monmouth, &c. The same author wrote an allegory of religious faiths, — *The Hind and the Panther*. Dramatic in form (*cf.* Chap. III. § 5) but full of a fine allegory is Milton's noble *Comus*.

(*b*) When the didactic allegory is bounded by very narrow limits, there results the *Fable*. The Fable is "the feigned history of a particular case, in which we recognize a general truth." The events are mostly taken from the life of beasts, birds, etc. One of the oldest English forms of this sort of allegory is a description of some animal and his habits, with a moral interpretation. A collection of such stories was called a *Bestiary* or *Physiologus*. But ordinarily, by fable we understand a short, pithy incident in animal life, intended to convey a moral. Jacob Grimm, it is true, thought there had once existed a regular *beast-epic*, like the human epic of early days, and he referred the later fables to such a source. There was, however, no Germanic beast-epic at all. The stories came from the East, from Byzantium, brought by word of mouth into Italy, and thence into the different nations of Europe. The "morals" were added by the monks. Such collections were very popular. Caxton printed in 1481 a prose history of *Reynard the Fox*. Gay's *Fables* in English — and Prior's also — are specimens of the light vein: in French, Marie de France among older writers, and the incomparable La Fontaine, are superior to the English, except that Chaucer's imitation of Marie de France (*The Nonne Prestes Tale*) far surpasses the original, and is one of the liveliest and most charming tales in our literature.

(*c*) Miscellaneous.

There are several kindred forms of allegory, such as *Poetic Parable*, which deals with human beings rather than with beasts. This sort of poetry came also from the East. In modern English we may cite a familiar example in Leigh Hunt's *Abou ben Adhem*. The *Gnomic Dialogue* is an old form of verse. Two persons tell in turn anecdotes intended to bring out some truth.

Such were the famous dialogues between the soul and the body, well known to our early literature: further, the dialogue between *Solomon and Saturn* (!) and others of the same type. This latter poem is related to the popular Riddle Ballads, in which difficult questions are put and answered. (See Child, *Eng. and Scot. Pop. Ball.*, Vol. I, p. 13, 2d ed.)

(3) REFLECTIVE POETRY.

The desire *to draw a moral* from the story of events was, we saw, practically unknown to the primitive epic. The later forms, as they grew fond of allegory, allowed the moral element to get the upper hand. At last arose a kind of poetry that is *all moral*, and not in any way story, — just the opposite extreme from the old epic. What allows us to class such Reflective Poetry in this place, is the fact that the poet bases his moralizing upon experience of life. Now the middle ages had a boundless affection for moralizing; they would have taken the excellent Polonius and his maxims very seriously indeed. Add a touch of melancholy, inherent in the Anglo-Saxon race, and we can readily understand how popular was the *Poema Morale* (about 1170), a good example of the reflective poem. It is a sermon in verse; perhaps with as much lyric tone as epic, but still well freighted with good advice in addition to the pathos. Much longer, epic in breadth, style, and plan, is Wordsworth's *Excursion;* shorter, his *Lines written above Tintern Abbey*. Another example is Cowper's *Task*. More directly appealing to the *intellect* is Pope's *Essay on Criticism;* to the *reason*, the same author's *Essay on Man*. With this kind of reflective and philosophical verse we touch the borders of poetry itself. Poetry purely didactic is not poetry; for poetry must, to a certain extent, exist for its own sake, as a work of art. There is brilliant verse in Pope's *Essays* above-mentioned; but when we come to the lower forms of so-called didactic poetry, we must deny the substantive. Thus rimed histories, catechisms, mnemonic verses, instructive literature generally, are not poetry. *Cf.* Furnivall's ed. of the *Book of Nurture* (E. E. T. Soc. 1868); Tusser's *Five Hundred Points of Good Husbandry;* Armstrong's *Art of Preserving Health*, and a host of the same kind: all of these could be much more simply and effectively written in prose. In fact, such verse is a survival from the days before prose was established, when poetry was maid-of-all-work to priesthood and the law. Yet we cannot say that all so-called didactic poetry is not poetry; even if we give up Vergil's *Georgics*, we have the great poem of Lucretius. In the latter case, a system of philosophy is taught in verse; but there is a vast remove from Armstrong's prattle about "The choice of aliment, the choice of air" to the "glittering shafts" of Lucretius' cosmic forces. We may say that the *De Rerum Natura* is poetical in spite of its subject.

(4) Descriptive Poetry.

This may be called a *Nature-epic*. It carries us not from one *event* to another, but from one *object* to another. It is generally combined with reflective poetry: *cf.* Goldsmith's *Traveller* and *Deserted Village*, or Thomson's *Seasons*. There is much descriptive verse in the *Excursion*, the *Task*, and like poems; also in the epic itself. A fine bit of description is the conclusion of M. Arnold's *Sohrab and Rustum*. In shorter compass, it appears in the famous epic *Similes* (*cf.* p. 109), and is familiar to lyric and dramatic verse. The one condition of descriptive poetry is that it shall have distinctively *human connections and human interest ;* else it becomes a catalogue. As a setting for the gem of human interest, it is omnipresent in poetry : the ballads open with a brief descriptive touch of the merry greenwood ; the lyric has its moonlight and rustling leaves ; the drama is set in actual scenery. It is this human interest combined with vivid description that gives success to Wordsworth's best work ; it is the lack of human interest that condemns from the start the effort of the verse-maker, who says (according to Carlyle), "Come, let us make a description !"

It is worth noting that the gorgeous pomp of description so common in the Elizabethan drama, and to modern taste often so superfluous, is due to the miserable scenery of the early stage. To beguile the imagination away from a bare space with a pasteboard tree and a label "Forest of Arden," the playwright had recourse to elaborate and highly colored description. Famous for this characteristic is the description of Dover Cliff in *Lear*.

(5) PASTORAL POETRY.

An odd mixture of narrative and descriptive, with a dramatic element added, is the so-called Pastoral Poetry. It was once believed that poetry originated among shepherds ; and in a corrupt or artificial age there is a reaction towards this primitive verse. Dwellers in crowded cities imagine themselves "silly" shepherds piping by the brookside among their sheep. But simplicity is, as a rule, the very last quality of this kind of poetry. Under such circumstances it is almost impossible to write naturally; there is too wide a gap between the singer and his song. The incongruity becomes evident when modern and ancient expressions are brought together, as in Pope's lines: —

> "Inspire me, Phœbus, in my Delia's praise,
> With Waller's strains or Granville's moving lays;
> A milk-white bull shall at your altars stand
> That threats a fight and spurns the rising sand."

But there is some very successful pastoral poetry; such is that of Theocritus and Vergil for the Greek and Latin, and of Spenser and William Browne for the English. This kind of poetry also had its origin in *worship of the gods,* and began in Greece with the worship of Pan and the Dorian Artemis. The Spanish pastoral poem *Diana,* by George de Monte Mayor, had considerable influence on Sidney in his *Arcadia.* Our earliest pastoral is the *Robyne and Makyne* of Robert Henrysoun, a Scotch poet of the Fifteenth Century.

Not so limited in range, though of the same character as the pastoral, is the *Idyll.* The Idyll must be simple, calm, more concerned with *situation* than with *action.* As a good example of this sort of poetry we should not instance the obvious *Idylls of the King* by Tennyson, which are more full of *action* than the title warrants, and belong to the legendary epic; but we should instance *The Cotter's Saturday Night* of Burns as an excellent short idyll. In German, *Hermann and Dorothea* (Goethe) is called an idyll; the quietness and simplicity of the poem, its exquisite grace, are more prominent than the action, which is very simple. It was the only one of his poems, Goethe told Eckermann, which pleased the author in his old age. — For the *dramatic* Idyll, see Chap. III. § 11.

(6) SATIRIC AND AMUSING POETRY.

The Latin word *Satura* (*lanx satura*, a plate heaped with various viands) meant a hodge-podge, or mixture of all things. A song was sung, made up of shifting subjects and metres, — a medley. At last it came to be a song ridiculing persons or events, and gradually gained dignity, till it ceased to *mock* its object, and began to *reprove*. The Romans were the greatest masters of this style of poetry, and Juvenal was its chief poet. Such satiric poetry as his, different from the milder satire of Horace, lashes public and private folly with a whip of indignant scorn. It does not aim to amuse; it is really didactic. Epic poetry was, we saw, objective; it mirrored the world, good or bad, without moral comment. Satiric poetry, on the other hand, judges events, and above all loves to belittle their importance, to show the reverse side of things. The epic loved to magnify its hero, to make him the special care of the gods; the satire delights to show him subject to petty ills and conquered by some ignominious fate. Thus Juvenal cries to Hannibal, "Go now, thou madman, scour the rugged Alps — that thou mayest please children (hearing his story) and be a good subject for compositions!" In order to make the satire keener, although the mixed and shifting treatment is retained, the poet adopts the form and manner of the epic: in Latin, the hexameter; in English, the heroic couplet. In the latter language we have vigorous satire from Marston, Donne, Bishop Hall, and many others. Butler's *Hudibras* is another kind of satire, in mock epic style. Dr. Johnson's two imitations of Juvenal are well known. — Dryden's *Mac Flecknoe* is a strong *personal* satire. There is much light and incidental satire in Chaucer; and in the old English poem called *The Owl and the Nightingale* (middle of the Thirteenth Century) the satire is softened to a delightful humor. This poem is in dialogue form, and may be compared with *The Twa Dogs* of Burns.

Amusing Epic Poetry.

Parody.—Here we look through a reversed spy-glass. The grand epic style is applied to petty subjects, and exact epic order and grouping are retained. One of the best mock-epics or parodies ever written is Pope's *Rape of the Lock*. Note especially the machinery of the sylphs, their punishment for neglect of duty (*cf.* the punishments in the *Odyssey*,— of Tantalus, Sisyphus, etc.); and the game of cards, described as the epic describes a battle.

A *Travesty*, on the other hand, is a noble subject treated in a ridiculous, ignoble way,— the opposite of the parody. Such are the Comic Histories.— But there is another sort of mock-poem which goes under the name *parody*, though really a travesty. It consists in copying a serious poem with comic effect, using, however, as far as may be, the same words, phrases, metre, and general plan. The best of this class is M. Prior's *English Ballad on the Taking of Namur by the King of Great Britain*, in which he parodies admirably Boileau's pompous ode, *Sur le Prise de Namur par les Armes du Roi, L'Annee*

1692. Prior wrote on its recapture by the English in 1695.

Humorous Epic. Not a parody or even a satire, but an easy poem, dealing with light events so as to form a connected story, and presenting generally some "philosophy of life," is the *Humorous Epic.* Byron's *Don Juan* is an example. With a far more serious undercurrent, but still outwardly humorous, is Clough's delightful *Bothie of Tober na Vuolich.* Byron and Clough had very different points of view, but the manner of the poems is in some respects the same.

Thence we descend to merry tales in rime, light poems written purely for entertainment. Such in France were La Fontaine's *Contes et Nouvelles,* many of which were based on Boccaccio's (prose) *Decameron;* England has Chaucer's lighter tales; and we may add for later literature (amid a host of 'comic' or 'humorous' poems) Burns' *Tam o' Shanter.*

Lastly, the *Riddle.* The Riddle is a short epic with the hero's name suppressed. Often the *form* of the poetry has great merit; *e.g.,* for older English, *Cynewulf's* Riddles; for later, *Praed's* so-called Charades.

(7) THE GRAND EPIC OF MODERN TIMES.

By "modern" is meant the period since poetical *composition* has taken the place of poetical *growth,* — since the epoch of the *Odyssey* or of *Beowulf.* The time is relative, and differs with different races. The splendid possibilities of the pure epic have not been disregarded by great poets, and in many lands there has arisen a later or imitated epic modelled on the early national epic. Vergil's *Æneid* is a not unworthy successor (inferior in many respects, it is true, and necessarily lacking the freshness and spontaneity of the original) of the *Iliad.* Ariosto and Tasso applied the manner and form of the grand epic to medieval subjects. For English, *Paradise Lost,* with its intense energy and lofty tone, ranks among the few great epic poems of the world. A bold venture on classic ground was the unfinished *Hyperion* of Keats, — an epic not far behind Milton's in that "high seriousness" which has been advanced of late as prime quality in a great poem. Further, there are countless English *translations of the great epics,* Pope's and Chapman's Homers being the most conspicuous. One great test of the old epic was its absolute belief in itself; there was no feigning. This sincerity is impossible in imitated epic; and what makes Dante's great poem almost worthy to rank with the old epic, is the intense belief of Dante in his own work. It so catches the spirit of the middle ages, is so intense in its sincerity, that in this respect it may well be called Homeric.

§ 4. THE BALLAD OR FOLK-SONG.

We see that from the original epic sprang many kinds of poetry that all had the common trait of telling something known, or supposed, or feigned to have happened. Other characteristics were simplicity, absence of personal property (authorship), truthful mirroring of nature, lack of a moral or reflective element. These qualities vanished in later epic poetry. But as in the natural world, when we have ploughed under some old wheat-field and planted a new crop of other grain, there will be crevices and corners where odd patches of wheat will spring up and flourish by the side of the regular crop, so it is in the world of literature. The old wheat-field of epic poetry, long after it was ploughed under, kept sending up scattered blades, which we call *ballads* or *folk-songs*. Except in authority, national importance, and kindred qualities, we may use the same definition for the (narrative) folk-song that we use for the early epic. Both names, ballad and folk-song, are suggestive: *ballad* means a song to which one may dance; *folk-song* is something made by the whole people, not by individual poets. Wright, in speaking of certain songs of the Fifteenth Century (Percy Soc., vol. XXIII.), says: "The great variation in the different copies of the same song shews that they were taken down from oral recitation, and had been often preserved by memory among minstrels who were not unskilful at composing, and who were . . . in the habit . . . of making up new songs by stringing together phrases and lines, and even whole stanzas, from the different compositions that were imprinted on their memories." The importance and influence and, we may add, the worth, of the folk-song are in inverse ratio to the spread of printed books. As the minstrel's welcome vanished from the baron's hall, and his audience degenerated to peasants and serving-people, we note a corresponding degeneration from the highest poetical merit to the level of modern street-songs.[1] It easily follows that much of the best folk-poetry must be lost,—not because, like the heroes before Agamemnon, it lacked the pious poet to sing it, but rather the 'chiel' to take notes and 'print it.'

[1] . . . "the usual marks of degeneracy [of ballads], a dropping or obscuring of marvellous and romantic incidents, and a declension in the rank and style of the characters." Child, Ballads, 2d Ed., vol. I., p. 48.

The folk-song is a complete satisfaction of the demand for "more matter and less art." It is very artless and full of matter. The passions jostle each other terribly, as they escape from the singer's lips: —

> "I hackéd him in pieces sma',
> For her sake that died for me."

The historical or narrative ballad is what we now consider. Like the early epic, it refers often to subjects made up partly of legend and partly of myth, — such as the Robin Hood ballads. But unlike the epic, the folk-song is often made immediately after a great battle or similar event. In the *Battle of Maldon, or Byrhtnoth's Death*, a stirring ballad of the later Anglo-Saxon period, the song follows the event so closely that the singer has not had time even to find out the name of the enemy's leaders. It is full of epic phrases and figures, and is thoroughly in the objective manner. The event seems to sing itself.

Professor Child has grouped our national ballads as follows: I. Romances of Chivalry and legends of the popular history of England. II. Ballads involving various superstitions; as of Fairies, Elves, Magic, and Ghosts. III. Tragic love-ballads. IV. Other tragic ballads. V. Love-ballads not tragic. In all these, and in the miscellaneous ballads, the tests we mentioned above will hold good for the genuine folk-song. It must be objective, filled with its story, adding no sentiment or moral, and breathing a healthy, popular spirit. Antique spelling and archaic phrases do not make a ballad. Many ballads, too, are not of native origin, but, blown from the East over Europe, dropped seed in many countries. Hence a number of similar ballads (*cf.* the extraordinary spread of a ballad known in English as *Lady Isabel and the Elf-Knight*) in the different literatures of Europe. Again, like fairy and nursery tales, like superstitions and folk-lore of every sort, many strikingly similar European ballads point to a common mythical source. But amid the diversity of subject and origin, the general spirit of the ballad or folk-song remains one and the same. The genuine ballad is one thing, and the imitated ballad — even such an imitation as Chatterton could make — is quite another. To understand this clearly, read a good specimen of each kind; compare, say, *Thomas of Ercildoune* with Keats' *La Belle Dame Sans Merci, a Ballad*. The latter is wrought by the fancy of a poet under certain influences of the past; the other, written in the Fifteenth Century, but older in composition than that, is the work of a single poet or minstrel only in the sense that this minstrel combined materials which had been handed down from remotest times. The study of these materials leads in all directions, — to the prophecies of Merlin, the story of the Tannhäuser, and so forth; the floating waifs of myth and superstition had gathered about the legendary (or historical) form of Thomas the Rhymer, and under one minstrel's hands take this definite shape as ballad. It is the old epic process in miniature. Even in the *style* we may distinguish the two. "I am glad as grasse wold be of raine" is the ballad style (*Marriage of Sir Gawayne*); "With kisses glad as birds are that get sweet rain at noon" is the imitated ballad style (Swinburne, *A Match*).

The ballad, with the spread of letters, degenerates

into the street-song or broadside. It bewails abuses in government, the wrongs of the poor, satirizes the follies of the day, and the like. For a collection of such, see (among others) the *Roxburghe Ballads*.

§ 5. LATER BALLADS.

As with the epic, so with the folk-song; poets soon saw how much could be done with the form and manner of the ballad. Prudentius wrote a sort of ballad on the death of the martyr Laurentius; it was in the metre of the Latin folk-song, and is called by Ebert the first example of a modern ballad. He compares the style, and even the metre, to the English popular ballads of later time. Of course, Prudentius purposely adopts this ballad style: "Hear," he cries to the martyr, "*a rustic poet.*" The nearer such *conscious* ballads approach the tone of genuine folk-song, the better they are. The old Anglo-Saxon ballad, *e.g.*, *Byrhtnoth's Death*, may be compared with Drayton's stirring *Battle of Agincourt*. The list of these imitated or conscious ballads, works of individual poets, would be endless. Any great occasion or situation can inspire such songs. Of martial ballads, we instance Campbell's *Battle of the Baltic;* of love-ballads (narrative, of course), *Maud Müller* or *Lord Ullin's Daughter;* gay ballads, like Burns' *Duncan Grey* or *John Barleycorn;* longer historical ballads, like Macaulay's *Lays of Ancient Rome*, in which there is more tinsel than true metal; the "dramatic," spirited ballad, such as Robert Browning delights in; and a host of others. Often a story is told in a story; *e.g.*, Coleridge's *Ancient Mariner*. *Comic* ballads are of two kinds. In one, the fun springs from the situation or event; *e.g., John Gilpin's* famous ride. In the other, the mind must work out the humor of the poem; there is nothing laughable in the event itself. Of this kind is Goldsmith's *Elegy on the Death of a Mad Dog.* To classify the great number of occasional ballads would be useless. They cover every conceivable situation. But we must note the gradual shading away of narrative ballads into ballads that are either *lyric* or *dramatic*. The tragic ballad is in its purity objective, — as *The Children in the Wood,* or *Sir Patrick Spens:* when it begins to let emotion outweigh narrative, then we have a lyric ballad. When the persons of the story speak for themselves, we have a dramatic ballad. Naturally, the lyric and epic are often closely blended. Thus a deep emotion — as of grief — finds expression by dwelling on certain events. *The Burial of Sir John Moore* is strongly objective; mingled with outbursts of feeling is the narrative in David's beautiful lament over Jonathan (2 *Sam.* 1. 17 ff.). This is closely allied to the lyric *Threnody;* but there is a tendency to dwell on events. There is much narrative in Milton's *Lycidas*, and at first we might call it chiefly epic in its lament; — what with the pastoral allegory, and the appeal to the nymphs, one is almost ready to add "artificial": but a deeper study shows us that the whole poem is a splendid burst of grief and indignation, — Milton's first strong cry against the evil of the times, against a degenerate priesthood. King's death is only the occasion for uttering those feelings. *Lycidas* is in every sense of the word a *lyric*.

CHAPTER II.—LYRIC POETRY.

The epic belongs to the outward world. Its business is to tell a story. It sings the wrath of Achilles, or the wanderings of Odysseus, or the feats of Beowulf; it reports simply what has happened. Quite the contrary with the lyric: it is subjective, proceeds from one individual; has to do, not with events, but with feelings. It belongs to a later stage of culture than the epic. "The lyric poets," says Paul Albert,[1] "are the interpreters of the new society. The field that is opened to them is vast, boundless, as the needs, desires, and energies of the people." Children, and the early world, content themselves with things about them,— events, objects of nature. Growing man becomes conscious of a world within him, of desires, hopes, fears. To express these is the business of lyric poetry. Consequently the test of a good lyric poem is *sincerity*. To show how important this is, read an artificial lyric like Rogers' *Wish* ("Mine be a cot beside the hill"), and compare it with the exquisite *Happy Heart* of Dekker. [Both lyrics are in Palgrave's *Golden Treasury*.] We ask, therefore, of the lyric that it be a real expression, an adequate, harmonious, and *imaginative* expression, of real feeling.

Hegel gives a good illustration of this subjective nature of the lyric as compared with the epic objectivity. Homer, he says, is so shut out, as individual, from his

---

[1] *La Poésie*, Paris, 1870. He is speaking especially of Greece, from 760–400 B.C.

great epics, that his very existence is questioned; though his heroes are safely immortal. The heroes of Pindar, on the other hand, are empty names; while he who sang them is the immortal poet. Lyric poetry tends to exalt the poet himself, to make his personality far more to us than the events which occasion his poem. Whether it be Horace or Robin Herrick who is singing, it is the poet who interests us, not the Mæcenas or Corinna to whom he sings, nor yet the villa or the May-day which he takes as subject.

Again, the epic moves slowly, majestically; it is a broad and quiet current. The lyric is *concentrated.* It is like a well-spring bursting out suddenly at one's feet.

So, too, epic and lyric differ in *form.* The epic has a traditional, uniform metre, such as the hexameter or the heroic couplet or blank verse. The lyric has its choice of a hundred forms, or may go further, and invent a new form. The epic was chanted; the lyric was sung. The old minstrel had his harp; the German Minnesänger accompanied their songs on the violin (not the harp, as often stated). This suggests the origin of the word lyric, — something sung to the lyre. Thus we have three elements: instrument, voice, words. In time a separation was brought about, so that now (1) the music is everything, and the words either altogether discarded (compare the *Lieder ohne Worte*) or else very subordinate and often foolish, as in opera; or (2) the words are the chief consideration and the music a *possibility.* When to a lyric of the second class (such as Goethe's charming songs), the music of a great master is added, we have revived the original conception of a lyric.

The Abbé Batteux says that *enthusiasm* is the basis

of lyric poetry, and he gives three divisions: the *sublime*, the *sweet*, and what lies between the two. But this is nothing more than what was said above, — the lyric comes from and appeals to *the feelings*. It stirs our emotions and purifies them, — a process to which in the case of the drama Aristotle applied the term *Katharsis*, a purifying or purging. Lyric poetry must therefore be divided according to the nature of the feelings aroused. But these same emotions may be (*a*) SIMPLE, and the poem may so become a natural expression of immediate feeling; or they may be (*b*) ENTHUSIASTIC, whence arises the dithyramb or ode; or lastly, they may be (*c*) REFLECTIVE, where the intellectual mingles with the purely emotional.

Many writers have proposed new classifications of lyric poetry; thus Carriere divides into lyrics of *feeling*, of *contemplation* (or the *symbolic*, *i.e.*, the poet traces his own sensations as manifested in the external world), and of *reflection*. Vischer has still another division; but the one given above seems the simplest, and needs no great array of philosophic terms to explain it.

§ 1. SACRED LYRIC.

The lyric here voices religious emotion. When this occurs (*a*) *simply*, when the feelings pour out unrestrainedly, we have such a hymn as Wesley's beautiful *Jesus, Lover of my Soul*. The world-old hymns on which mythology and religion were based were more epic than lyric. Otherwise with the purely emotional character of the Psalms of David: *cf.* XLII., *As the hart panteth after the water-brooks*. To these, as to Wesley's hymn, may be applied a phrase which De Quincey quotes from the Greek, "*Flight of the solitary to the Solitary.*" The spirit of Christianity is an individual spirit; it appeals to the single human soul. Hence many beautiful hymns of the church.

(*b*) The second class of lyrics, the *Ode*, is where "any strain of enthusiastic and exalted lyrical verse [is] directed to a fixed purpose, and [deals] progressively with one dignified theme." (E. W. Gosse.) — For purely sacred lyric, an instance of this kind would be the Ode, "God," by Derzhavin, the Russian; translated by Bowring. With slight epic leaning is Pope's *Messiah*.

(*c*) The reflective sacred lyric is well represented in the poems of George Herbert, where, however, the passion for 'conceits' often clogs the lyric flight. Whittier's *Eternal Goodness* may be mentioned among modern poems of this class.

§ 2. PATRIOTIC LYRIC.

National hymns flourish in every country, and the feeling of love for one's native land has found frequent and various expression in the lyric. "*Scots wha hae wi' Wallace bled*" (Burns); *The Isles of Greece* (Byron); *The Marseillaise;* the exquisite little "Ode," *How Sleep the Brave* (Collins); *Give a Rouse* (R. Browning, 'Cavalier Tunes'); *Ye Mariners of England* (Campbell) — are all examples of this sort. Then there is the fine *Ode* by Sir W. Jones, *What Constitutes a State?* the sonnet *To Milton* by Wordsworth; Coleridge's *Ode to France;* and the masterpiece of lofty reflection joined with intense feeling flashing out in the "higher mood" of *Lycidas*. In patriotic lyrics are, of course, included lyrics of *war*. Several have been mentioned. Poems like *The Destruction of Sennacherib* (Byron) and *The Charge of the Light Brigade* (Tennyson), though narrative in form, are really lyric; the feeling is the main thing, not the story. They are subjective, not objective.

Lastly, we must not forget that in the best *dramatic* poetry there are bursts of feeling so strong as to make them lyrical, despite the chains of blank-verse and the dependence on the rest of the play. Such a patriotic outburst is the part about England in the dying speech of old John of Gaunt (*Rich. II.*, II. 1), or the famous exhortation of King Harry (*Hen. V.*, III. 1).

§ 3. LOVE-LYRICS.

These are the lyrics *par excellence*. Our literature is wonderfully rich in this respect. We think of such a simple love-lyric as *Take, O take those lips away* (in *Measure for Measure*), or *O my love's like a red, red rose*, or *Whistle and I'll come to you, my lad* (Burns); of such an ode as Spenser's *Epithalamion;* of such a fine 'reflective' love-lyric as *She was a phantom of delight* (Wordsworth), and, though we have combined most widely sundered points of view, we have by no means exhausted the "many moodes and pangs of lovers . . . the poure fools sometimes praying, beseeching, sometime honouring, auancing, praising: an other while railing, reviling, and cursing; then sorrowing, weeping, lamenting: in the ende laughing, rejoysing and solacing the beloued againe, with a thousand delicate deuises, odes, songs, elegies, ballads, sonets and other ditties, moouing one way and another to great compassion." (Geo. Puttenham, *Arte of Eng. Poesie,* ch. 22.) Or we may sum up the two prevailing moods — hope and despair — of love-songs, in Chaucer's line : —

"Now up, now doun, as bokets in a welle."

The *troubadours* (or *trouvères, i.e.,* finders, inventors of poetry) flourished in France, and the *Minnesänger* (*Minne* = love) in Germany, some six centuries ago, and made a golden age of love-lyrics. To compose a love-song, and then sing it effectively, was every noble's accomplishment. Richard the Lion-heart is credited with a French love-lay. Then, too, the gay "clerkes," the wandering scholars of the middle ages, sang love-songs enough, from the reckless tavern-catch (such as may be found in modern collections of the medieval Latin songs) up to the passionate outburst of love to the holy and gracious Virgin of heaven. [See Kennedy's translation of Ten Brink's *Hist. Eng. Lit.,* p. 208.] Another great cycle of love-lyrics is found in the time of Elizabeth ; *e.g.,* Marlowe's "smooth song," *Come live with me and be my love.* Popular collections were printed ; *e.g.,* "England's Helicon," Tottel's "Miscellany," &c. — The *Madrigal* was originally a *shepherd's* song, but came to mean a love-ditty; "airs and madrigals," says Milton, "which whisper softness in chambers." It must be short and fanciful ; *e.g., Take, O take those lips away* (see above), or *Tell me where is fancy bred* (*Merch. of Ven.*). Reckless or amusing love-lyrics are plentiful : Suckling's *Why so pale and wan, fond lover?* and Wither's *Shall I, wasting in despair* are good examples. An admirable love-lyric, swaying between jest and earnest, is Drayton's sonnet, *Since there's no help, come let us kiss and part;* the sudden turn of the last two lines is of the highest merit. Grave entirely, and gracious, is Lovelace's *Tell me not, sweet, I am unkinde.* With Herrick, Carew and the rest, we come to *Vers de Société,* which will be treated below. It is folly to attempt any minute classification of love-lyrics: each good one should make a class for itself. We must, however, note the wonderful revival of the Elizabethan lyric by William Blake; *e.g.,* in his song *My Silks and Fine Array.* The *tragic* side of love represented in this song is more appropriately treated under lyrics of grief, though we may here mention the exquisite ballad *Fair Helen,* Wordsworth's *Lucy* (that beginning *She dwelt among the untrodden ways,* and also *A slumber did my spirit seal*); while there is what Mr. Arnold calls a "piercing" pathos in the stanza of *Auld Lang Syne:*—

> "We twa hae paidl'd i' the burn
> From morning sun till dine;
> But seas between us braid hae roar'd
> Sin' auld lang syne."

§ 4. LYRIC OF NATURE.

The good poet ought to feel with Chaucer:—

> " When that the monethe of May
> Is comen, and I here the foulës synge,
> And that the flourës gynnen for to sprynge,
> Fairewel my boke, and my devocioun!"

Out of very early times comes down to us a fresh little "Cuckoo-Song," a refrain to welcome Summer; it is an excellent example of the simple nature-lyric:—

> "Sumer is i-cumen[1] in,
> Lhude[2] sing cuccu!
> Groweth sed
> And bloweth med,[3]
> And springth the wde[4] nu[5];
> Sing cuccu."

Simple, too, is the song in *Cymbeline*, "*Hark, hark, the lark,*" and the song in R. Browning's *Pippa Passes*, "*The Year's at the Spring.*" A little reflection (nature is ever suggestive) is mingled with Shelley's *Cloud*, Blake's *Tiger*, Wordsworth's *Cuckoo* and *Daffodils*, Keats' *Autumn*, Beaumont and Fletcher's *Now the lusty Spring is seen* and *Shepherds all and maidens fair*, and Swinburne's fine chorus *When the hounds of spring*, in "Atalanta in Calydon."

Of the *odes*, we instance Collins' beautiful *Ode to Evening;* and Wordsworth's *Ode on Intimations of Immortality*, etc., is also in great part a praise of nature.

With *reflective* lyrics of nature we come upon a boundless field. Man's life and the life of nature are so mutually suggestive, we so perpetually express one in terms of the other, — the oak dies, hope fades, and so on, — that there can be no end to the variety of emotions called forth. Burns ploughs up the daisy, and the analogy with his own fate bursts out in song. Even light-hearted Herrick reminds Corinna (*Corinna's Going a Maying*) that life ebbs fast, and nature must be enjoyed while May is with us. When the feelings come still further under the influence of the intellect, when we allow analogies to be suggested which lead us hither and thither, there results the reflective lyric of the

[1] come.   [2] loud.   [3] meadow.   [4] wood.   [5] now.

graver cast. The lyric tends to be less spontaneous; but it gains in breadth and often in beauty. Take the process in little. Wordsworth says:—

> "My heart leaps up when I behold
>   A rainbow in the sky:
> So was it when my life began:
> So is it now I am a man;
> So be it when I shall grow old,
>   Or let me die!
> The child is father of the man;
> And I could wish my days to be
> Bound each to each by natural piety."

Here we note (1) a pure emotion, a simple, unmixed influence of nature; then (2) memory, and a wish born of reflection; finally (3) an intellectual conclusion, a result of that reflection. This process, extended or brief, makes a reflective nature-lyric. Shelley's *Skylark* and *Ode to the West Wind*, Andrew Marvell's *Garden*, and especially Milton's *L'Allegro* and *Il Penseroso*, may be read with profit as excellent examples of this class. Mr. Pattison has shown, as regards Milton's two poems, that they are not "descriptive";—that descriptive poetry (as Lessing proved in his *Laocoön*) is "a contradiction in terms. . . . Human action or passion is the only subject of poetry." The charm of nature-poetry is not its description, its rivalry with a painting of the scene; it is the suggestive power of objects to stimulate the imagination,—in Marvell's fine words, often

> "Annihilating all that's made
> To a green thought in a green shade."

The perfection of this sort of poetry is perhaps reached in Keats' two odes *To a Nightingale* and *On a Grecian Urn*.

Finally, nature may serve as mere mirror for intense feeling. Such a poem is Tennyson's *Break, break, break*.

§ 5. LYRIC OF GRIEF.

There is pure grief expressed in the last poem cited above; and indeed, classification of lyrics is often arbitrary and uncertain, for a poet does not confine himself in one poem to one feeling. But *death* is the prime mover of grief, and we consider here the lyric that deals with death. Such a lyric should be the result of *immediate* feeling. Malherbe, the French poet, took three years to compose an ode to a friend who had lost his wife. When the ode was ready, the friend was again married.

The old-time lament was epic; it sang the deeds of the dead. So the end of Beowulf tells us how twelve warriors rode around the hero's tomb and sang his praise. Nowadays the lament is lyric. Examples are: *Dirge in Cymbeline;* Shelley's *Adonais* (in memory of Keats); Tennyson's *In Memoriam* (Hallam). These will fairly represent the simple (also expressed in Wordsworth's *Lucy* and in Poe's *Annabel Lee*), the impassioned, and the philosophic or reflective. But *In Memoriam* has three distinct moods: (1) epic, memories of old friendship; (2) lyric, bursts of pure grief; (3) reflective, philosophic — as in the canto 117, *Contemplate all this work of time.* See, further, Milton's *Lycidas* and Arnold's *Thyrsis*. A calamity involving many deaths is bewailed in Cowper's *Loss of the Royal George*.

The words *elegy* and *elegiac* must be used with caution. The classical lament was written in alternate hexameter and pentameter; this was called elegiac verse. It came to be used for any reflective poetry; hence "elegiac" refers more to the metre than to the subject. In English we understand it generally to mean solemn or plaintive poetry; but the *Roman Elegies*, for example, of Goethe are anything rather than solemn or plaintive. Still, in general terms, an elegy is a song of grief, whether acute or mild. It can also look forward to death, as well as back. Thus Nash has some beautiful lines on Approaching Death (in *Summer's Last Will and Testament*) : —

> " Brightness falls from the air : —
> Queens have died young and fair;
> Dust hath clos'd Helen's eye;
> I am sick, I must die. —
> Lord, have mercy on us!"

Less immediate is Shirley's *Dirge* ("The glories of our blood and state"), or Beaumont's lines *On the Tombs in Westminster Abbey.*

On the contrary, personal and full of terrible suffering are those saddest verses of Cowper, *The Castaway.* Like Beaumont's lines in beauty, and more read than any other poem in our language, is Gray's famous *Elegy.* There is no passion; it is simply the language of the heart that comes face to face with the wide and impersonal idea of death. There is no individual grief, nor is there appeal to tumultuous sorrow, as in Hood's *Bridge of Sighs.*

Again, the *living* can cause grief; there can be a living death. So Whittier in *Ichabod* laments the fall of Webster; so R. Browning, in the *Lost Leader*, bewails — as it is generally understood — Wordsworth's ' secession ' to the Tories.

Finally, one must draw a sharp line between the sentimental and the really pathetic. To the former class belong many vulgar but popular songs about blind people, drunkards, dead sweethearts, and so on; to the latter, Lamb's *Old Familiar Faces*.

§ 6. PURELY REFLECTIVE, AND MISCELLANEOUS.

Purely intellectual verse is too apt to be didactic. It easily drifts away altogether from the domain of poetry. Still, there are poems filled with exalted thought which deserve a high place. Such is Sir H. Wotton's *How Happy is he Born and Taught* (simple); such is, for more elaborate work, the *Ode to Duty* of Wordsworth, full of high enthusiasm. Much of Matthew Arnold's poetry is purely reflective. Here, too, we may mention such lyric poems with a strong epic leaning as Gray's *Progress of Poesy*; *Alexander's Feast* is of the same nature. Further, we note the ode *addressed to a certain person*, like Marvell's 'Horatian Ode' to *Cromwell*; Ben Jonson's *Ode to Himself*; and many other poems more or less filled with the reflective, philosophical element. Here belong such half allegorical lyrics as George Herbert's *Pulley*, — ("When God at first made man"). As a reflective ode, pure and simple, wrought up to the highest fervor, there is nothing better than George Eliot's one poem, "*O may I join the choir invisible.*"

Didactic poetry, as hinted above, can hardly be called in the strict sense, poetry. The difference between it and the reflective lyric may be thus stated: the latter allows the poetic suggestion of the senses or imagination to lead the mind in certain channels (*e.g.*, a dead leaf, our mortality). The didactic poem *forces* our poetic instincts, as well as suggestions of the senses, into certain channels of its own. But this is putting Pegasus to the plough.

§ 7. CONVIVIAL LYRICS; VERS DE SOCIÉTÉ.

Man is social by nature, and from most ancient time he has had convivial songs. Drinking choruses and songs in honor of wine and good fellowship over the bowl, are found in every literature. The wandering "clerkes" of the middle ages were very skilful with this sort of lyric; there are certain famous lines attributed to Walter Mapes: —

"Meum est propositum
In taberna mori," etc.

In our own literature, drinking songs are numerous: thus in Bishop Still's play, *Gammer Gurton's Needle*, there is a song inserted (probably taken from some popular ballad-collection of the day) in praise of ale, "*I cannot eat but little meat.*" The Dutch wars during Elizabeth's reign greatly increased drinking-excesses among the English; and hence the frequent allusions to heavy drinking made by such writers as Shakspere; the passages in Hamlet (I. 4) and Othello (II. 3) are well known. — One of the best short songs of this kind is in *Antony and Cleopatra* (II. 7), with the refrain, *Cup us, till the world go round;* though for sheer Bacchanalian glee and reckless merriment, the prize must be given to Burns' *Willie brew'd a peck o' maut.* In Beaumont and Fletcher's *Valentinian*, there is a fine drinking-song, *God Lyæus ever young.* Anacreon was the master of this sort of poetry, — all his songs praise love or wine, — and the name *Anacreontic* is often applied to the convivial lyric. Thomas Moore has both translated Anacreon and also written many songs in the same vein.

From strictly convivial lyrics we pass into that wide realm covered by the term *Vers de Société*. Locker, in his collection of such poems (*Lyra Elegantiarum*, London, 1867) quotes a definition of *Vers de Société:* "It is the poetry of men who belong to society . . . who amid all this froth of society feel that there are depths in our nature which even in the gaiety of drawing-rooms cannot be forgotten. Theirs is the poetry of sentiment that breaks into humour. . . . When society ceases to be simple, it [*i.e.*, *Vers de Soc.*] becomes sceptical. . . . Emotion takes refuge in jest, and passion hides itself in scepticism of passion." Locker thinks Suckling and Herrick, Swift and Prior, Cowper and Thomas Moore, Praed and Thackeray, the representative men of this class of poetry. This *vers de société* spreads itself over a wide area, and must, of course, cover some ground already marked off, — love, reflective, and other lyrics. The lower forms of this sort are lines in an album, a short note in verse, asking pardon for some blunder or omission, hits at passing folly, a valentine, and the like. Higher are poems like Clough's *Spectator ab Extra*, where sad earnest is hidden beneath a mocking tone. The poets of the Seventeenth Century were particularly apt in the former sort of verse; besides Herrick, we have a number of graceful writers, such as Carew, and later, Prior, whose Ode, *The Merchant to secure his treasure*, is a brilliant specimen of the *Vers de Société*. Carew and Herrick, 'pagan,' as Mr. Gosse calls them, were the poets whose joyous, indolent verses made the Puritan Milton sigh a moment over his more serious task, and query if it were not perhaps better after all, "as others use, To sport with Amaryllis in the shade, Or with the tangles of Neæra's hair." These lines from *Lycidas* admirably define a great part of the sort of poetry treated in this division, as opposed to the 'high seriousness' of Milton's own work.

§ 8. OTHER LYRICAL FORMS.

As a rule, the lyric is of no fixed length or form. But there are certain kinds of lyric which are bound by absolute limits as to quantity and confined to specified forms of verse. Such, for example, is the *Sonnet*. The Sonnet is often reflective, but the prevailing tone is lyric. Its chief advantage lies in the compression of thought in the compass of fourteen lines, in which the changes of rime are also limited. Wyatt, Surrey, Sidney, and Daniel were among the first to use the sonnet, which was introduced from Italy into England. Shakspere's so-called sonnets are not of the strict form, being three 'quatrains' followed by a 'couplet.' The true sonnet has two parts, — the *octave* and *sestette:* in the first eight lines the subject is introduced and expanded; in the last six the conclusion or result is drawn out; but both parts must relate to one main idea. [For further particulars as to form, *cf.* Part III.]

As an outburst of pure feeling, Milton's splendid sonnet *Avenge, O Lord, thy slaughter'd saints* is perhaps the best in our tongue. Wordsworth (*e.g., To Milton*) and Keats (*e.g., On first looking into Chapman's Homer*) are masters of this form. The host of poor sonnets is enormous, the form seems so easy to handle; but the really great sonnets are few. A sonnet must be transcendently good, or it ought not to exist.

Lately we have seen a number of new lyrical forms brought into English by the younger modern school of poets. The *Rondeau*, the *Rondel*, the *Triolet*, the *Ballade*, the *Villanelle*, were invented by French poets of the Fourteenth and the Fifteenth Centuries. They depend, like the sonnet, on arrangement of rimes in a fixed number of verses, and tend to be even more intricate. When handled by a master, however, they are very agreeable, and lend themselves admirably to the purposes of *Vers de Société*. [*Cf.* E. W. Gosse, *Foreign Forms of Verse*, Cornhill Magazine, 1877.]

The *Epigram* is less rigid in form than the above, but it rarely exceeds four lines. The name defines purpose and origin: verses *written on* something,—say with a diamond on a window-pane. An *antithesis* or *pun* is likely to be the base of the epigram. An *Epitaph* is something written on a tombstone, or supposed to be so written. Both epigram and epitaph may be *serious* or *mocking*. Serious is Landor's beautiful quatrain:—

"I strove with none, for none was worth my strife;
Nature I loved, and next to Nature, Art;
I warmed both hands before the fire of life—
It sinks, and I am ready to depart."

Mocking is Rochester's combined epigram and (quasi) epitaph on Charles II.:—

"Here lies our sovereign lord the king,
Whose word no man relies on:
Who never said a foolish thing
Nor ever did a wise one."

A *Cenotaph* may be inscribed with verses as if it were the actual tomb;—or else the fact may be told, as in those fine verses of Tennyson in Westminster Abbey on Sir John Franklin: "Not here! the white north holds thy bones," etc.

§ 9. LYRICAL BALLAD.

We use this term, not in the sense of Wordsworth's Lyrical Ballads, but to indicate the folk-song, or ballad, that is lyrical rather than historical. Even the lyrical folk-song, like other forms of poetry, can be detected slipping back into the domain of religious rites and ceremonies. Thus we find *rimed charms*— verses sung to expel sickness, drought, tempest, etc. These were once parts of public worship; Christianity banned them into all out-of-the-way corners, village customs, peasants' firesides, etc. They generally had an *epic* beginning, telling how the sickness was caused; this was followed by the regular lyric, meant either to curse or to flatter the evil out of the possessed subject. The Indian "Medicine-man" with his charms [*cf.* etymology of *charm*] is a case in point.

But the pure lyric was early developed among the people. Thus the *Cuckoo Song*, quoted above [*cf.* § 4] is a joyous folk-song to the spring. — Prefixed to a song of the Thirteenth Century is a little refrain to be sung after each stanza. This refrain is not by the author of the song, but must have then been an old catch, sung by the peasants time out of mind:—

> "Blow, northerne wynd,
> Send thou me my swetyng.
> Blow, northerne wynd. blow. blow. blow!"

Still, the lyric is essentially *individual*. We cannot claim, even for the so-called folk-lyric, or ballad, that spontaneous growth in the popular heart that we claimed for the epic folk-song. In nearly all cases we must assume individual authorship. So that the lyrical ballad is different from the lyrics we have just examined only in so far as the former catches a simple and popular tone. Thus, in the verses —

> "O waly waly, but love be bonny
> A little time while it is new;
> But when 'tis auld it waxeth cauld
> And fades awa' like morning dew"—

we can very plainly hear this simple, popular tone; whereas in Byron's famous lines —

> "My days are in the yellow leaf;
> The flowers and fruits of love are gone;
> The worm, the canker, and the grief
> Are mine alone"—

we recognize plainly the individual tone, though the sentiment is the same. And yet it is not impossible to put into a lyric that popular and simple beauty, as it is to put into an imitated ballad the sentiment of a whole people. Burns has caught the Scotch 'flavor,' if we may use such a term; and his best poems are truly national, truly popular. As soon as he leaves his native dialect he is flat, and full of uninteresting mannerisms. The lyrical ballad is judged by its *simplicity* and *sincerity;* in these qualities Burns and Wordsworth excel, though in very different ways. According to a German critic (Carriere), "in lyric poetry the highest result is reached when a great poet sings in the popular tone." This, certainly, is true of Burns. — as it is of Goethe.

CHAPTER III. — DRAMATIC POETRY.

The Epic deals with the *past*, the Lyric with the *present*. The Drama unites the two conditions, and gives us *the past in the present*. Events are the epic basis; but they unroll themselves before our eyes. We have the epic *objectivity* — *i.e.*, the sinking of the author's own thought and feeling in the work itself — in the lifelike course of events; we have lyric fire in the different *characters*. What lyric can match, for example, Hamlet's beautiful tribute to friendship [*Ham.* III. 2]; what love-songs compare with the passion of the exquisite little *Tagelied*, in *Romeo and Juliet* [III. 5] where the lovers part at daybreak? What reflective lyric strikes a deeper note than Hamlet's famous soliloquy on death? — A drama, then, may be called *an epic whole made up of lyric parts*. Aristotle's definition is *imitated action;* which is about the same thing. The lyric element in the drama makes it more rapid, more tumultuous than the epic, which, at its best, holds an even and stately pace.

§ 1. BEGINNINGS OF THE DRAMA.

The drama is no exception to the rule concerning the origin of poetry; it begins in religious rites. We shall here confine ourselves to the modern drama, particularly the English, and trace its beginnings and development up to the time of Shakspere. [For a wider survey of the drama in general, see Ward's article "Drama" in the *Encyclopædia Britannica;* for the

English, see the same author's *English Dramatic Literature.*]

The Greek drama began in the Dionysian feasts; our modern drama in the rites of the early Christian church. These were elaborate and impressive. By certain ceremonies — such as the Mass — effort was made to change the past history of the church into a present fact. The epic part, as Ward points out, was the reading of the Scripture narrative; the lyric was the singing; to these was added the dramatic. On certain church festivals, the clergy were wont to bring in actual form before the people the events which the day commemorated; *e.g.*, the marriage at Cana. At first the dialogue was in Latin; but little by little the speech of the folk was brought in. "The French mystery of *La Resurrection* (Twelfth Century) is regarded as the first religious drama in the vulgar tongue." Thus arose the so-called *Mysteries* and *Miracle-Plays*. (The name should be *mistery*, as it is a corruption of *ministerium*.) Later than these — which were dramatic representations either of the Gospel narrative or of legends of the church — came the *Moralities*, where virtues, vices, and other allegorical figures appeared in appropriate costume.

The only drama which our race knew before the Norman Conquest was of a rude kind. Until then, the old dialogues between Summer and Winter, and kindred attempts at dramatic representation, were all that English literature could boast in that direction. But when the churchmen brought in the Sacred Drama, there soon arose a class of secular performers. These secular performers were the successors to such as may have presented the rude drama of heathen origin. True, a dialogue is not a drama; but there was enough action in some of the dialogues to justify, despite Mr. Ward's assertion, the adjective 'dramatic,' as applied, *e.g.*, to *The Strife between Summer and Winter*, preserved in German folk-song. Compare, further, two fine English dialogue-ballads: *Lord Randal* and *Edward, Edward*. They are throughout in dialogue. There is no narrative verse. The two speakers bring out the whole story; though of course they do not *act* a story. Gervinus has shown the popular character of the English drama, and its close connection with the ballad. We know how much dialogue there is in many of our old narrative ballads: *e.g.*, *Sir Patrick Spens;* and there are dialogues in Anglo-Saxon poetry. Ward's distinction is far too sharp to hold good, when he says: "Before the Norman Conquest there are no signs in our own literature of any impulse towards the dramatic form."[1]

The drama meets a popular craving; it gratifies that wish felt by all men to see their own life, its hopes and fears, pictured in the acts and life of another. So the rude miracle-plays took a human and even local coloring. The minor characters now and then bore English names; there were English oaths, — rough, popular wit, — drastic acting: — all these means were used to bring the play home to men's "business and bosoms." Shakspere's clown, as well as the traditional 'fool' of our comedies to-day, goes back in direct line to the 'Vice,' whose business it was to plague and worry Satan in every conceivable way. The drama, so devel-

---

[1] Vol. I. p. 6, *Hist. Eng. Dram. Lit.*

oped, could not possibly continue to be a mere part of the church ceremonies. It attained an individual existence, and grew to be a department of literature.

The elements of this new drama were all present in these old Miracles and Moralities — but sadly confused, and jostling each other in a now intolerable fashion. Tragedy and Comedy were not sharply defined. "*The Murder of Abel*" is in subject a tragedy; half the action, even in the critical part, is roughest horse-play. The miracle of "*Noah's Flood*," however, was nearly all comedy: the patriarch flogs his wife because she will not go into the ark. Finally, there is the drama often called Reconciliation-Drama, because a *threatened danger* is suddenly and unexpectedly removed. Of this class was the play "*Abraham and Isaac.*"

If imitated human action alone made a drama, a prize-fight would come under that head. But the mind of the spectator craves more: he demands that the actors shall be *individuals of a sharply marked character*. The action and the characters are the two great elements of the drama. In the best plays there must be a thorough blending of the two; the action must at once shape and be shaped by the characters that take part in it. A distinction is usually made between the classical and the modern drama in this respect: in the former, we see a gigantic action, a manifestation of fate, dragging along with it characters whose struggling is in vain; in the latter, the individual characters are the central interest, and the action seems more the result than the cause of the characters. Shakspere alone unites the advantages of ancient and modern drama. — In the old plays from which the Elizabethan drama sprang, there was a rude but marked distinction on the above principle: where the action took precedence, the play was called a *Mystery* or a *Miracle;* when the characters attracted the main interest, the result was the so-called *Morality* or *Moral Play.*

§ 2. MIRACLE-PLAYS AND MYSTERIES.

The highest form of the drama, the tragedy, is where human will and human action come in conflict with a higher power. Rough as they were, the Miracle-Plays fulfilled the demands of such a drama; for there were both elements — human action and divine interposition. The fault was that this latter element was enormously exaggerated, and the only way to retain human interest was to introduce the low comedy noticed above. Still, there were many human attributes. The biblical heroes were human enough, and the interest of the spectators was easily aroused by the rude pathos of Abel's death, or by the edifying spectacle of a quarrel between man and wife. Scenery, too, was attempted; and the costumes were regulated by dramatic consistency [*cf.* the word *properties*]. There are three well-known collections of these plays: the Towneley, the Chester, and the Coventry collections. From various sources we compile the following brief notice of the plays — their manner and matter.

Each play was called a "pageant"; such was the name of the vehicle on which the play was exhibited (Ward). In Rogers' Account of the Chester Plays, written about the end of the Sixteenth Century, we are told that "every company had his pageant, which pageants were a high scaffold with two rooms, a higher and a lower, upon four wheels. In the lower they apparelled themselves, and in the higher room they played, being all open on the top, that all beholders might hear and see them. The places where they played them was (*sic*) in every street. They began first at the Abbey gates, and when the first pageant was played, it was wheeled to the high cross before the Mayor, and so to every street." As to costumes, the good souls wore white; the condemned, black ("Black is the badge of hell" says the king in *Love's Labour's Lost*); and the angels wore "gold skins and wings." The sacred personages had golden beards and hair. Hell-torments were represented with considerable effect; and mechanical devices were known — as where the cherry-tree miraculously bends down its branches at the command of Mary.

As to the contents, actual stories from the Bible, or else legends of the church, were the common material to be dramatized. The action was not well knit together into a harmonious whole; but tended to be a mere series of situations. Thus in the murder of Abel, the tragedy does not from its central point spread over the play, in anticipation and result, but is confined to the scene where Abel is killed. Cain and his ploughboy indulge in comic dialogue after the murder; there is allusion to the constable; and the play ends with a travesty of an English royal proclamation. The *Harrowing of Hell* was one of the earliest subjects treated by the Miracle-Plays, — the well-known story, founded on the false gospel of Nicodemus, how Christ went down to hell, subdued it (harrow = harry), and released the patriarchs. The metre of these plays is rough; and is often full of the old alliterations: *e.g.*, the opening passage of Parfre's *Murder of the Innocents* — for Candlemas Day —

> "Above all *k*ynges under the *c*lowdys *c*ristall,
> *R*oyally I *r*eign in *w*elthe without *w*oo,
> Of *p*lesaunt *p*rosperytie I lakke non at all;
> *F*ortune I *f*ynde, that she is not my *f*oo.
> I am kyng Herowd" ——, etc.

These rude plays utterly failed to satisfy the higher dramatic laws. As moving situations, as a patchwork of bald conversation, stiff action and occasional pathetic elements, they show a beginning, — but nothing more. The most wonderful fact in Elizabethan literature is the sudden leap made by the drama from such depths to the height of *Edward II.*, of *Lear* and of *Hamlet*. The miracle-plays satisfied only the rudest dramatic instinct. Higher in every way was the effort made by the so-called Moralities — a second step toward the finished drama of Shakspere. — The Mysteries flourished chiefly from the Thirteenth to the Sixteenth Century, and were mostly presented by the different guilds or trading-companies.

§ 3. MORAL PLAYS, OR MORALITIES.

What the didactic allegory is to the epic, so is the morality to the drama. There is a decided attempt to portray *character* and to enforce a moral. But we find the same defect as in the Miracle-Plays. There we saw that bald representation of events satisfied the demand for action; we look in vain for the finer art of a connected plot, a thread of purpose running through all the sayings and doings of the play. So, too, here; instead of *a person with a character*, there is simply an *abstract character* or *quality*. Take the well-known Morality called *Every Man*.

Every Man is one of the best of the Moral Plays. It is purely didactic, and shows, as the messenger or Prologue announces, —

> " how transitory we be all daye.
> Her shall you se how Felaweship and Jolyté,
> Bothe Strengthe, Pleasure and Beauté,
> Will fade from the as floure in maye;
> For ye shall here how our heven kynge
> Calleth every-man to a generall rekenynge."

Then God appears, calls "Dethe," and bids him go summon Every-man to make his pilgrimage and bring with him his 'reckoning'—*i.e.*, of good and evil deeds, etc. Every-man is fain to evade this command, but cannot. Fellowship, called to help, promises to do anything and go anywhere; but when he learns what the journey is, utterly refuses. Kindred, likewise, will not venture on such an expedition. "Goodes" is summoned; but he lies in chests and bags and cannot stir. Every-man is desperate, but bethinks himself of "Good-dedes." Good-deeds lies 'colde in the grounde' on account of Every-man's sins, and cannot move; but Good-deeds' sister, Knowledge, goes with Every-man to that holy man Confession, who dwells in the 'hous of salvacyon'; Every-man confesses his sins, does penance, and so releases Good-deeds, who can now 'walke and go.' Discretion, Beauty, Strength, are called together, and also Five-wits. But they all refuse to go with Every-man, although they give good advice enough; for Beauty and the others run as fast as they can when they see Every-man begin to fail in death. Good-deeds, however, remains; Knowledge tarries till the last moment. Every-man, after commending his soul to God, dies (on the stage); and there is an epilogue which further enforces the very palpable moral.[1]

Not so good is the Moral Play *Lusty Juventus*, which attacks the church. Among the characters are *Abhominable Livyng*, *God's Mercyful Promises*, and the like. It was written under Edward VI., for whom *Good Councel* makes a prayer at the end of the play.

The Moralities are an advance on the Miracles; they humanize the characters to a considerable degree, and the nature of the play makes consistency of action more imperative than in the loose progress of a Mystery, where a serious character may suddenly wax comic. The development of the drama was now rapid: action and character were to be woven together and made into a dramatic unity. A step in this direction is a sort of *historical morality* called *King John*. It has been attributed to Bishop Bale. King John is asked by the widow England to help her against her oppressors. Other characters are Sedition, Clergy, etc., but it is important to note that now and then a real name is used instead of an abstraction. Thus, Sedition becomes Stephen Langton. Compared with Shakspere's play of the same name, *King John* is crude to the last degree. But it is an advance from the older plays. There is still a yawning chasm between it and the Elizabethan drama; to bridge this chasm, materials were soon supplied. Chief of these are the *foreign impulses and influences* and the *Interlude*.

[1] For the subject and sources of this play, see an interesting treatise, *Every-Man, Homulus und Hekastos*, by Carl Goedeke, Hanover, 1865.

§ 4. FOREIGN MODELS.

The revival of learning found a hearty welcome in England. Greek and Latin were carefully studied; and under Henry VIII., men like Erasmus, Colet and Sir Thomas More made the "new learning" famous. The *Latin plays of Plautus and Terence*, — comedies, — and the *tragedies of Seneca*, were studied, translated, and even acted in the original before the universities. The *Italian imitations* of these plays were likewise read with interest. The Mysteries and Moralities ceased to please. A better taste arose. General history was eagerly studied. People demanded that the drama should treat of human life in a concrete way. But not only *subject-matter*, — the *form and style* of the drama were greatly influenced by the study of foreign models.

Here, then, was a public with its insipid miracle plays; a learned class with its foreign dramas. Neither was national. But working mightily in both classes was the strong intellectual life that rose with the English national spirit and reached its height under Elizabeth. The task was to find a common ground for the learned and the popular taste. This was found in the *Interlude*.

§ 5. THE INTERLUDE.

John Heywood was the genius of the Interlude. It was a play performed, as its name implies, in the intervals of feasts or other entertainments. It was of a light character. Take, for example, Heywood's *Four P's*. A *palmer*, a *pardoner*, and a *'pothecary* meet and, after some dialogue, contend who is the greatest liar of the three. The *pedler* is judge. Each tells his test-tale;

the 'pothecary wins the prize, for he says he has seen hosts of women, but never one out of patience. Here at last are actual human characters, with a thoroughly human action.

This is not very high comedy, it is true; but it is a great advance upon the fleshless abstractions of the moralities, from which the comedy is really descended. Further interludes of later origin are such as Shakspere introduces in *The Tempest, Love's Labour's Lost* and *Midsummer Night's Dream.* Some of these interludes are called "Masques" or Masks. The Mask proper was an Italian importation, brought over early in Henry VIII.'s reign. Men and women, disguised as shepherds, shepherdesses, and the like, went through a certain amount of acting, mixed with a great deal of dancing. Often classic deities were represented. The Mask as developed by Ben Jonson became very elaborate. The greatest English Mask is, of course, Milton's *Comus.*

These Interludes and Masks raised the popular taste. Now that the public demanded such work, the playwright could avail himself of classical models, and put into English settings the jewels of Seneca and Plautus. *The dividing lines of tragedy and comedy were now sharply drawn.* Tragedy appears in its first English guise in the play (about 1562) by Thomas Norton and Lord Buckhurst, called *Gorboduc* or *Ferrex and Porrex.* The characters are human, the interest human. The plot is from the (mythical) history of Britain. The play resembles the old miracles in its rough action, its love of violence and blood; it differs from them in its carefully drawn and consistent plot, its division into acts, its more elaborate form. As in Greek plays, the murders are here announced by a messenger. There is a dumb-show prefixed to each act, showing what is to follow; and at the end of each act is a chorus. (For the dumb-show, compare the play in Hamlet, where the poison is poured into the ear of the player-king.) — *Gorboduc* is an imitation of Seneca. Plautus's well-known comedy of "The Braggart Soldier" (*Miles Gloriosus*) is imitated in the *First English Comedy*, entitled *Ralph Roister-Doister*, written by Nicholas Udall, of Eton, about 1550. But the names, scenes, etc., are all English. There is an elaborate plot and spirited action. A pretty song is woven into the play, — forerunner of those exquisite lyrics that sparkle in the drama of Shakspere and Fletcher.

We have thus come to the threshold of our national drama. The task before its early artists is plain enough. All the rude remnants of the old plays must be worked out; simplicity, vigorous action, whatever was best in the old must fit itself in the new to a finished art, a sympathetic study of human nature. Marlowe, Shakspere, Fletcher and Jonson tell how this was done.— We can, therefore, now treat the finished drama, its forms and rules.

§ 6. THE DIFFERENT KINDS OF DRAMA.

First, however, a word about certain *general rules* for the drama. The drama is imitated human action. Now, human action is a complex affair; it is by no means the province of a dramatist to imitate any action or series of actions just as they occur in daily life. A confused mass of human action may be subordinately used — as in Schiller's *Wallenstein's Camp*, or a mob-scene, — but it must be a help to a higher purpose. The action is grouped about *a single controlling purpose;* in short, there must be *Unity of Action*. This restriction on the nature of the action is the first of the so-called *Three Unities;* and in the observance of this rule all great dramatists agree. For it is not at all necessary that the action should consist *of one event*, as some have understood the rule. Many events may go together; but each — not necessarily in a conscious way — must have its share in the development of the central dramatic purpose. Nor does unity of action compel a unity of person. Thus the dramatic unity of *King Lear* is not broken by the introduction of Gloster, Edmund and Edgar with their subordinate action. Several heroes are allowable in a play, provided only that they do not so change places or importance that one part of the play differs in spirit and purpose from the other.

The second and third " unities " are by no means of equal importance with the first, nor are they so generally acknowledged. Thus (2) the Unity of *Time*. The structure of the Greek drama was of such a nature as to call for far stricter treatment in this regard than is demanded by the modern drama. But the French critics of Louis XIV.'s time made the classical standard their own, and scoffed at Shakspere as a barbarian because he disregarded the second and third unities. It was Lessing, the great German critic and man of letters, who finally drove the French school from their dictatorship in dramatic composition. True, some observance of the spirit of these rules is to be desired in all dramatists. The strict rule forbade the supposed time of the play to cover more than twenty-four hours. So boldly did the modern drama transgress this rule that in 1578 George Whetstone (in his *Promos and Cassandra*) complained that the playwright "in three hours runs through the world, marries, makes children men, men to conquer kingdoms, murder monsters, and bringeth gods from heaven and fetcheth devils from hell." In the *Winter's Tale* we have some similar liberties. The Greek drama took for its time the central moment of the action; and by narration in dialogue brought out the preceding steps that led up to the main situation. The result is announced by a messenger, — *e.g.*, the death of the protagonist, or chief actor. In other words, the Greek tragedy goes at once to the catastrophe. In the modern drama we begin with the elements of the catastrophe or, if in a comedy, of the entanglement, and let the action and the characters develop under our eyes. The modern play has less intensity, but more human interest.

The third Unity, that of *Place*, demanded that the events should occur in one and the same place. This is what Hamlet (II. 2) calls "scene individable." Undoubtedly this rule sprang from the peculiar construction of the Greek stage, which was not at all adapted to change of scene. But in modern drama the Unity of Place is practically disregarded — except in certain comedies and farces; and Shakspere especially changes his scenes with the greatest freedom. Sir Philip Sidney in his *Defence of Poesie* laughs at this ceaseless shifting of scene and the inadequate stage machinery to help the illusion. The Germans take a middle course, keeping the same scene as long as possible, but changing it when absolutely necessary.

So much for the Three Unities. It is folly to insist on the literal observance of these rules; but it is important to heed their spirit. Every playwright should be regulated by the spirit of unity, first of all in *action*, but also to some extent in time and place.

Further rules are laid down for the drama, — *e.g.*, that *the action should be complete in itself*. It must stand out clearly as a dramatic whole. To make the action complete, there must be, as parts of the organic whole, *causes, development* of these causes, a *climax*, or height of the action; — then the *consequences* and general *conclusion*. The technical division into *five acts* is simply a convenience, and is taken from the Latin plays; Horace says, *A. P.* 189: *Neve minor neu sit quinto productior actu*. The further division into scenes is more with regard to persons (especially in German and French plays), while the acts regard the action or plot. We may name the real divisions of a play as follows: 1. *The Exposition;* 2. *The Tying of the Knot;* 3. Conclusion, — *The Untying*. Prologue, epilogue, etc., are mostly outside the action of the play; although *cf.* "the prologue in heaven" in *Faust*, and, in another fashion, the prologue to Ben Jonson's *New Inn*. We noted also the *Dumb-Show* in *Gorboduc*.

The Exposition is mostly contained in the first act. The second, third, and sometimes the fourth, develop the action up to a climax. This is what Aristotle calls the tying of the knot. Lastly, in the fifth comes the *denouement*, the untying. Here great skill is required. Says Mr. Ward, "the climax concentrated the interest; the fall must not dissipate it." And here we note that this close or catastrophe *must always be a consequence of the action*.

In tragedy, the conclusion (mostly a *death*) is foreshadowed through the whole play; in comedy, the conclusion (mostly a *wedding*) is a sudden surprise. Thus in *Othello*, we feel that the hero's jealousy must lead to some great evil, and overwhelm him.[1] While, on the other hand, we cannot always call the marriage of heroine with hero something totally unexpected, still we are surprised to find what seemed insuperable barriers to such a consummation suddenly removed.

Again, *the action ought to be probable.* Here belongs the famous dictum: *prefer probable impossibilities to improbable possibilities.* The impossible is permitted if it harmonizes with the action. Thus we may introduce ghosts, fairies, and so on; though in Shakspere's time ghosts were by no means commonly regarded as impossibilities.

Consistency of character and fitness of the actors to the action need not be insisted upon. Here is Shakspere's greatest triumph. Instead of mere types of character like the lady's-maid and valet of French comedy, his men and women are flesh and blood, who do not merely follow a set model, but stand as ideals of their sort: we can say *Romeo* — and a distinct personage leaps before the mind. Emerson has finely said of this wonderful power of Shakspere in creating characters: "What office, or function, or district of man's work has he not remembered? What king has he not taught state? . . . What maiden has not found him finer than her delicacy?

---

[1] The climax and the conclusion must, of course, be held apart. In *Othello* the conclusion is Othello's death; the climax is where he becomes sure of his wife's guilt. "Why did I marry?" he cries in his first doubt; then, with certitude, comes to sheer violence.

What lover has he not outloved? What sage has he not outseen?"—The Greek drama concentrated itself upon the action, and drew its characters in more shadowy outline: they were not so much individuals as Shakspere's men and women were.

Finally, the *surroundings* of the action must be consistent. They need not be chronologically faithful—else *Lear* and *Julius Cæsar* would be condemned; but they must not make a violent contradiction with the general action.

§ 7. TRAGEDY.

Tragedy presents a mortal will at odds with fate. This conflict and the final overthrow of the individual make up a tragic drama. There must be a central character (or there may be more than one,—a group). The motive of this character may be either *mistaken* or *criminal* (*Othello*—*Macbeth*); but the end is in either case tragic.

The effect upon the spectator is, as Aristotle said, to produce in the mind *pity* and *terror;* — sympathy for the victim, fear that a like fate may overtake us. This emotion excites the mind, "purges" it of smaller and unworthy thoughts, and so works a *katharsis*, a purification. It leaves one in "calm of mind, all passion spent."

When all this danger is only apparent, when we see that only every-day blunders, without lasting consequences, are at work, we feel no pity, no terror; we are amused:—it is a *Comedy*.

The name Tragedy is an accident. The Greek drama began with a mere chorus, or dithyrambic refrain, sung at the feasts of Dionysos, and the singers were dressed in goat-skins: hence (probably) tragedy (= "goat-song," from *tragos*, a goat). To such a chorus was added some one who chanted epic poems; this person *acted* more or less, and addressed his chant to the leader of the chorus, who answered singly or with the whole chorus: so, little by little, the tragedy (or drama) was developed. Æschylus and Sophocles added more actors. The modern tragedy is far more complex than the ancient; and there is also a charming trait in Shakspere's tragedies which was unknown to the sterner drama of Greece, — the gleam of hope, of a new dawn, following on the night of ruin and despair. Thus in *Hamlet*, as a German critic has pointed out, we have young Fortinbras, who will doubtless "set right" the times that Hamlet found so "out of joint." So with Richmond in *Richard III.*, with Malcolm in *Macbeth;* in *Romeo and Juliet* it is the reconciliation of the rival houses. And yet the Greeks, too, recognized in their way that a true tragedy always ends in the triumph of the good over the evil. The hero may perish, but his death brings about good in the end. The tragedy purifies emotion, chastens the impulses, teaches men to accept the order of things and to believe that all is for the best: —

> "Men must endure
> Their going hence, even as their coming hither:
> Ripeness is all."

Lowell ably sums up the difference between classical and modern tragedy: "the motive of ancient drama is generally outside of it, while in the modern . . . it is within."

§ 8. IMITATIONS OF THE GREEK TRAGEDY.

The noblest English example of these is Milton's *Samson Agonistes*. The time is limited to twenty-four hours; there is a Chorus; the catastrophe is announced by a messenger. In our day, Swinburne has closely followed a Greek model in his *Atalanta in Calydon*, and in his *Erechtheus* — the latter a splendid piece of work, with elaborate arrangement of the chorus (in Strophe, Antistrophe, and Epode), and a pure and lofty diction.

§ 9. COMEDY.

Tragedy sets forth the triumph of the general over the particular, of law over individuals. In Comedy, it is the individual who triumphs over the complications of life. — But the term "Comedy" needs definition; the above will not explain all the uses of the word.

Dante called his great work a comedy, and simply meant that it was not a tragedy, that it had no *unhappy* ending. *Cf.* Chaucer's use of the word "tragedy." The name Comedy is not absolutely clear as to its origin. Probably it was derived from the songs sung by bands of men who thus celebrated the Dionysian feasts. In these songs, people and customs were held up to ridicule. From the Greek word for such a festal procession or band, we have the name Comedy. A chorus was joined to these single songs, and thus the Greek Comedy was begun. English Comedy, on the other hand, sprang from the Moral Plays, passing first into the Interludes, and also aided by the models of classical as well as modern Italian Comedy, — but especially by Plautus and Terence. These, in their turn, had imitated the later Grecian Comedy.

Comedy takes a cheerful view of things. The sense of *perplexity*, so common in our lives, is rendered sorrowful by tragedy, mirthful by comedy. In one case, tears; in another, laughter, is what "purges" the mind. — In tragedy we hold as doomed and guilty even those who innocently mistake. In comedy we are tender toward human frailty. Falstaff is a coward: as Dowden says, he is "a gross-bodied, self-indulgent old sinner, devoid of moral sense and of self-respect, and yet we cannot part with him."

Comedy lies either in the *characters*, or in the *situation*, or in both. The best is where both are blended in a mellow atmosphere that has no kindred with sorrow, nor yet with uproarious laughter. Such a comedy is found in *As You Like It* or in *Twelfth Night*. — The comedy that relies entirely on situation is called a *Farce*. — English comedy since Shakspere has been handled with great success by Congreve, by Goldsmith, and by Sheridan; but at present seems utterly dead. Most of our modern plays are adapted from the French.

Under Comedy are often included plays which really are not comic, and yet are not tragic, for the ending is happy. *A threatened danger* is at last averted, but not until near the end of the play. This sort is sometimes called *Tragi-Comedy*, which is an absurd name. Shakspere and Fletcher's *Two Noble Kinsmen* has an ending at once sorrowful and happy: one hero is killed, the other is finally married to the heroine. The Germans call the drama which is neither tragedy nor comedy *Versöhnungsdrama*, the reconciling drama; this we consider below. — Comic scenes are often woven into tragedy; and, *vice versa*, though rarely, tragedy is found in some one scene of a comedy. But we shall find that such a mixture is successful only when some particular end of the plot is to be served.

Comedy is the grand field for "poetical justice." The miser is tricked, caught in his own snare; the proud is brought low; honest merit is crowned; true love — though it never runs smoothly — comes to a happy union; and even the fool is made happy. In fact, Shakspere's clowns often teach us the lesson that a fool's wisdom is about as near the mark as the world's wisdom. In *Lear*, this is a tragic and bitter lesson; but in *As You Like It*, we acknowledge the truth of it in a laugh. — The comedy is the tragedy *with all elements of danger removed*. We feel this from the beginning; we do not weep, but laugh. Like the tragedy, therefore, comedy has its exposition, development, climax, and conclusion. Instead of death and ruin which close the tragedy, we have in the comedy, as the curtain falls, the group of characters all united and happy. Even the villain, after he has been soundly punished for his wickedness, often turns over a new leaf, and announces resolutions of prodigious virtue.

As to the *form*, tragedy is fond of verse; — comedy inclines to prose. The tragedy is full of resounding lines, is further removed from the ways of real life, — uses more elaborate diction, figures and general construction. The comedy — notably in Congreve, Goldsmith and Sheridan — tends to be *brilliant*, especially in the direction of rapid and sparkling dialogue. There is also much of this word-fencing in Shakspere.

§ 10. RECONCILING-DRAMA.

The name Tragi-Comedy is, as we said, absurd. No play can be at once tragedy and comedy. To be sure, life is made up of the two elements, and the drama is a copy of life; but, as Lessing pointed out, only Infinity could be spectator of this infinite variety, and man is bound to take a definite point of view — either the comic or the tragic. Dryden (*Essay on Dramatic Poetry*) says sharply but truthfully: "There is no theatre in the world has anything so absurd as the English Tragi-comedy. . . here a course of mirth, there another of sadness and passion, and a third of honor and a duel: thus in two hours and a half we run through all the fits of Bedlam." And he goes on to say that mirth, the result of comedy, is incompatible with compassion, the end of tragedy: the two results destroy each other. — Dryden, in principle, is perfectly right. And we shall find, in spite of a superficial mingling of comic and tragic in some of Shakspere's plays, that each play has a uniform spirit and tendency running through every scene. Thus in *Hamlet*, the clown's joking by the grave awakens no real mirth: it deepens the sense of tragedy.

But there is nevertheless a third sort of drama. It is not made up of tragic and comic elements, but it is a *harmony*, a reconciling of the two. The tragic conflict is softened to a triumph of earnest will over heavy obstacles; the wantonness and wilfulness of comedy are dignified into serious purpose. So *Henry V.* is made by Shakspere to represent a serious and lofty purpose that gains its object; but the cheerfulness of life is also admitted. Another example is Goethe's

Iphigenie. Carriere further names, under this head, *The Merchant of Venice, Cymbeline,* and *Measure for Measure.* In these a threatened danger is averted, partly through Providence, partly through the energy of the characters themselves. In these plays, too, we have some of Shakspere's noblest women put in the forefront of the action : — Portia, Imogen and Isabella. — With Goethe's *Faust,* finally, we reach the *subjective drama.* It is the development of a human soul: not tragedy, not comedy, — but the subjective drama, teaching the lesson of incessant individual struggle to higher stages of life and action, — "evermore to strive towards the highest existence."[1] This poem comes as near as a poem well can to perfect reconciliation of tragedy and comedy: it is a drama of the human soul wrestling with all the problems of life.

§ 11. OTHER FORMS OF THE DRAMA.

Not strictly dramatic, but tending in that direction are such forms of poetry as the *Idyll.* The Idyll is mainly literary — for reading, not for acting. It is originally a dialogue of shepherd and shepherdess, or of similar characters, and has a strong epic flavor [*cf.* I. § 5]. A charming example of the dramatic Idyll in its highest form is the famous Fifteenth Idyll of Theocritus. Then there are *Eclogues* — much like the last, except that Eclogues are confined to shepherds and their friends, while the Idyll just noted had for characters a couple of city dames, and contained a song and abundant action. The *Eclogue* is quiet and rural. In English we have Spenser's *Shepherd's Calender.*

---

[1] "Zum höchsten Daseyn immerfort zu streben." *Faust,* II. Act I.

Finally, there arose a regular *Pastoral Drama*, whose origin "was purely literary." Famous as models of this sort were Tasso's *Aminta* and Guarini's *Pastor Fido*. Love and Allegory were the main ingredients. In England there were two branches:—the *Mask* (already noticed) and the regular Pastoral Drama, of which the best examples are Fletcher's *Faithful Shepherdess* and Ben Jonson's *Sad Shepherd* (fragmentary). The splendid Mask of *Comus* soars above its fellows by reason not only of its exquisite versification and diction, but also of its lofty moral tone. Properly speaking, this sort of poetry should be only a dance-song with masks. But the masks give a *character* to each dancer—he must sing, or speak, in conformity with this character—and so comes the dramatic element.

Nowadays this Pastoral Drama is unknown. But *combined with music* it is still common enough. We mean, of course, *The Opera*. The opera, says Schlegel, is "the anarchy of the arts; since music, dancing and decoration, struggling to outrank one another, make up [its] real character." Recently, Wagner has tried to reconcile the best poetry—both in subject and treatment—with the best music. But in general the opera has no literary merit.

We need not consider at length the minor forms of dramatic poetry. Such are the *Tagelieder* (Provencal, *Alba*) or *Daybreak-Songs* of parting lovers, very popular among the troubadours and certain German Minnesänger:—for example, the bold figures and masterly diction of Wolfram. A specimen in English is the parting scene of *Romeo and Juliet*, III. 5. Similar is the *Serenade*, where lover and mistress sing alternate stanzas: there is a pretty specimen by Sir P. Sidney. With more epic treatment, the same dramatic form is shown in R. Browning's *In a Gondola*.

Lastly, we have what may be termed *Mock-Tragedy*. All dramatic forms are used, but in broad burlesque. Carey and Fielding mocked the stilted tragic style of Lee and others in two amusing plays;—the title of Fielding's is " *The Tragedy of Tragedies,* or the Life and Death of Tom Thumb the Great. With the Annotations of H. Scriblerus Secundus." It is to be borne in mind that the fact of two persons talking to each other does not constitute a drama, is not even necessarily dramatic in any degree. Hence a dialogue, or exchange of opinions in verse, belongs to the didactic class, and is, as a rule, not even poetry (*cf.* Chap. I. § 4).

§ 12. OUTWARD FORM OF THE DRAMA.

We saw that Tragedy tends to verse, and Comedy (though not always) to prose. Further, the drama may avail itself of the *Chorus,* the *Monologue,* or the *Dialogue.* The first, as we saw, is much used in the classic, especially the *Greek* drama. In modern drama it is not common (*cf.* § 8); though here and there met with,—as in *Gorboduc,* where it is imitated from the tragedies of Seneca; or in *Henry V.,* where it is a chorus only in name, and simply helps to explain the action. The Monologue is more common. *Hamlet* is remarkable in this respect. But the great favorite is the Dialogue, which, in its rapid movement and shifting character, lends itself better to the purposes of imitated action than any other form of speech.

Part II.

STYLE.

CHAPTER IV.

POETRY, then, may treat its subject-matter as an Epic, — by narration : or as Lyric, — by addressing it, expressing certain feelings about it : or as Drama, — by letting it speak for itself.

We now ask whether there is anything noteworthy in the words and phrases by which poetry treats its subject; that is, we consider Poetical Style. In the third and last division of this book we shall treat the harmony of sounds, the laws of verse. So that of the three elements of poetry, we have considered the Thought, have yet to consider the Sounds, and now busy ourselves with Words — whether separately or in combination. Prof. Sylvester calls these elements Pneumatic, Rhythmic, and Linguistic.

The study of poetical style must be to some extent a study of words and their origin. Comparative Philology has shown us that all our words go back to descriptions of natural things, to pictures. With the currency of words, their pictorial suggestion wears away. They become mere counters for the game of conversation; thus *caprice* is now for most of us (though *cf. As You Like It*, III. 3. 6) a symbol of an abstract thought, not the picture of a lively animal. So, too, with that old word "daughter": it is now a class-name, whereas once, we are told, it meant "milkmaid." Even words brought into our speech in later times suffer a like process, and lose their color and force. We are not prepared to talk with Herrick about the "candor" of Julia's teeth; or as Bacon does, about the *ejaculations of the eye*, or even with Milton, about "elephants *endorsed* with towers."

Poetry instinctively shrinks from colorless and abstract talk. Prose concerns itself with the *sense* alone; but poetry always seeks a concrete image. Therefore it tries to restore a fresh and suggestive force, a pictorial force, to our speech. It leaves the beaten track of language, turns away from it. Hence the word *trope*, from the Greek *trepo*, — to turn.

Now we may turn away from the ordinary meanings of words, that is, we may use a different *kind* of word, to make up our poetical style; or we may adopt a different *arrangement* of words. In ordinary speech we say directly: "A troop came swinging their broadswords." In poetical, vivid style, we say: "Came a troop with broadswords swinging." There is a turning from the ordinary arrangement, and a consequent vigor of style. Inversions like this are also used in vivid conversation; but no one would ever say in common speech, as Milton says in poetry —

"Erroneous there to wander and forlorn."

Poetical style is therefore distinguished from ordinary speech by the use (1) of a different *kind*, and (2) of a different *arrangement* of words. The two terms which we shall employ to distinguish these two kinds of style are terms not always held apart. But this arbitrary use is convenient. We call the first (a different *kind*), which refers to the meaning, *Trope;* we call the second (different *arrangement*), which refers to the order, *Figure.*

Tropes and Figures make up the bulk of those peculiarities of style which we are wont to call poetic. But there are other means by which we make expression more vivid; and though these latter, like many figures and tropes, are frequently used in an ordinary prose style, still they must be briefly mentioned as aids to poetic language. Thus instead of the *variation* from ordinary expressions, we may have *additions.* Familiar are the "poetic" adjectives and adverbs. As a rule, an abundance of adjectives means poverty of imagination. But often an adjective may "connote" so much as to make a positive addition to the vividness which is the object of poetry. When Marlowe speaks of "*shallow* rivers by whose falls Melodious birds sing madrigals," the imagination registers a gain. "Shallow" suggests clearness, murmurs, ripples, etc. So, too, Shakspere's "*multitudinous* sea." Springing from the same intense and abiding wish of poetry to avoid the commonplace, the cold, the abstract, is the use of *Epithets* (*cf.* below § 1, under *Kenning*). The epic cannot mention even a hero's name without attaching to it a concrete notion: it is "crest-tossing Hector," "swift-footed Achilles." From this to trope is only a step; we next make an object more vivid, more individual, by the aid of another object (*cf.* below, *Metaphor*). The limit of this process is reached, when, instead of a rapid confusion of one object with another, the poet places them both before our eyes and thus makes the original thing compared as individual and important as possible (*Simile*). [An attempt to explain the superiority of poetic style to prose style will be found in § IV. of H. Spencer's *Philosophy of Style.*]

§ 1. HISTORICAL SKETCH.

Professor Heinzel[1] has shown that many traits of poetical style are common to the Indian Vedas and our own early Germanic song. We consider briefly some of the prominent traits. First, there is the *love of repetition*. This affects words (subject or object) and phrases. In the Vedas: "now will I sing Indra's hero-deeds, that *the lightning-hurler* has done." Indra is repeated under another name — a descriptive name. Something like this is Lear's —

>"I do not bid the *thunder-bearer* shoot,
> Nor tell tales of thee to *high-judging Jove.*"
>
> Act II. Sc. 4.

Look at *Beowulf*, and we have a similar figure; as in 3111 ff. : —

>"Then straightway bade   the son of Wîhstân,
> the man battle-keen   many of the heroes,
> of the house-owners,   that they hither should bring
> from far the bale-wood,   the folk-shielders."

In prose: "Wîhstân's son, the battle-keen man, bade many of the heroes, the house-owners, that they, the folk-shielders, should bring funeral-wood." The result of this repetition in Anglo-Saxon poetry is to give a restless, forward-and-back motion to it, so that, as has

---

[1] Ueber den Stil der altgermanischen Poesie, Strasburg, 1875.

been said, we seem to be very active, but do not move forward. This is in strong contrast to the quiet movement of the Greek epic.

Sometimes this "Variation" is applied to a whole clause. Thus *Beowulf*, 48 ff. : —

>   "They let the wave bear him,
> they gave him to ocean;   grave was their heart,
> mournful their mood."

But there are also tropes in the stricter sense of the word. Our oldest poetry has almost no *formal comparisons* or *similes* (*cf.* below). It had no time to turn to a quite foreign object and describe it, leaving, meanwhile, the matter in hand, as the Homeric poems are so fond of doing. But our poetry makes up for this lack by its profusion in *Epithets*, or characteristics. For the thing itself is substituted a characteristic of the thing. This trope is often called by its Norse name, *Kenning*. Thus the sea was the "whale's bath," the "water-street," the "path of the swan," the "foamy fields," the "wave-battle," and so on. Arrows are "battle-adders." See too the above extracts from *Beowulf*. A wife is prettily called "the weaver of peace," for marriage often put a stop to feuds and wars.

It is to be noted that the Anglo-Saxon trope was confined to a few words. It did not take long flights. Extended metaphorical phrases are unknown. A short, vivid epithet, — often several such, not at all harmoniously joined, — much repetition, variation, ceaseless forward-and-back : such are the chief characteristics. Speaking of a sword, the poet tells us "the battle-gleam was unwilling to bite." "Battle-gleam" is a vivid trope for literal "sword"; but by the time the poet reaches his verb, he has forgotten his noun, and does not stop to ask how a "gleam" can "bite," but uses another vivid word simply with regard to the common (*cf.* below) personification of weapons. Here lie at once the merit and the defect of our old poetical style. There is also something of this haste in *Hebrew* poetry.

It is a long journey from the style of those poets who sang of their Germanic heroes to the finish and brilliancy of a modern singer who can not only "take all knowledge for his province," but also use a hundred smooth roads through it. The style of *Beowulf* differs from the style of Tennyson just as a prairie of last century differs from the wheat-field of to-day. The enormous change is due chiefly to the influence of the Greek and Latin classics, in which flourished every sort of trope and figure. Modern literature is essentially "Gothic"—*i.e.* Germanic; but its style of expression is overwhelmingly classical in all external qualities. A writer in one of our journals recently remarked that the history of the development of modern poetical style remains to be written. It is here our business simply to treat that style as we find it in our best poets.

§ 2. TROPES.

This turning out of the beaten track of language is confined to the meaning, and does not concern the form and order of words. The poet wishes to put in a vivid, palpable way some thought or idea which he has in his mind. To express this vividly and at the same time beautifully,—for beauty, harmony, is the object of all art,—he chooses some picture that shall at once interpret the thought and also in itself satisfy our instinct for beauty. Instead of saying that a pleasant idea comes without labor into his mind, the poet turns aside from these colorless words and gives us a picture:—

> "There *flutters* up a *happy* thought,
> *Self-balanced* on a *joyous wing.*"

Or take the following stanza of Whittier's *Ichabod*, and see how, in his intense feeling, the poet uses the vivid trope rather than the literal symbol of thought:—

> "O dumb be passion's stormy rage,
> When he who might
> Have lighted up and led his age,
> Falls back in night."

. That is, it is best to endure in silence the sorrow and shame that one feels when a great man betrays his trust. Even in this prose rendering, we slip into a trope — but it is not vivid and concrete, as in the poem. The more intense, the more true to nature a concrete trope is, the stronger its poetical effect. Thus Dante, *Inferno*, 33,—"I did not weep, *I was so turned to stone within.*" The terrible fidelity of this trope is what gives it force. A moment's reflection will show how this instinct runs through all speech. "Hard" or "soft" heart; "sweet" disposition — and so on; — are tropes that are no longer thought of as tropes. In this way, all language has its poetical elements; and it has been said that every word was at its beginning a poem. Brush off the dust of common use, and the poetry of any word whose etymology we know will at once flash out. Poetry uses tropes *consciously*, *boldly*, and *systematically;* restores, as far as it can, color and freshness to language, and vividness to expression. The rich array of pictures satisfies the intellectual eye, just as the harmony and music of metre satisfy the ear. When these combine in interpreting a noble or beautiful idea, we have poetry. Poetical style, poetical language, under the control of metrical law, is therefore the material in which the poet expresses himself. It is not a mere *ornament*. It is the material — useless without a vivifying idea, but none the less necessary to that idea. This is why we lay such stress on the *imagination* as chief gift of the poet. He puts thought into images or pictures.

The Trope is a substitution of one thing for another, on the basis

   A. Of RESEMBLANCE; which may be
      1. ASSUMED.
      2. IMPLIED.
      3. STATED, —
         a. Stated *positively*.
         b.   "   *negatively*.
         c.   "   *in degrees of comparison*.
   B. Of CONNEXION; which may be
      1. LOGICAL.
      2. MATHEMATICAL.
   C. Of CONTRAST.

§ 3. THE METAPHOR.

The trope based on likeness or resemblance is extremely common. Where this likeness is *assumed*, and the picture or comparison is put directly in place of the thing itself, we have what is commonly known as the *metaphor*. We do not state the resemblance of x to y; we simply assume it, and give x in terms of y. Hence metaphor, from the Greek word meaning "transfer." All speech, as we saw, is based on metaphor. It is the first of all tropes. — It is important to remember that in the metaphor the comparison and thing compared *are not both named*, but only the former. When both are named, we have either the implied or the stated *simile*.

The metaphor may deal with *objects*; — may give one in terms of another, and so gain in vividness of expression. Instead of literal "sun," Shakspere says "the eye of heaven"; the likeness of the heavens to a human countenance, the sun to a human eye, is first assumed, and then the more vivid expression is used for the literal. So in *Merch. of Ven.* the stars are called "blessed candles of the night." Further: "a *forest* huge of spears" (Milton); "the *surge* of swords" (Swinburne); "Each in his narrow *cell* for ever laid" (Gray).

The metaphor may deal with a *process* or a *situation*. In Keats' *Eve of St. Agnes*, the taper's "little smoke in pallid moonshine *died*." "Died" is far more vivid than "went out." This sort of metaphor is very common in descriptive and narrative poetry. Milton's Satan "throws his swift flight in many an aery wheel"; the gates of Hell do not simply give a jarring noise, but "grate harsh thunder." In description of nature, *personification* (see below) plays a very important part; but metaphor is used in abundance. Thus the dawn, sunset, etc., have given rise to a number of metaphors, —

" . . . the golden Orientall gate
Of greatest heaven gan to open faire." — Spenser.

Wordsworth makes the sun "bathe the world in light." Moonlight is "silver"; rays of light — as in Shelley's *Skylark* — are "arrows."

The commonest metaphors, however, are where *physical processes in man* are likened to those of *the outer world*. This class is common in the drama and in lyric poetry. "The tackle of my heart," cries King John, "is crack'd and burnt." Wordsworth says:—

> "The good die first,
> And they whose hearts are dry as summer's dust
> *Burn to the socket.*"

Macbeth laments that his

> " May of life
> Is fallen into the sear and yellow leaf;"

and in *Lear* Kent says: "I have years *on my back* forty-eight." Shakspere's famous passage about sleep (*Macb.* II. 2) has a number of metaphors, combined in the figure of Variation, already described as common in our old poetry. *Cf.* further his beautiful Sonnet (73) "That time of year thou mayst in me behold."

Again, *Mental Processes* may be so treated. Thus for "royal anger and ambition," we have the metaphor in *King John*:—

> "Ha, majesty, how high thy glory towers,
> When the rich blood of kings is set on fire."

Or *Macb.* v. 3 :—

> "Canst thou not minister to a mind diseased;
> Pluck from the memory a rooted sorrow;
> Raze out the written troubles of the brain;
> And, with some sweet, oblivious antidote,
> Cleanse the stuff'd bosom of that perilous stuff
> Which weighs upon the heart?"

To use the processes of the outer world to describe our feelings; to attribute to natural objects a personality like our own:—these are the chief factors of poetical style. The latter is known as *personification*, and though a metaphor, deserves separate treatment.

In like manner with the above metaphors, we may render *abstract* by *concrete*. This is *unconsciously* done whenever we speak of abstract ideas, for they can be expressed only by concrete words: such a case is the word *attention*, which passes as abstract, but really means a *stretching toward*. Or we may do it *half consciously*, as in the expressions "deep thought," "cool determination." But in poetry we do it *consciously*, as in the following:—

"The very head and front of my offending."—*Othello*.

"Shake patiently my great affliction off."—*Lear*.

"Mine eternal jewel (*i.e.* his *soul*)
Given unto the common enemy of man."—*Macbeth*.

Sometimes we express an abstract term by another such term, but fresher, less used. Thus, instead of saying "O ruined man!" we may say (*Lear*) "O ruined *piece of nature!*" So Shakspere in his 87th sonnet, instead of the common terms "sympathy," "claims of affection," puts it all in legal phrase:—"the charter of thy worth," "bonds," "patent," and so on. Tennyson asks sleep if it have "such *credit* with the soul" as to make present the past.

Concrete expressed by abstract is a rare metaphor There are some classical imitations. Gray says:—

"Now the rich stream of music winds along, . . .
. . . Through verdant vales and Ceres' golden *reign*."

He means the fields over which Ceres' reign extends. Milton calls Scipio "the height of Rome" (*Par. Lost*, 9. 43).

In the old poem of *Exodus*, wrongly attributed to Cædmon, we have a strikingly bold use of this metaphor. Speaking of the Red Sea in storm, after the drowning of the Egyptians, the poet says: "*the mightiest of sea-deaths* lash'd the sky." That is, "the sea, which had slain the Egyptians, rose to the clouds." This trope may also be referred to *Metonymy* (*cf.* below).

§ 4. THE ABUSE OF METAPHORS.

The rhetoricians call the bad use of metaphors *Catachresis*. But we cannot lay down too positive a law. Dante says that as he descended into the second circle of hell, "he came into a place *mute of all light*, which bellows as the sea does in a tempest."[1] Now, at first glance, we say light cannot be "mute"; nor, again, can a mute place "bellow." But the vividness of the trope, its splendid effect, "gloriously offend." It pictures admirably the way in which that desolation and that darkness worked upon the poet. Furthermore, we may refer to another passage in Dante where the beast drives him back *dove il sol tace*, — "where the sun is silent;" and we remember the old idea that approaching light — say of dawn — makes a great tumult. Again, Hamlet's query whether "to take arms against a sea of troubles" is blamed as mixed metaphor, because we do not arm ourselves against the sea. But how well the metaphor pictures the troubles rushing upon the speaker from all sides. It would be more correct, but infinitely

---

[1] Longfellow's translation.

less vivid, to use a *simile* in the second case, and say "to take arms against troubles that rush upon me as a sea." But, after all, it is a very safe and useful rule that one should not "mix" metaphors. The usual example quoted for warning is the couplet:—

> "I *bridle* in my struggling muse with pain,
> That longs to *launch* into a nobler strain."

This assumes a likeness of the main object to objects that are themselves mutually incongruous. The picture is confused. We can hardly justify Hamlet's "*fruitful river* of the eye" for "tears."

Metaphor can be so constant as to be wearisome. We tire of a rapid and ceaseless succession of pictures. George Chapman, for example, though a vigorous poet, is so full of "conceits" as to tire the reader and mar the general effect of the play in which they occur. Shakspere often yielded to the intense desire felt by his age for this piling up of metaphors, and especially of far-fetched ones; but he understood the power of simple vigor.

Goldsmith's distinction is sound,—"between those metaphors which rise glowing from the heart, and those cold conceits which are engendered in the fancy."

Again, we may have *disgusting details*, or *ridiculous associations*. Dryden, when a young man, wrote about a nobleman who had died of the small-pox:—

> "Each little pimple had a tear in it
> To wail the fault its rising did commit."

Crashaw, the religious poet of the Seventeenth Century, in a poem on Mary Magdalen, speaks of Christ as

> "Followed by two faithful fountains,
>   Two walking baths, two weeping motions,
>   Portable and compendious oceans."[1]

This is the abuse of the conceit. On lighter themes the conceit can be happily employed, as Carew and Herrick have shown us.

Finally, as is well known, the poet should never mingle metaphorical with literal; that is, his image or picture should be complete as far as it goes.

§ 5. PERSONIFICATION.

As we saw, the two chief factors of poetical style are (1) the *Metaphor*, which imposes nature on personality, *i.e.* describes human action in terms of a natural process, as "his life ebbed away"; and (2) *Personification*, which imposes personality on nature.

In the metaphor we turn back to the vivid and concrete force of early language, which was made up of pictures. In personification we turn back to the early belief of mankind, a belief that saw personal act and motive in every occurrence of nature. Personification works also in the mental world. Here, too, we restore the old belief, which was full of visions and spiritual voices. A dream was a person, a messenger from the gods: *cf.* the dream sent to Agamemnon, in the *Iliad*. In our modern poetry, we can treat the expression "misfortune overtook him" as a personification. With our forefathers, however, fate (Wyrd) was a real being: she seized a man unawares. Even a sudden thought was a message from the gods, then a messenger; "it

---

[1] This same poet, however, made the line about Christ's first miracle:
"The conscious water saw her God, and blushed."

ran into his mind," says the singer of *Beowulf*, speaking of a sudden determination of King Hrôthgâr, "*it ran into his mind* to build a banquet-hall." Even weapons, utensils, etc., were personified. The warrior chid his sword for refusing, at a critical moment, to "bite." But the great field for early personification was nature and its processes. Then the poet *believed*, now he *assumes*, animism in nature. This belief was the mainspring of mythology; the assumption is the mainspring of poetry. Every right-minded child, even nowadays, believes devoutly in that once-upon-a-time when trees and beasts and birds, and even pots and pans, could talk.

Primitive mankind made its deities of the personifications that lay nearest to it. (Grimm.) Violent forces of nature were made gods; mild and loving powers, goddesses. Air and fire — Woden, the god of rushing wind, the storm-god; and the fire-god, the devourer — these were, of course, masculine; but earth and water were goddesses. Feminine, too, were what we now call the "abstractions," — Love, Truth, Virtue, Fortune. Other abstractions were Wish, Hunger: but the feminine outnumber the masculine. So we see that man's early worship, like man's early language, was an unconscious poetry. The task of modern poets is to restore not only the semblance, but also the spirit of this old poetry, and as far as possible make the fields and woods, the outer world, even thoughts and fancies of the inner world as well, personal and animated. On a large scale this is done by such poems as Wordsworth's *Ode*, where the "meanest flower that blows" has a sympathetic message; on a smaller scale it is done by that trope which we call personification.

This personification may be (1) IMPERFECT. We are told, the voice of Abel's blood cried from the ground. That is an imperfect personification; for we cannot picture any person. We simply have a human *attribute* joined to the blood; speech is lent to it, but not a full personality.

This attribute may be either *physical* (as above) or *mental*. The vassals of Scyld lay their lord (*Beo.* 35) "in the *lap* of the ship." Further (physical) examples are: "bosom of the deep" (Milton); "wide cheeks of the air" (Shaks. *Coriol.*); "Mountains on whose barren breast the laboring clouds do often rest" (Milton, *L'All.*). So in common speech we use personal attributes like back, foot, face, head, etc., as applied to objects. But often we can go directly to mythology in these tropes and need assume no deliberate personification. Thus, take Lear's "Blow, winds, and crack your cheeks!" In the uncouth pictures of the *Sachsenspiegel*, the oldest German book of custom and law — composed about 1200 A.D. — the winds are represented by faces or heads with puffed cheeks, as if blowing furiously. And this notion of the winds goes back to remotest times; so that the expression in *Lear* is a bit of fossil mythology. On the contrary, there is no trace of the old weapon-personification in the sarcastic remark of Gloster when he has slain the King (3 *Hen. VI.* v. 6), —

"See how my sword weeps for the poor king's death."

A close approach is made to full personification in *King John*, II. 1 : —

"That pale, that white-faced shore,
Whose foot spurns back the ocean's roaring tide."

The attribute may, however, be not *physical*, but *mental*. Exquisite is the passage in Spenser's *Epithalamion*: —

> "Behold, whiles she before the altar stands,
> Hearing the holy priest that to her speakes,
> *And blesseth her with his two happy hands,*
> How the red roses flush up in her cheekes."

The "happy hands" is a most happy touch. Further (*Rom. and Jul.* III. 5) : —

> "Look, love, what *envious* streaks
> Do lace the severing clouds in yonder east."

The white rose of York (1 *Hen. VI.* II. 4) is "this pale and angry rose."

Further, this imperfect personification may be applied to *abstractions*. In the passage (*Macb.* v. 5) —

> "To-morrow, and to-morrow, and to-morrow,
> Creeps in this petty pace from day to day," —

we hardly get the picture of a person — only a personal attribute, which illustrates the slow course of time. And the speaker immediately proceeds to a personification that is still fainter : —

> "And all our yesterdays *have lighted fools
> The way to dusty death.*"

Imperfect, too, is the personification in Keats' line, —

> "And Madeline asleep in *lap of legends old*,"

and in Pope's, —

> "At every word a reputation dies."

Secondly, we have PERFECT PERSONIFICATION, — and this, again, may be of *concrete* objects or of *abstract* ideas. In concrete objects we have the vast range of nature. Often a complete personification is undesirable. Milton is especially happy in his description of natural forces: he gives touches of personality here and there, but leaves a vagueness about the picture that adds greatly to its power. Thus *P. L.* I. 174 ff. :—

> . . . "and the thunder,
> Wing'd with red lightning and impetuous rage,
> Perhaps hath spent his shafts, and ceases now
> To bellow through the vast and boundless deep."

Still more powerful is this vagueness in the picture of Superstition in Lucretius (I. 62 ff.) :—

> "humana . . . cum vita jaceret
> *in terris* oppressa gravi sub religione
> quæ caput *a cæli regionibus* ostendebat."

Superstition (religio), with her foot upon mortals, shows nevertheless her head from among the clouds of heaven. The suggestion of indefinite vastness and power is very strong. — But in most cases we demand from the poet a full and satisfying personification. We have imperfect, uncertain personification in the changing epithets applied to the sun by Shakspere in his 33d Sonnet. There is no clear-cut personality : it shifts — is now a monarch, now a lover, now an alchemist. More distinct is the 7th Sonnet, — "Lo in the orient when the gracious light." But the fullest satisfaction is given by those passages in which the old mythology flashes forth : —

> "Night's candles are burnt out, and *jocund day*
> Stands *tiptoe on the misty mountain-tops*."
> —*Rom. & Jul.* III. 5.

> "But look, *the morn in russet mantle clad,*
> Walks o'er the dew of yon high eastern hill."
> —*Hamlet*, I. I.

> "When the gray-hooded Even,
> Like a sad votarist in palmer's weed,
> Rose from the hindmost wheels of Phoebus' wain."
> — Milton, *Comus*.

Further, *cf.* Sidney's sonnet: —

> "With how sad steps, O moon, thou climbst the skies!"

The blithe young morning peering over the hills, the sober-robed evening, the wandering moon, — all are mythological.

So in our oldest poetry. In the *Genesis* (called the first book of "Cædmon") we have such phrases as "In its (the evening's) footsteps *ran and pressed* the gloomy shadow," or "they saw the *light stride away*." — Finally we must add to these natural personifications our inheritance from the classic literatures. Greek and Roman mythology has left us a countless host of such tropes. — Modern poets should use these with great caution; it is better to make fresh tropes. Thus Pope and his school are never tired of Sol and Phœbus and Luna. Keats, with all his love for classic beauty, catches the spirit and neglects the letter — as in his *Isabella:* —

> "Ere the hot sun *count*
> *His dewy rosary* on the eglantine,"

which also contains a fine metaphor.

Finally, we have complete personification of *abstract* ideas. In early times, imagination — the power to picture a definite object — was much stronger than the intellectual power of grouping classes and qualities, and forming abstract ideas. Instead of scientific classification of will and thought and feeling, early psychology knew only a changing inner world whose processes it pictured in concrete terms (metaphor) and whose powers it personified. We revive this latter instinct when we say with Lear: "Down, *climbing Sorrow!*" Further, such an abstraction as our word Fate (=that which is spoken, irrevocable) was to our forefathers, under another name, the goddess of destiny, *Wyrd* (="accomplished," "finished"). "Wyrd wove me this," cries the hero; that is, "here is my fate." In the Old-Saxon (not Anglo-Saxon) poetical version of the gospel, the *Heliand*, Christ says to Judas: "Thy Wyrd stands near thee." — Even such an abstract idea as *hunger* was personified, and was not felt as at all abstract. This is well shown by a passage in the *Genesis:* —

"When from thy heart   *hunger or wolf*
Soul and sorrow   at the same time tears."

Observe the co-ordination of abstract "hunger" and concrete "wolf." In modern poetry we perform the process consciously, not in a mythological belief: —

"Methinks it were an easy leap
To pluck bright honour from the pale-faced moon,
Or dive into the bottom of the deep . . .
. . . And *pluck up drowned honour by the locks;*
So he that doth redeem her thence, might wear,
Without corrival, all her dignities." — 1 *Hen. IV.* 1. 3.

Examples lie everywhere. Take all of Collins' *Ode to the Passions.* Further: —

"Slander, whose whisper . . ." — *Hamlet.*

"Strong War sets hand to the scythe, and the furrows take fire from his feet." — Swinburne, *Erechtheus.*

§ 6. ALLEGORY.

Allegory, as we know, is "where more is meant than meets the ear" — or eye. One thinks immediately of

Gulliver's Travels, of the *Pilgrim's Progress*, or of the *Faery Queene*. That is in subject-matter. But in point of *style*, allegory is *a sustained metaphor*, one extended into several phrases or clauses, *so that we do not think so much of the object as of the illustration*. Often, however, *abruptness* makes up for length. Hamlet, thinking of his counter-plot against the king (III. 4), says:—

> " For 'tis the sport to have the enginer
> Hoist with his own petar: and 't shall go hard,
> But I will delve one yard below their mines
> And blow them at the moon."

Cf. Jul. Cæs. II. I :—

> " 'tis a common proof
> That lowliness is young ambition's ladder," &c.

Imperfect allegory goes not quite so far away from the object. King Philip points to Arthur (*King John*, II. 1), and says:—

> " Look here upon thy brother Geffrey's face ;—
> These eyes, these brows, were moulded out of his;
> This little abstract doth contain that large
> Which died in Geffrey: and the hand of time
> Shall draw this brief into as huge a volume."

Sometimes the allegory is, for the sake of clearness, introduced or ended by a *simile* (*cf.* below); thus in the well-known *Epitaph in Croyland Abbey* :—

> " Man's life is like unto a winter's day.
> Some break their fast, and so depart away.
> Others stay dinner, then depart full-fed.
> The longest age but sups and goes to bed."

There is a finely sustained allegory near the end of Cowper's *Lines on the Receipt of my Mother's Picture*.

The seasons furnish abundant occasion for allegory. Out of many examples, we instance Clough's *No More* — "My wind has turned to bitter north, etc." Further, instead of a prolonged metaphor, allegory may be a prolonged *personification*. Milton describes the peace prevailing on the earth at Christ's nativity, in an allegorical way: —

> " But he her fears to cease,
> Sent down the meek-ey'd Peace, etc."

A beautiful allegory is contained in the 80th Psalm. In fact, metaphor slips easily into allegory. Naïve is Chaucer's explanation at the beginning of Book II. of *Troylus and Cryseyde* : —

> " Out of these blake wawes for to saylle,
> O wynde, O wynde, the weder gynneth to clere;
> For in this see the boot hath swiche travaylle
> Of my connynge, that unneth I it stere:
> *This see clepe I the tempestuous matere*
> *Of desespeyre, that Troylus was inne.*" . . .

Like the simile, allegory was introduced into our poetry at a very early date. In the Anglo-Saxon *Physiologus* (*cf.* Ch. I. § IV.), in the poem "Christ" (Grein's *Bibliothek*), and in other old poems, it often occurs. But it is an importation from classic and sacred writings, and is not native to our oldest literature.

§ 7. THE SIMILE — IMPLIED.

The trope based on resemblance of two objects may *assume* that resemblance, as in metaphor, personification, allegory: in metaphor, the ship "ploughs the sea." We assume that the action of a ship resembles the action of a plough. But when we *name* the action of the ship, and then compare it to the action of the plough, we have simile. The *likeness* may be stated frankly, or it may be implied. Most writers on poetics place the implied simile under the head of metaphor. Thus Nichol (*Eng. Comp.*) says that "He fought like a lion" is simile; "He was a lion in fight" is metaphor. Surely the latter is implied simile. Every one understands by "was" just about what one understands by "was like." The idea of comparison and likeness is present in both cases. But the metaphor boldly expresses *one thing in terms of another*, does not place the two objects before the mind. A simile, then, is where two objects are presented to the mind for comparison.

An implied simile is not a metaphor, and yet is bolder than the stated simile. It may be implied in several ways. Thus, by *apposition:* —

"The noble sister of Publicola,
The moon of Rome." — *Coriol.* v. 3.

"And those eyes, the break of day,
Lights that do mislead the morn." — *M. for M.* iv. 1.

"Those green-robed senators of mighty woods,
Tall oaks." — Keats, *Hyperion.*

"Northumberland, thou ladder wherewithal
The mounting Bolingbroke ascends my throne."
— *Rich. II.* v. 1.

A splendid succession of comparisons, too long to quote, is the eulogy of England that Shakspere puts into the mouth of the dying Gaunt (*Rich. II.* II. 1); one is, — "this precious stone set in the silver sea."

The simile may be implied by a *dependent genitive case:* "The dew of sleep"; "The milk of human kindness"; "The nunnery of your chaste breast." Here note particularly that the two nouns are *co-ordinates.* "Dew" and "sleep" are co-ordinate, of equal value, — comparison and compared. Different would be the case with such an expression as — "the quiet of sleep," where "quiet" is simply a part or quality of "sleep." Further *cf.* "In cradle of the rude imperious surge" (2 *Hen. IV.* III. 1).

More distant is the implying by means of *adjectives:* "Passionate, pale, cold face, *star-sweet on a gloom profound*" (Tennyson, *Maud*); "Golden sleep"; "This working-day world." — There are many other ways of implying likeness. For instance (*Merch. of Ven.* II. 5), "But stop my house's ears — I mean my casements." Then, approaching the stated simile, we have the connection of comparison and compared by the "copula" *is* or *are:* —

"He is the brooch indeed
And gem of all the nations." — *Hamlet.*

"A jewel in a ten times barred-up chest
Is a bold spirit in a loyal breast." — *Rich. II.*

"Love is a sickness full of woes." — S. Daniel.

Other equivalents of *is* or *are* may be mentioned besides the one from *Merch. of Ven.* just given: —

"Then her voice's music, — *call it*
The well's bubbling, the bird's warble." — R. Browning.

"The sullen passage of thy weary steps
Esteem a foil, wherein thou art to set
The precious jewel of thy home-return."
— *Rich. II.* 1. 6.

With a *gesture* Cleopatra implies the comparison, as she points to the asp on her bosom, and asks (*A. and C.* v. 2): —

"Dost thou not see my baby at my breast,
That sucks the nurse asleep?"

§ 8. THE SIMILE — STATED.

This marks the extreme stage of the trope based on likeness. In development, the metaphor precedes the simile. The former can rest on a picturesque confusion of names[1] — as in calling the bird's nest his "house": so Tennyson, speaking of the vanished inmate of a sea-shell, asks: "Did he stand at the diamond door of his *house?*" Our early poetry is full of this metaphor; it calls the sky "the people-*roof*," the sea "foamy *fields*," and so on. All that was required was a common quality, and the immediate substitution of one object for another. Hence a great confusion, "mixing" of metaphors, as when the "mouth" (*sc. door*) of the ark is "locked." Much more art, more balance, is needed to pause in the current of poetry and hold two objects apart, painting carefully the details of the comparison, then returning to the main subject and proceeding quietly with the interrupted narration. This demands a higher poetic faculty, a more analytic, self-contained faculty. Hence the superiority, in point of style, of the Homeric poems over our old English epos. The former are famous for their sustained similes; the latter has scarcely a simile worthy of the name, setting aside, of course, the later poems, where classical and sacred models now begin to exert their influence. We are, therefore, not surprised to learn that Lessing, the experienced man of letters and brilliant critic, disliked, as a poet, the metaphor, and used in preference the sim-

[1] Goldsmith ("Essay on the Use of Metaphors") calls metaphor "a kind of magical coat by which the same idea assumes a thousand different appearances."

ile. Hegel notes that the simile is essentially oriental, the metaphor occidental. The simile came into our literature through the influence of Latin models and the love of sacred literature for allegory. The Bible is very fond of similes: "As the hart panteth after the water-brooks, so panteth my soul after thee, O God!" But our primitive poetry ventured, at the best, only on such a timid flight as when it says that the ship glides over the water "most like a bird" (*fûgle gelícost*). This fact, that the simile stands on a higher plane of poetical development than the metaphor, must be borne in mind when one is told that the metaphor is a "condensed" simile. *It is so logically; not, however, chronologically.*

The simile may be stated *positively:* —

"Like the winds in summer sighing,
Her voice is low and sweet."

"Ponderous syllables, like sullen waves
In the half-glutted hollows of reef-rocks." — Keats.

"Her feet beneath her petticoat,
Like little mice, stole in and out,
As if they feared the light." — Suckling.

The simile, being a formal comparison, should not state the familiar and obvious. The poet must give us an unexpected, yet fit and beautiful comparison. In general effect, the two things compared should be as unlike as possible, so that the one common trait shall gain in intensity from the general contrast. This is finely brought out in a passage of Browning's *Paracelsus:* —

"Over the waters in the vaporous west
The sun goes down as in a sphere of gold,

> Behind the outstretched city, which between,
> With all that length of domes and minarets,
> Athwart the splendor, black and crooked runs
> Like a Turk verse along a scimetar."

See, too, the deposed Richard's famous simile of the well and buckets, *Rich. II.* IV. 1.

The simile may be stated as a *negative*, or in *degrees of comparison*. This adds emphasis: —

> "The sea enraged is not half so deaf,
> . . . . as we to keep this city."
> — *King John*, II. 2.

> "O Spartan dog,
> More fell than anguish, hunger, or the sea!"
> — *Othello*, V. 2.

> "That she may feel
> How sharper than a serpent's tooth it is
> To have a thankless child." — *Lear*, II. 4.

The simile best fits the stately motion of epic poetry. A short simile is used with great effect in lyric poetry, or the drama; but when it is sustained and carried into detail, it is out of place in these, and belongs to the epic. So we find the famous Homeric similes of a most elaborate finish; *cf.* that at the end of the eighth book of the *Iliad*. In English, Milton has best followed this path. The fallen angels stand (*P. L.* I. 612 ff.) —

> "Their glory withered. As when Heaven's fire
> Hath scath'd the forest oaks, or mountain pines,
> With singed top their stately growth though bare
> Stands on the blasted heath."

More like the Homeric simile and longer — too long to quote — are such as that (*P. L.* III.) where Satan, as he looks down on the world, is compared to a military scout. The Sonnet often makes an elaborate simile in its octave, then in the sestette draws the moral or shows the application. So, too, the *Epigram*, as in the stanza by Waller, given below.

It is to be remembered that *a mere instance is not a simile* : —

> "Thais led the way
> To light him to his prey,
> And *like another Helen, fir'd another Troy.*"

Nevertheless, the simile is often combined with *Allusion*. Thus the poet takes for granted our knowledge of classical mythology when he says that Portia's

> "Sunny locks
> Hang on her temples like a golden fleece;
> Which makes her seat of Belmont Colchos' strand,
> And many Jasons come in search of her."

The simile may be stated in *words equivalent to* "*like*" or "*as*": —

> "It *were all one*
> That I should love a bright particular star,
> And think to wed it, he is so above me."
> — *All's Well.*

Or take Waller's conceit : —

> "The eagle's fate and mine *are one*,
> Which on the shaft that saw him die,
> Espied a feather of his own
> Wherewith he wont to soar so high."

The great similes of classic poetry find frequent imitation. Thus we may trace one simile (of dead leaves falling in frosty weather) from Chaucer (*Troilus*, 4. 29) back to Dante (*Inferno*, 3. 112), and from him to Vergil (*Æn.* 6. 309).

§ 9. TROPES OF CONNEXION.

One expression is here used for another on the basis not of *resemblance*, but of *connexion*, or association. In the former (resemblance), two things may be sundered in space and in thought; yet a common quality, a likeness in one point, may allow one to be used for the other: *e.g.*, "her roses" for "her cheeks," because both are red, or "rosy." But when we say: "the bottle will be his death," we see no *likeness* between what we say and what we mean (the liquor); but we do see a *connexion*. The two are associated in space as containing and contained: therefore we use one for the other. Connexion in space is sometimes called *mathematical;* connexion in thought, *logical.*

When one thing is put for another on account of connexion in space, we have the trope called *Synecdoche;* the word means to understand one thing by another. It is mainly based on the relation of *whole to parts*. Thus a part is taken for the whole.

> "That cursed *head*
> Whose wicked deed." — *Hamlet.*

Here "man" is meant.

> "*Cheeks* of sorry grain will serve to ply
> The sampler." — *Comus.*

In the next example, a singular proper noun expresses the collective idea of "nation"; note the plural pronoun:—

> "*The Spaniard*, tied by blood and favour to her,
> Must now confess, if *they* have any goodness," etc.
> — *Hen. VIII.* II. 2.

A favorite use of this trope among our Germanic forefathers was to take some striking part of an action and use it instead of the general expression. Instead of saying "they went ashore," the poet of *Beowulf* puts it thus: "They bore their armor to the strand." The vividness of the picture is much increased. A fine modern use of this is in Marc Antony's famous speech about Brutus and the others "*whose daggers have stabbed Cæsar.*" How infinitely stronger this is than "murdered," any one can see. So our forefathers did not simply "sail"; they "*drove the keel over the sea-street.*"

Similar to this trope is *Distribution*. Instead of simply naming the whole action or thing, one part after the other is named in detail. Instead of "They shall nevermore come to their homes at evening," the poet says: —

> "For them no more the blazing hearth shall burn,
> Or busy housewife ply her evening care;
> No children run to lisp their sire's return,
> Or climb his knee, the envied kiss to share."

See also the ghost's picture of Hamlet's abhorrence at the tale that might be told, —

> "whose lightest word
> Would harrow up thy soul," etc. — *Hamlet*, I. 5.

Another similar trope, known as *Periphrase*, puts a certain prominent habit for the thing or person meant: —

> "Ye that in waters glide, and ye that walk
> The earth, and stately tread, or lowly creep."
> — *Par. Lost*, 5. 200 f.

"The filmy shapes
That haunt the dusk, with ermine capes
And woolly breasts and beaded eyes."
— Tennyson, *In Mem.*

"Where sailors gang to fish for cod" = Newfoundland.
— Burns, *Twa Dogs.*

The above substituted part for whole. We may also have *whole for part*. As "the Spaniard" was used for Spain, or all Spaniards, so conversely, the whole country is used for its monarch. This is common in Shakspere. "Good Hamlet," says the queen, "let thine eye look like a friend on *Denmark*"— meaning Claudius, king of Denmark. So, too, in *King John*, Faulconbridge's pun, when Hubert lifts the dead body of Arthur, rightful heir to the crown : —

"How easy dost thou take all England up!"

Material is used for *thing made*.

"*Sonorous metal* blowing martial sounds." — *Par. Lost*, 1.

Our old poets were fond of this trope : "curve-necked wood" for "ship"; "glee-beam," or "glee-wood," for "harp"; and many more. Wolsey says (*Hen. VIII.*) he will "sleep in dull, cold marble."—"Not to taste that only *tree*," *i.e.* fruit of the tree (*Par. Lost*, 4. 423).

Finally, one object is put for another connected with it in space. This is not like the case of part for whole, since the two objects are separable. Thus : —

"Costly thy habit as thy *purse* can buy."

"For the four winds blow in from every coast
Renowned suitors."— *Merch. Ven.* I. I.

LOGICAL ASSOCIATION. — This relation is that of cause and effect, substance and attribute, and all such as are grasped, not by the senses, but by thought. The trope is called *Metonymy*, — change of names. In the Anglo-Saxon *Genesis* we are told that "God created for the false ones *groans of hell*," *i.e.* pains that would cause groans. "Savage clamor drowned both *harp and voice*," — *sound* of the harp (*Par. Lost*). "I know the *hand*," quibbles Lorenzo, when he sees Jessica's letter (*Merch. of Ven.*): "in faith, 'tis a fair hand." So *Hen. VIII.* II. 3 : —

> "'tis better to be lowly born
> Than to be perk'd up in a *glistering grief*,
> And wear a *golden sorrow*."

Prince Henry calls the crown a "polish'd perturbation," — *cause* of perturbation; and the Dirge in *Cymbeline* tells us that

> "The sceptre, learning, physic must
> All follow this and come to dust,"

a case of attribute and symbol instead of substance.

Quality for *person* or *thing:* "To fawn on rage" = raging man (*Rich. II.* v. 1). "*Bondage* is hoarse" (*R. and J.*). "When thus the *angelic Virtue* answered mild," = virtuous angel (*Par. Lost*).

So, too, relations of *time:* —

> "Nor wanting is *the brown October* drawn
> Mature and perfect, from his dark retreat
> Of thirty years." — Thomson.

> "And on her (*sc.* the table's) ample square from side to side
> All *Autumn* piled." — *Par. Lost*, 5. 391.

§ 10. TROPES OF CONTRAST.

In order to express something in a very forcible way, we can use a phrase entirely unexpected, making a sharp contrast with the literal statement. It does not deceive the reader; it simply draws his attention, as by a violent gesture, to the real object.

1. *Hyperbole.* — This trope (the word means to "cast beyond") states a fact in words that we know to be impossible or extremely improbable. It shows that we must believe as far as we can in the direction indicated. "*Countless* houses" is a term by which we understand houses so numerous that it would be *very difficult* to count them, or would take a long time. The hyperbole is common in all speech. In poetry it is also abundant.

> "I was all ear,
> And took in strains that might create a soul
> Under the ribs of death." — *Comus.*

> "Will all great Neptune's ocean wash this blood
> Clean from my hand? No: this my hand will rather
> The multitudinous sea incarnadine,
> Making the green one red." — *Macbeth.*

> "When I lie tangled in her hair
> And fettered to her eye." — Lovelace, *To Althea.*

Hyperbole easily degenerates into *rant.* Shakspere intentionally ridicules this in Hamlet's wild speech at Ophelia's grave. Unintentionally, Lee, the tragedian, rants in his well-known passage: —

> "Pouring forth tears at such a lavish rate,
> That were the world on fire, they might drown
> The wrath of heaven, and quench the mighty ruin."

This, as Blair remarks, is "mere bombast." But a slight step makes the trope forcible in Macbeth's nervous words: —

> "Shall blow the horrid deed in every eye
> That tears shall drown the wind."

The hyperbole, as Lord Kaims pointed out, must not contain an absurd and contradictory statement. On this ground we condemn Pope's couplet:—

> "When first young Maro in his boundless mind
> A work *t' outlast immortal* Rome designed."

2. *Litotes.*—This is the opposite of the hyperbole. It *understates.* It stops far short of the actual truth. We feel the sharp contrast between the insufficient statement and the literal fact, and we hasten to do the subject right and justice. Thus Chaucer, describing a fat, jolly, rosy, ease-loving monk, says:—

> "He was not pale as a forpyned gost."

So in *Par. Lost:*—

> "Whereof in Hell
> Fame is not silent."

3. *Euphemism.*—There are certain forms of religion in low stages of culture where the good gods are neglected — they will do no harm — and the bad gods are overwhelmed with gifts and flattery. To these are given *good names:* the wish is father to the thought,— they are called good in hopes that they will *be* good. Even the Greek word *Eumenides* was given to the Furies, who, as Æschylus tells us, spoil the growing corn and fruit. There are similar names in our own mythology. Now this same spirit crops out in the disguise of modern *Euphemism.* This term ("speaking well of") is applied to that trope which, in contrast to the literal badness of the object, gives it a good name. In exalted style, we use Euphemism for harmful, destructive things; in familiar style, for disagreeable things. Especially is it used of *death.*

"How *sleep* the brave who *sink to rest*
By all their country's wishes blest!"— Collins.

"After life's fitful fever, he sleeps well."— *Macbeth*.

"Ah, Warwick, Montague hath breathed his last."

For the second case, in *Hamlet* (II. 1), instead of "intoxicated" we have the polite "*o'ertook*." *Cf.* such colloquial and rather vulgar expressions as "appropriated" for plain "stolen."

4. *Irony.*— The contrast here consists in our believing the opposite of what is said. Irony may be light, almost harmless, as in Sterne; merciless and biting, as in Swift. Poetically it is often used:—

"Go teach eternal wisdom how to rule."

"Enjoy the thoughts that rise
From disappointed avarice,
From frustrated ambition."

"Now get you to my lady's chamber," says Hamlet to Yorick's skull, "and tell her, let her paint an inch thick, to this favour she must come; *make her laugh at that.*" A most admirable example of compliment shading into irony, and irony into bitter sarcasm, is Marc Antony's speech about the "honorable men." Finally, we get the plain statement with the word "traitors."

In epic poetry, irony alternates with direct abuse,— as in speeches of warriors about to fight. So Gabriel calls Satan "courageous chief."

CHAPTER V. — FIGURES.

The terms Trope and Figure have often been confused. Metaphors are called "figurative" language, and Trope is often just as loosely understood. But the distinction is useful and just. A trope deals with the expressions themselves; a figure, with their relations and arrangement.

Figures may be based on *Repetition*, on *Contrast*, or on *Combination*.

§ 1. FIGURES OF REPETITION.

The repetition of certain relations of sounds is, as we shall see, the basis of metre; there is also a harmony and poetic effect gained by repetition of words and phrases.

1. *Iteration.* — Single words are repeated. This is very common in dirges and in passages expressive of deep emotion. The tendency is to dwell on one name or thought. *Lycidas* is very remarkable in this respect: —

> "For Lycidas is dead, dead ere his prime,
> Young Lycidas, and hath not left his peer.
> Who would not weep for Lycidas?"

The poem is full of such iteration.

So in *Paradise Lost:* "though fall'n on evil times, On evil times though fall'n and evil tongues." The strong passion and wonder of Hamlet find expression by dwelling on two words: —

> "Oh villain, villain, smiling, damned villain!
> My tables — meet it is I set it down
> That one may smile and smile and be a villain."

For sacred poetry, see the song of Deborah, *Judges* v. 26-28.

Without any reference to emotion, iteration is used for the harmony of verse.

> "Sweet is the breath of morn, her rising sweet."

> "See golden days fruitful of golden deeds."

Both are from *Paradise Lost*. Milton thoroughly understood such cadences and harmonies. More involved iteration is seen in the following : —

> "Increasing store with loss and loss with store."

> "Might hide her faults, if belles had faults to hide."

Or George Puttenham's example : —

> "Much must he be beloved that loveth much;
> Feare many must he needs, whom many feare."

In these latter examples we find *antithesis* also. *Cf.* § 3 of this chapter.

2. This iteration may vary the application of the word.

> "Treason doth never prosper. What's the reason?
> If it doth prosper, none dare call it treason."

> "When thou hast done, thou hast not done;
> For I have more." — Donne.

> "And every fair from fair sometimes declines." — Shakspere.

> "How beautiful, if sorrow had not made
> Sorrow more beautiful than beauty's self." — Keats.

3. Finally, this becomes *word-play*. So Antony, when he looks upon the body of Cæsar, cries out : —

> "Here wast thou bay'd, brave hart;
> Here didst thou fall. . . .
> O world! thou wast the forest to this hart;
> And this indeed, O world! the heart of thee."

Thence we come to the regular *pun*. The prince of pun-makers in verse is, of course, Thomas Hood. Where the pun is confined to one word, as is usual, it is not an example of repetition. But otherwise with

> "They went and told the sexton,
> And the sexton tolled the bell."

4. Whole sentences are repeated. The arrangement and matter are generally the same, but the expression is slightly changed. This figure is called *Parallelism*. It is very common in the Bible and in our Anglo-Saxon poetry : —

> "The voice of the Lord is upon the waters;
> The God of glory thundereth. . . .
> . . . The voice of the Lord breaketh the cedars;
> Yea, the Lord breaketh the cedars of Lebanon."

In Anglo-Saxon poetry, this figure is combined with the trope of *Variation*. An example from Milton of Parallelism, though with order reversed for metrical reasons, is the beginning of the Morning Hymn (*Par. Lost*, 5. 153) : —

> "These are thy glorious works, Parent of good,
> Almighty, thine this universal frame,
> Thus wondrous fair."

§ 2. FIGURES OF CONTRAST.

Here the arrangement is different from the expected and ordinary arrangement. Hence, through surprise, a stronger impression. Thus, we usually speak of an absent person or thing in the third person. If we suddenly address it in the second person, as if it were present, we have *Apostrophe*.

1. *Apostrophe.* — Literally, this means a turning away from something. Quintilian says its origin was in the custom of orators, pleading in court, who were wont to turn from the judge and suddenly address some one else. Cicero, as we know, was pleading for Ligarius, when unexpectedly he broke off his argument and turned to the accuser, who was present, saying: — " Quid enim, Tubero, tuus ille destrictus in acie Pharsalica gladius agebat ? "

This stricter sort of apostrophe abounds in poetry.

> " Within a month, —
> Let me not think on't — Frailty, thy name is woman —
> A little month," etc.

In a wider sense, apostrophe is any case where an absent person or thing is addressed as if present. Banquo, in his soliloquy, turns to Macbeth as if the latter were present : —

> " Thou hast it now, King, Cawdor, Glamis, all
> As the weird women promised ; and I fear
> Thou playd'st most foully for it."

So Macbeth, about to murder Duncan, who sleeps in another room, hears the bell ring, and cries : —

> " Hear it not, Duncan ! "

The figure is used also of things: —

> "Hold, hold, my heart;
> And you, my sinews, grow not instant old,
> But bear me stiffly up." — *Hamlet.*

2. Apostrophe was a change of person. We may also have a change of *number*. For singular, we have the plural. Such is the "royal 'we.'" So the ordinary second-person plural is now used altogether for the older "thou."

3. The change may be in *tense*. Present is used for past, — the *historical present*. Events are narrated as if taking place before the eye.

> "Behind the arras hearing something stir,
> H' whips out his rapier, cries 'A rat, a rat!'
> And in this brainish apprehension, kills
> The unseen good old man." — *Hamlet*, IV. I.

This figure is effectually used in *The Cotter's Saturday Night* of Burns. — Present may be used for future. So in ordinary talk: "I go away to-morrow." In poetry we have such pronounced examples as (*Ham.* v.): —

> "Horatio, *I am dead;*
> *Thou livest;* report me and my cause aright."

4. The speaker describes an absent thing, not in the second person, indeed, as in *apostrophe*, but as if it were present, though the third person is retained. The speaker seems to see the thing. Hence the figure is called *Vision*. Famous are the stanzas in *Childe Harold*, beginning

> "I see before me the gladiator lie."

In Gray's *Bard*, in Pope's *Messiah*, are fine examples of continued Vision. Naturally, the figure is not restricted to what one sees. The poet looks upon the rows of muskets in an arsenal and "hears even now the infinite fierce chorus," that has been sung in all ages by the voices of war. — In imperative form, this figure is very common. The *Nativity Hymn* affords an example : —

"See how from far ... the star-led wizards haste."

5. Instead of the simple *order* of words, as we naturally form any proposition, with subject, predicate, and so on, some other order is adopted. This is just as familiar to prose as to poetry. "Great is Diana of the Ephesians" is infinitely more forcible than "Diana of the Ephesians is great."

But in poetry there is far greater freedom of inversion and involution than in prose. The imitators of Milton found it easy to make up a quasi Miltonic style, simply by scattering inverted constructions broadcast through the verses. But Milton could be simple and direct when there was need for naked force : —

"He called so loud that all the hollow deep
Of Hell resounded."

On the other hand, take that description of the gate of lost paradise : —

"With dreadful faces thronged and fiery arms."

In neither case can we change without infinite loss.

There is one poetical inversion, however, that needs special notice. Besides such cases as Abbott (*Shakspere. Gram.* § 423) notices, *e.g.*, "thy cause of distemper" for "the cause of thy distemper," we have inversions like

"The fond husband strove to lend relief
In all the *silent manliness of grief*."

Goldsmith means "manliness of silent grief." So Tennyson's Princess moves to the window "Robed in the long night of her deep hair," *i.e.*, "deep night of her long hair." When Milton speaks of "flowering odors" he means "odorous flowers"; and a somewhat similar figure is, "The *flowing gold* of her loose tresses," unless we take it as implied simile.

Shakspere is fond of this construction: *cf.* Son. 77: "by thy dial's *shady stealth*," = stealthy shade.

6. Almost touching the trope Hyperbole, is a figure in which the statement taken as literal grammatical construction is impossible, but in loose construction is possible and intelligible.

> "Adam, the goodliest man of men since born,
> His sons, the fairest of her daughters Eve."
> —*Par. Lost*, 4. 323 f.

> "Of all men else I have avoided thee."—*Macbeth*, v. 7.

> "So these two brothers *with their murdered man*
> Rode past fair Florence."—Keats, *Isabella*.

In the last example, the meaning is 'the man whom they were about to murder.' This anticipation, or *Prolepsis*, can be a mere matter of grammar, not of sense. Thus in Byron's *Giaour:*—

> "These scenes, their story not unknown,
> Arise, and make again your own."

Shakspere often used this figure: "What is infirm from your sound parts shall fly" (*All's Well*, II. 1); what is infirm will fly, and the part thereby *become* sound.

7. Instead of the *kind of sentence* that we expect, we find some other: as a question instead of a statement.

"Hath not a Jew eyes," asks Shylock, "hath not a Jew hands, organs, dimensions, senses, affections, passions?" This is stronger than the statement, "A Jew hath eyes," etc.

> "Am I not, am I not here alone?" — Tennyson, *Maud*.

> "Is it not monstrous that this player here
> But in a fiction," etc. — *Hamlet*.

We expect an affirmative answer to these. Otherwise with

> "Lives there who loves his pain?" — *Par. Lost*, 4. 888.

8. The *Parenthesis* is common everywhere.

> "For I this night
> (Such night till this I never passed) have dreamed,
> If dreamed," etc. — *Par. Lost*, 5. 30.

9. Finally, the most abrupt contrast arises when the construction comes suddenly to an end, is broken off violently, and a new sentence begins in a new direction. The famous Vergilian example is where Neptune rebukes the winds, and begins to threaten, but leaves the threat unfinished: —

> "Quos ego — sed motos præstat componere fluctus."

> "Ay me, I fondly dream!
> Had ye been there — for what could that have done?"
> — *Lycidas*.

> "But her eyes —
> How could he see to do them?"
> — *Merch. of Ven.* III. 2.

§ 3. FIGURES OF COMBINATION.

Here the effect is made by the arrangement and mutual relations of the different parts of the sentence.

There is no repetition; there is no turning from the proper tense or number; but the joining of the parts differs from that of common speech.

1. Chief of these figures is *Antithesis*. Two expressions are placed in close relation, so that each throws the other into strong relief. Sometimes we have two verses; sometimes the antithesis is shut in a single verse. In prose, the figure should be sparingly used; a case of undue abundance is John Lyly's *Euphues and his England* (1579) which riots in antithesis and alliteration. But sparingly used, antithesis has a pleasant effect. Keats says (*Endymion*) he will

" . . . *Stammer* where old Chaucer used to *sing*."

" Have eyes to wonder but lack tongues to praise."
— Shakspere, *Sonnet*.

" And my large kingdom for a little grave."
— *Richard II*. III. 4.

" His back was turned, but not his brightness hid."
— *Par. Lost*, 3. 624.

" Saw undelighted all delight." — *Par. Lost*, 4. 286.

" New laws from him who reigns new minds may raise
In us who serve." — *Par. Lost*, 5. 680.

This figure was carried to excess in the formal poetry of Dryden and Pope. Still the theme may often excuse the figure. So in Pope's masterpiece: —

" Slight is the subject, but not so the praise,
If she inspire and he approve my lays."

Pope is very fond of *parallel constructions:* —

" Hang o'er the box and hover round the ring."

" When music softens and when dancing fires."

> "On her white breast a sparkling cross she wore
> Which Jews might kiss and infidels adore."

So Dr. Johnson : —

> "All Marlborough hoarded or all Villiers spent."

Dryden : —

> "He had his wit and they had his estate."

Prior : —

> "If 'tis not sense, at least 'tis Greek."

> "They never taste who always drink:
> They always talk who never think."

So Swift and many other poets of the Eighteenth Century.

Another use of the antithesis is to sharpen satire. It brings incongruous things together as if they were congruous. Pope : —

> "Forget her prayers or miss a masquerade."

> "Or lose her heart or necklace at a ball."

Another use is to point a moral. Dryden : —

> "Resolved to ruin or to rule the state."

> "But wild ambition loves to slide, not stand,
> And Fortune's ice prefers to Virtue's land."

> "He left not faction, but of that was left."

The antithesis is much used in the *Epigram:* —

> "On parent's knees, a naked new-born child,
> Weeping thou sat'st, while all around thee smiled
> So live, that, sinking in thy long last sleep,
> Calm thou may'st smile, while all around thee weep."

A peculiar antithesis is the sneer of Richard after he has murdered the king : —

> "What, will the aspiring blood of Lancaster
> Sink in the ground? I thought it would have mounted."
> —3 *Henry VI.* v. 6.

The antithesis generally brings out an *opposition* in the meaning — as in the foregoing examples. But there is a similar figure which brings out a likeness — a sort of parallel. Thus Chaucer: —

> "Up roos the sonne and up roos Emelye."

> "When that the poor have cried, Cæsar hath wept."
> — *Julius Cæsar.*

The great merit of the antithesis is the same as the merit of its chief masters, Dryden and Pope, — *conciseness* and *clearness*. It presents an idea in brief but forcible expression. But its faults are also the faults of Pope and Dryden, — lack of naturalness, a tendency to labored manner, a striving after effect. In poor hands (imitators of Pope) it becomes intolerable.

2. The antithesis is not necessarily a contradiction. But there is a figure (something like the hyperbole among tropes) where a seeming contradiction in terms brings out vividly the general idea.

When the contradictory terms are brought sharply together, the figure is called *Oxymoron;* when they are not so closely joined, *Paradox.* Keats is a poet fond of such figures: —

> "... and then there crept
> A little *noiseless noise* among the leaves
> Born of the *very sigh that silence heaves.*"

> "A half-heard strain
> Full of *sweet desolation, — balmy pain.*"

To these striking examples we may add : —

"O heavy lightness, serious vanity!"
— *Romeo and Juliet*, I. I.

Chaucer : —

"And smale fowles maken melodie
That slepen alle night with open eye."

Pope : —

"And sleepless lovers just at twelve awake."

Milton : —

"By merit raised to that bad eminence."

"With wanton heed and giddy cunning."

Shirley : —

"Upon death's purple altar now
See where the victor-victim bleeds."

Mrs. Browning : —

"He denied
Divinely the divine."

Example of Paradox is : —

"Stone walls do not a prison make,
Nor iron bars a cage." — Lovelace.

3. *Climax* and *Anticlimax*. — The great art in prose or verse is to leave on the reader's mind the most distinct and sharp impression possible (*cf.* H. Spencer *On the Philosophy of Style*). To do this, great care must be exercised in the arrangement of thought and expression. The most important part should, as a rule, come last, and thus leave itself in the mind without anything following to mar the impression. So Eve says to Adam : —

> "But neither breath of Morn when she ascends
> With charm of earliest birds, nor rising sun
> On this delightful land, nor herb, fruit, flower,
> Glistring with dew, nor fragrance after showers,
> Nor grateful Evening mild, nor silent Night
> With this her solemn bird, nor walk by moon
> Or glittering starlight, *without thee is sweet.*"
> — *Par. Lost*, 4. 650 ff.

We see how far better is this arrangement than if Eve said, "Nothing without thee is sweet, — neither," etc.

This figure of *Climax*, — a gradual rising in power to a conclusion that towers above all that precedes, — is very common. Note the order of terms in the following: —

> "The cloud-capp'd towers, the gorgeous palaces,
> The solemn temples, the great globe itself,
> Yea, all which it inherit, shall dissolve,
> And, like this insubstantial pageant faded,
> Leave not a rack behind." — *Tempest*, IV. 1.

One form of climax is that which leads us, by one particular after another, up to the main fact of a statement: —

> "When, fast as shaft can fly,
> Bloodshot his eyes, his nostrils spread,
> The loose rein dangling from his head,
> Housing and saddle bloody red, —
> Lord Marmion's steed rushed by." — Scott, *Marmion*, VI.

For *oratorical climax*, Nichol calls Marc Antony's speech to the citizens, the most remarkable instance in English. "Of more purely poetical climax," he says, "there is no finer example than the concluding lines of Coleridge's *Mont Blanc.*"

We may add that the finest *dramatic* climax is the last speech of Othello. — The conclusion of Pope's *Dunciad* is another famous climax, and was especially admired by Dr. Johnson.

Climax, we see, strengthens the impression of any great or striking part of a statement. But it is also used to make littleness appear yet more little, the laughable or mean still more laughable or mean. This is called *Anticlimax*. We ascend nearly to the height of the climax, the sublime, — then fall either to the absurd, mean, or to some other unexpected end.

"Not louder shrieks to pitying heaven are cast
When husbands or when lapdogs breathe their last."
— Pope, *Rape of the Lock*.

"Is it not monstrous that this player here,
But in a fiction, in a dream of passion,
Could force his soul so to his own conceit,
That from her working all his visage wann'd,
Tears in his eyes, distraction in's aspect,
A broken voice, and his whole function suiting
With forms to his conceit? And all for nothing!"
— *Hamlet*, II. 2.

"The wisest, brightest, meanest of mankind." — Pope.

For purposes of *sarcasm*. Pope: —

"Go teach eternal wisdom how to rule,
Then drop into thyself, and be a fool."

For purposes of mere wit: —

"When late I attempted your pity to move,
What made you so deaf to my prayers?
Perhaps it was right to dissemble your love,
But, — why did you kick me down stairs?"

These examples of intentional anticlimax are, of course, to be held apart from the *rhetorical fault* of the same name, — which is simply a bad climax. With the infinite blunders and bad uses of figurative poetry we are not concerned, as the aim of our study is to find out all that is peculiar to the style of good poets.

Part III.

METRE.

Chapter VI.

The science of verse is the most difficult part of Poetics, and yet it is the most important; for metrical form is "the sole condition ... absolutely demanded by poetry." The chief difficulty lies in the great confusion of opinion about the essential laws and tests of verse. There is no fixed use of terms, no full agreement even on some of the simplest elements of the science. We must therefore proceed carefully, accepting only the more generally admitted facts, and refusing to follow those sweeping changes of recent writers, which are in so many cases merely destructive of old theory without offering solid basis for new rules.

§ 1. RHYTHM.

A *Syllable* is a body of sound brought out with an independent, single, and unbroken breath (Sievers). This syllable may be *long* or *short*, according to the time it fills: compare the syllables in *merrily* with the syllables in *corkscrew*. Further, a syllable may be *heavy* or *light* (also called *accented* or *unaccented*) according as it receives more or less force or *stress* of tone: compare the two syllables of *streamer*. Lastly, a syllable may have increased or diminished *height* of tone, —*pitch: cf.* the so-called "rising inflection" at the end of a question. Now, in spoken language, there are infinite degrees of length, of stress, of pitch. If phonetic spelling come to be firmly established, we shall also have a phonetic versification to note these degrees. But while some new systems have been advocated (*e.g.*, Ellis's plan for a new metrical terminology; or see a report, in the *Academy*, Jan. 10, 1885, of a paper read before the Philological Society in London: it advocates a "phonetic notation, providing signs for all the significant sounds, as well as for at least three degrees of stress and five of length") none has been established. Our conventional versification recognizes only accented and unaccented, long and short syllables.

It is a well-known property of human speech that it keeps up a ceaseless change between accented and unaccented syllables. A long succession of accented syllables becomes unbearably monotonous; a long succession of unaccented syllables is, in effect, impossible. Now when the ear detects at regular intervals a recurrence of accented syllables, varying with unaccented, it perceives *Rhythm*. Measured intervals of time are the basis of all verse, and their *regularity* marks off poetry from prose; so that Time is thus the chief element in Poetry, as it is in Music and in Dancing. From the idea of measuring these time-intervals, we derive the name Metre; Rhythm means pretty much the same thing, — "a flowing," an even, measured motion. This rhythm is found everywhere in nature: the beat of the heart, the ebb and flow of the sea, the alternation of day and night. Rhythm is not artificial, not an invention;[1] it lies at the heart of things, and in rhythm the noblest emotions find their noblest expression. Rhythm, or metre, made itself known very early in the history of our race. Just as one who walks briskly in a cheerful mood, involuntarily marks his steps with a song, whistling, humming, or the like, so at the primitive religious rites of our ancestors the usual solemn dance[2] was accompanied by a song. As the dancing lines swayed back and forth, they marked their steps by chanted words, — a syllable for each step: the words were rude enough at first, but little by little gained in precision and meaning (*cf.* p. 9). Two steps, right and left, made a unit; for with the third, the first motion was repeated. We may thus assume the double beat of left-right as metrical unit: *cf.* the term "foot." Westphal has shown that the original Indo-European metre consisted of a measured chant accompanying a dance of eight steps forward and eight backward; the whole making one verse, divided into halves (*cf.* the classic *Cæsura*) by the pause and return. We shall see below that in *Germanic*[3] poetry these half-verses were firmly bound together by *Rime*. The alternation of

---

[1] Hence much of the talk about "barbarous metre" and "apt numbers" is absurd so far as it assumes to treat rhythm as a constantly increasing accomplishment of civilized man. "Any *Volkslied*," writes in a private letter one of our leading English scholars, "any *Volkslied* shows as good an ear as any Pindaric ode by Gray or whomever else."

[2] This dance was regular; it was developed from the *march* and consisted of steps, not of irregular leaps.

[3] It is perhaps necessary to insist on the meaning of this term: it includes High and Low German, Gothic, Norse, Anglo-Saxon, etc.

stronger right and weaker left gave the accented and the unaccented beat (= syllable) of the foot. With the end of the *verse* (*verto*), the dancers *turned* again to repeat their forward-and-back. [For further particulars, see Westphal, *Metrik der Griechen*, Vol. II.; or Scherer, *Zur Geschichte der deutschen Sprache*, 2d ed. p. 623.]

Or, we could imagine a quicker rhythm, in which there should be *two* syllables to each step: one syllable light, with the lifting of the foot; the other heavy, as the foot struck the ground again: *cf.* the classic terms (inconsistently used) *arsis* and *thesis*. One thing is certain: in this combination of song and dance we see the origin of rhythm as applied to connected words. Thus, rhythm is the harmonious repetition of certain fixed sound-relations: time being the basis, just as in dancing or music.

This brings another question:—what relation is there between the rhythm of music and the rhythm of poetry? The further back we go, the more closely music and poetry are connected. For modern times, we may state the difference thus: Music has for distinctive characteristic, *melody*,—the variations of pitch, of "high" and "low" notes, but speech has, in effect, no such fixed variations; that is, they furnish no special, definite mark to speech, except in questions, surprise, etc. But speech has *quality*,—what the Germans call *tone-color*. Infinite variety is imparted to speech by the combinations of different vocal effects,—the full or thin vowels, the diphthongs, the consonants. This tone-tint is to poetry what melody is to music: common to both poetry and music is *rhythm*.

Our business, therefore, is to consider verse in its

rhythm and in the quality of its tones. Rhythm has two branches: *time* and *stress*, or *quantity* and *accent*. Both are familiar to music, but time more especially. Hence, *that poetry which depends, for metrical effect, chiefly upon detailed time-relations (quantity) will come nearer to music than the poetry which depends chiefly on stress-relations (intensity, accent)*.

§ 2. QUANTITY.

Quantity deals with the relative length of a syllable; that is, with the time required to utter it. The Greeks adopted quantity as principle of their metre, and based their verse upon the relation of long and short syllables. A syllable was long which contained a long vowel or a diphthong, or a final consonant coming before another consonant in the next syllable; a long syllable was equal to two short ones. For such poetry, the term "metre" is very appropriate: the verse was really *measured*. In the Germanic languages, and in nearly all modern poetry, *accent* is made the principle of verse: we *weigh* our syllables, we ask how much *force*, not how much time, they require. Meanwhile, we do not utterly refuse to recognize quantity as an element of verse, nor was classic poetry unfamiliar with accent. In the latter, an "ictus," or stress, fell upon the long syllable; in modern verse, while the main principle is the alternation of heavy and light syllables, we nevertheless admit quantity as a "regulative" element. It is a secondary factor of verse.

First, as to the principle of quantity in classic verse. Take the famous line of Vergil:—

"Quadrupedante putrem sonitu quatit ungula campum,"—

and a verse of *Evangeline*: —

"This is the forest primeval, but where are the hearts that beneath it," —

and at first sight we call each a dactylic hexameter verse. We give a scheme : —

$$\acute{-}\smile\smile\ \acute{-}\smile\smile\ \acute{-}\smile\smile\ \acute{-}\smile\smile\ \acute{-}\smile\smile\ \acute{-}\smile$$

In one sense, this scheme fits both verses; but there is a radical difference in the application. In the Latin, contrast of long (–) and short (⌣), a fixed relation of time within the foot as well as within the verse, gave exquisite pleasure to the sensitive ear. This time-relation was the chief metrical factor, although an "ictus" (´) or stress undoubtedly marked the long syllables. In the English verse there is no fixed relation of quantity within the foot: "this" requires practically no more time than "is" or "the," and not as much as the metrically short but actually long *pri-* in "primeval." The time-intervals of the whole verse are marked off by the recurrence of the stress, just as in Latin by the recurrence of the long syllable. This is an important difference. We may say that in classic metres, quantity is the mistress, while quality (stress) plays a handmaid's part. The result was a harmony more musical than can be given by our verse, in which stress is chief metrical factor, and quantity has only a *regulative* office. Some writers say that modern verse does not recognize quantity at all. This is a mistake. "Long and short syllables," says Schipper in his *Englische Metrik*, "have no constant length, no constant relation, — but they depend on their place in the verse, and on the context; though they do not determine the rhythm of verse, they still act as regulators of our metre in a very important degree." That is, while no precise rules prevail, the skilful poet avoids an excess of unaccented long syllables or accented short ones. It is not the proportion of long and short within the foot that we heed, but the proportion in the whole verse. Further, quantity is used to help the meaning —a sort of *onomatopœia:* as in

"The lowing herd wind slowly o'er the lea."

It is very important to hold apart this special, classical principle of quantity, or the time of separate syllables, from the general principle of time-intervals underlying all rhythm (*cf.* p. 134). Thus Tennyson's two verses: "Break — break — break" — and "On thy cold, gray stones, O Sea!" are rhythmically harmonious, since the time-intervals agree; as may be seen by any one who will tap off the accented syllables, allowing for the pauses in the first verse. But we can arrive at no metrical result by simply applying the test of quantity to the individual syllables. It is not the length of the word "break" (of course, elocutionary motives may prolong the sound at will) which makes it metrically equal to "on thy cold"; it is the heavy *accent*, followed by a *pause*.

§ 3. ACCENT.

Accent, then, is the chief factor of modern verse. But there are two kinds of accent which we must consider before we can fully grasp the difference between classical and modern metres: the word-accent and the verse-accent. (1) WORD-ACCENT. — When a word has two syllables, one of these receives a marked increase of tone as compared with the other. In words of more than two syllables, there is generally a secondary accent: *i.e.*, one of the remaining syllables receives less tone, indeed, than the accented syllable, but more than the rest: *cf. shépherd, shépherdèss, shépherdèsses.* Of course, there can be a third accent, if the word have syllables enough; for, as said above, speech tends to alternate accented with unaccented.

Of the same nature as the word-accent are, further, the *syntactical* and the *rhetorical* accent, which concern relations of words in a sentence. The accent lifts certain words into prominence, leaving others without special stress of tone, and without the added distinctness of articulation which often accompanies accent.

These two accents — of the word and of the sentence — are of great importance in modern verse; but in the classic metres, which had more of a musical character than our own, they exercised less influence. Especially is this the case with word-accent; and this we must look at more closely, in order to see what difference there is between ancient and modern languages in their methods of selecting, in a given word, the syllable to be accented. This applies, of course, to prose as well as to poetry. (1) *The Grammatical Accent.* — This is the principle in Sanskrit, and, to a certain extent, in Greek. Taking a given word, we find its accented syllable shifting with different grammatical forms of the word. In Sanskrit this word-accent is not even confined, as it is in Greek, to the last three syllables. Thus we have a *Movable Accent.* (2) *The Rhythmical Accent.* — The word-accent tends to fall upon a *long* syllable, as in the Latin. In Greek, the accent was indifferent to the quantity of the syllable on which it fell: thus the Greek *chímaira* became Latin *chiméra*.

(3) *The Logical Accent.* — A brilliant piece of research by Carl Verner has proved the existence of a movable accent in the oldest forms of the Germanic languages. This has left its mark in a few sound-changes with which we are not here concerned. But it is certain that at a very early period, before the date of any Germanic literature known to us, *this movable accent was given up, and the word-accent became a fixed one.* It chose and clung to a certain syllable, and this was *the syllable which gave meaning to the word.* Hence the term "logical accent." In all original English words, and in many words derived from foreign sources, we bring out with additional stress the syllable which bears the real weight of the word, the root-syllable. Instead of the shifting Greek accent which changed from a nominative to a genitive of the same word (*ánthrōpos: anthrṓpou*), we have such persistence as *sheep, shepherd, shepherdess, shepherdesses.*

(II) VERSE-ACCENT. — We have seen that verse is now marked off by the regular recurrence of a stress or accent falling on certain syllables; and that even in classic metres a stress fell upon the long syllables. We naturally ask how this verse-accent agrees with the word-accent just described. Looking, first, at the different ways in which we could make verses, we find the simplest plan to be a mere counting of syllables, with absolute ignoring of word-accent. Each syllable would be a verse-accent. Thus, if we slowly count off "one — two — three — four," then repeat the words with the same slowness, accenting each like the rest, we shall have a metrical result. Fragments of verse said to be based on this bare syllable-counting are found in the Old-Persian, the language of the *Avesta*. But such a system tends to pass into something else; for the impulse to pairs (as in the ticking of a clock), and to alternation of strong and weak tones, is inherent in language.

Or, again, we may have a regular system of verse in which (as in the pairs of steps in the primitive dance noticed above) certain syllables are accented for metrical reasons, and others are left without accent. The metre will thus be regarded at the sacrifice of the word-accent. As a *license* of verse, this is common enough in our modern poetry; but does not extend beyond isolated words. We have two kinds of this license: the "Hovering Accent" and the "Wrenched Accent." In the former, word-accent and verse-accent simply divide the stress between them: the accent "hovers" over both, — as in : —

"That thróugh the gréen còrnfìèld did páss."— Shakspere.

The "wrenched accent" throws the stress on an inflexional syllable : —

"For the stárs and the wínds are únto hér
As ráiment, as sóngs of the hárp-*playér*."— Swinburne.

So, too, the *portér* and *countrée* of the ballads. Of this license Puttenham speaks (*Arte of English Poesie*) in a chapter headed : "How the good maker (*sc.* poet) will not wrench his word to helpe his rime, either by falsifying his accent, or by untrue orthographie." Gascoigne (*Notes of Instruction*) lays down the same law, and observes it carefully in his *Steele Glas;* and it is quite clear that we cannot extend this license to a whole verse; no harmonious system can result from a mere ignoring of one kind of accent to suit another. Some other metrical element must come in. This new element is furnished in the shape of *quantity.* Suppose, now, we do push word-accent out of the question, but make a rule that the verse-accent, the ictus, must fall exclusively upon those syllables which have a stated quantity — the "long" syllables. This is the rule of Greek and Latin metre. But in this scheme we need not ignore the word-accent: for the Greek word-accent was an *increase of pitch*, an added *height* of tone, not added stress. "In the Indian, in the Greek, and in the Roman verse, there was no conflict between the ictus, by which the verse was measured, and the accent of the words which made up the verse" (Scherer).[1] The fact that our Germanic race, and, later, most modern languages, made stress of tone necessary for the word-accent, renders it now impossible to distinguish a word-accent by height of tone (pitch) and give the stress to a neighbor-syllable. But the Greek combined musical and metrical effects where we cannot. As was hinted above, the recitation of the Greek minstrel must have been a sort of chant: the speech was more musical on account of its pitch; the metre was more musical on account of its time-relations.

But early in the history of the Germanic races, stress-accent for words pushed into the foreground. They gave up the fixed relations of quantity, as well as the

---

[1] So, too, Westphal. It is only fair to state that some writers on metre oppose this view, and contend that the Greek verse simply ignored word-accent.

pitch-accent. They *weighed* their syllables. Their verse depended on the contrast of heavy and light, not long and short. Accent became, as Daniel puts it in his *Defense of Ryme* (1603), "the chief lord and grave governour of numbers." This choice of accent rather than quantity lay, thinks Scherer, in the passionate and vehement nature of our Germanic race. Our ancestors were disposed to extremes, and lacked the quiet, artistic sense that adopted the placid rhythm of Greek verse. The German could not *linger* on his verse-accent; he put into it all the strength of which he was capable; and he helped his voice by strokes on some loud instrument, the strokes being timed by verse-accents. Now, we remember how the Germanic *word-accent* was chosen: it had to rest on the root-syllable. Perhaps this word-accent was once, as in Greek, a variation of pitch, not a stress; but early in the history of the race, *stress* was adopted as sole mark of the word-accent. But here is a conflict. The same word might have on one syllable the verse-accent, on another syllable the word-accent; and both were marked by stress, by strength of tone. This was intolerable. Hence a rule which became the fundamental principle of all Germanic verse: THE WORD-ACCENT AND THE VERSE-ACCENT MUST FALL ON ONE AND THE SAME SYLLABLE; AND THIS COMMON ACCENT CONSISTS IN STRESS OF TONE.

Compared with Greek and Latin metres, our verse gains in intensity and force, loses in grace and flexibility. This is especially true of our earliest verse, before the influence of the classics had added so much grace and freedom, and, at the same time, regularity, to our rhythm. The Greek verse sped swiftly and lightly, like an Olympian athlete; the early Germanic verse had the clanging tread of a warrior in mail.

As to the agreement of the verse-accent with the *rhetorical* or the *syntactical* accent, there is no fixed rule. The agreement may lie on the surface, as in Pope's or Dryden's verse, where a rhetorical effect is always evident:—

"When music softens or when dancing fires."

But in other verse there is not the same effort to bring out a rhetorical accent; *cf.* Keats:—

"His eyes from the dead leaves, or one small pulse."

In general, the metrical stress and the syntactical accent must agree; for otherwise an intolerable emphasis would be thrown upon the unimportant words.

We may here note that traces of accentual verse are found in the oldest Latin literature. Latin poetry of the classical period took its metres from the Greek; but in the so-called Saturnian Verse we have undoubted accentual rhythm, and also *rime*, which, indeed, is a natural product of the accentual system.

§ 4. PAUSES.

The foundation of rhythm is a regular succession of equal time-intervals. In English verse these are marked off by accented syllables. A *group* of such "bars" or "feet" may be marked off by a regular stop in the sense; another group follows, repeating the conditions of the first,—and so on. But this would be intolerably monotonous. Variety is obtained not only by license in the distribution of heavy and light syllables, but also by the use of *pauses*. There are two kinds of pause : the *compensating* and the *rhythmical.* The compensating pause takes the place of a syllable. While in general the rule holds that modern verse regularly varies accented with unaccented syllables, *i.e.*, gives at least one light to every heavy syllable, there are cases where the accent is preceded or followed by a pause in place of the light syllable. This omission of the unaccented syllable may be *regular,* — as in the already quoted "Break, break, break," where the pauses are very evident; or it may be somewhat irregular, as in the lines quoted by Ruskin (*Prosody*, p. 34) : —

> " Till' said' to Tweed':
> Though' ye rin' wi' speed',
> And I' rin' slaw',
> Whar ye' droon' ae' man
> I' droon' twa'."

The metrical effect, say of the first line, would be the same if we read : " The Till, it said to Tweed." — Or the omission may be isolated and quite irregular. *Cf.* the witches' song in *Macbeth :* —

> " Tóad, that únder *cóld stóne,*
> Dáys and níghts hast thírty-óne," etc.

> " Lét your ódour *drive hénce*
> *All mists* that dázzle sénse." — Fletcher.

Guest condemns this license between syllables of one word — as " sún-beám," " moón-líght " (Spenser). It may be said in general terms of this compensating pause that the spirit of our modern verse is against its isolated use, but allows it when it is employed with regularity. Compare expressions like " Aúld láng syne," or Cowper's "Toll' for' the brave'." Dramatic verse is very familiar with this pause. Dowden speaks of the dramatic pause "expressing surprise or sudden emotion, or accompanying a change of speakers, and leaving a gap in the verse, — a gap through which we feel the wind of passion and of song." One famous line in *Measure for Measure* goes so far as to let the pause compensate for a (technically) heavy syllable : —

> " Merciful heaven!
> Thou rather, with thy sharp and sulphurous bolt,
> Splitt'st the unwedgeable and gnarled oak,
> *Than the soft myrtle. But man, proud man,*" etc.

Certain editors have even proclaimed this verse corrupt because hopelessly unrhythmical. Scanned by the fingers, it *is* unrhythmical. But let any one read it carefully aloud, give due weight to the (technically light) syllable "soft" (which is naturally emphatic as opposed to "unwedgeable and gnarled"), and also to the decided pause after "myrtle,"— and the line will be musical enough.

The Rhythmical Pause. — Here there is no dropped syllable in the case. It is simply a pause in the verse which generally, but not always, corresponds to a pause in the sense. The compensating pause allowed the omission of a syllable: the rhythmical pause frequently is followed by an extra syllable. Of course, the end of the verse furnishes the chief rhythmical pause. When the sense also pauses here, the verse is called "end-stopt" (the technical term used by Shakspere scholars): when the sense does not so pause, the verse is called "run-on." But there is another pause after either the accented or the unaccented syllable, commonly about the middle of the verse (called in classical metres the *cæsura*), which increases in importance with the number of accents contained in the verse. This pause naturally tends to agree with the logical pause; but such is not always the case.   Thus (*L'Allegro*)

"When rocking winds are piping loud"

has no pause in the sense, but there is a slight rhythmical pause after "winds." It is stronger and equally independent of logical pause in (Dryden, *A. & A.*)

"Usurp'd a patriot's | all-atoning name;"

and it is absolutely importunate in (Drayton, *Polyolbion*)

"The yellow kingcup wrought | in many a curious shape."

But in most cases it is logical as well as rhythmical; and here we distinguish (*a*) the pause that breaks a single verse into two or even three groups, — as in (Pope, *R. of L.*)

"When husbands | or when lapdogs | breathe their last;"
"When music softens | and when dancing fires;"

and (*b*) the pause in run-on lines, breaking up a series of verses into new groups, so that the logical divisions of phrases and sentences, and the rhythmical divisions of feet and verses, do not coincide. In both these cases (*a* and *b*) there is produced that exquisite strife between unity and variety, the type and the individual, which is characteristic of our best poetry. There is great freedom in the use of the pause. Whereas Gascoigne thinks that the pause "in a verse of tenne will best be placed at the end of the first foure sillables," our later blank-verse does not follow the stiff example of *The Steele Glas*. Thus with Milton, the *stateliness* is due to the sonorous march of accents, their arrangement and proportion; the *variety* is due to the constantly shifting pause within the verse. In Shakspere's verse we can trace the progress towards a free handling of pauses. His earlier plays are full of "end-stopt" verses,—*i.e.*, the sense pauses at the end of each verse. But the later plays abound in "run-on" verses. In *Love's Labour's Lost*, an early play, Mr. Furnivall counts one run-on verse to 18.14 end-stopt; in the *Tempest*, a late play, the proportion is 1 : 3.02.

The pause occurs in different parts of the verse, and may be "masculine" or "feminine,"—*i.e.*, it may occur after an accented or an unaccented syllable. Note the pauses in the following extract from *Paradise Lost*, 3. 80 ff. : —

    "Only begotten son, | see'st thou what rage [1]
    Transports our adversary, | whom no bounds
    Prescribed, | no bars of hell, | nor all the chains
    Heap'd on him there, | nor yet the main abyss
    Wide interrupt can hold, | so bent he seems
    On desperate revenge, | that shall redound
    Upon his own rebellious head? | And now
    Through all restraint broke loose, | he wings his way
    Not far off heaven, | in the precincts of light,
    Directly toward the new-created world."

In the third line there are *two* pauses; in the last line there is *none*. In the first, the pause is "masculine";

---

[1] None of these "run-on" lines is a "weak ending." Example of such a weak ending is (*Tempest*, I. 2) : —

        "Thy father was the Duke of Milan, *and*
        A prince of power."

Here we approach the freedom of prose.

in the second, "feminine." The pause can even come in the first foot, halving it:—

> "Not to me returns
> Day, | nor the sweet approach of even or morn."— 3. 42.

Or in the *last* foot:—

> "Where no shadow stays
> Thy coming and thy soft embraces; | he," etc.— 4. 470.

Schipper notes that in lyric verse, and verse of four accents, or less, the sense-group and verse-group generally (not always) coincide; while for verse of more than four accents, the sense-group falls within the limits of the verse,— as in examples just quoted.— Often the pause in heroic verse has an exquisite harmony with the sense. Thus, Mr. Seward, quoting from Beaumont and Fletcher, notes such a use of the pause in giving a suspended or incomplete image; and also quotes Milton:—

> "Despair
> Tended the sick, busiest from couch to couch,
> And over them triumphant death his dart
> Shook | —— but delayed to strike."— 11. 480.

§ 5. RIME.

Our oldest English verse depended for its rhythm on the recurrence of accented syllables; the number or position of the light syllables was not strictly regulated. There must be so many accents in each verse. But the bare recurrence of accents was not enough for the ear, especially when the light syllables were so irregular. It was hard to establish the unity of the verse. Further, there must be something to afford the same sort of pleasure that was given to the Greek by the quantity of his syllables. Germanic verse had discarded quantity as a metrical factor; but at a very early period it must have taken up *quality*. It gave to its accented syllables *Rime*, which (*a*) brought new emphasis to the accents, and (*b*) bound the verse firmly together as a strict unit. In Greek, the verse-accents agreed in quantity; in early Germanic verse, they agreed in quality. In general terms, then, rime is where two syllables or combinations of syllables, agree in the quality of their sounds. But this agreement is of different kinds; and in treating rime, we must make a distinction between our earliest (Anglo-Saxon) verse and that of later times. In regard to the former, we note that rime was *confined within the limits of a single verse;* that *it affected the beginning, and not as now the end, of syllables;* and that it was an absolute necessity of verse,—whereas now, thanks to the more regular alternation of heavy and light syllables, and the consequent harmony, we can often, as in blank-verse, dispense with rime. It is most convenient to treat the three kinds of rime separately.— 1. Beginning-Rime.— This is commonly known as *Alliteration*, but the term misleads us, and makes us think it something different from rime. The initial sounds of two syllables agree in quality of tone. We leave the details of Anglo-Saxon verse to be discussed later, and for the present look at beginning-rime in itself. It is of great antiquity. Our Germanic ancestors used it to make still stronger the already word-accented and verse-accented syllables. It had practical uses. In Chap. I. § 1, we noted its application to religious and legal ceremonies; and rimed phrases still survive, as "man and mouse," "bed and board," "house and home"; *cf.* the chieftains Hengest and Horsa, and the riming tribe-names Ingævones, Istævones, Herminones (= Irmin-). It is seen at its best in *Beowulf;* Cynewulf uses it with masterly effect. With the conquest, Norman minstrels brought in end-rime, already familiar in sacred Latin poetry, and, as extra ornament, in the native verse; but the old rime still flourished here and there. Layamon (about 1200) employs it to a great degree in his *Brut;* and in the famous *Vision concerning Piers the Plowman*, it is used with regularity and force. But it dropped out of fashion. The old rules relaxed and it fell into anarchy, or became a mere accident of verse. Chaucer laughs at it as a North-of-England trick (Prol. *Persone's Tale*) : —

> "But trusteth wel, I am a sotherne man,
> I cannot geste rom ram ruf by my letter."

In 1550, Robert Crowley printed *Piers the Plowman*, and felt compelled to explain how the verse "runs upon the letter." This noted, he says, the metre "shal be very pleasaunt to read." Beginning-rime thus became a mere adornment of verse, — and even of prose, for Lyly's *Euphues* riots in "alliteration." Early Elizabethan lyric poetry is full of it, — but as an ornament, not as a principle. George Gascoigne tells the poet not to "hunte a letter to death." Shakspere makes Holofernes, his pedant (*Love's Labour's Lost*, IV. 2), "something affect the letter" in his "extempore epitaph," because it "argues facility." In modern times, Swinburne is very persistent with it; though no one will quarrel with his "lisp of leaves and ripple of rain." It is best not to thrust beginning-rime forward in verse; the poet should let it often lurk in unaccented syllables, — as in Coleridge's lines: —

> "The *shadow* of the *dome* of *pleasure*
> Floated *midway* on the *waves*,
> Where was heard the mingled measure
> From the fountains and the caves." — *Kubla Khan.*

Rime that includes *both beginning and end* of the syllable or combination of syllables, and thus makes the agreement absolute, is not looked upon with favor. This "perfect rime" was used sporadically by Chaucer, and is still popular in French poetry; but is now entirely foreign to English verse. 2. END-RIME. — This sort of rime was well known to the Latin Hymns of the Church, and thus crept into the learned literature of Europe. Rime had always been a mark of the (accentual) Latin folk-poetry, and for this popular quality it was adopted by the church; in the hymns it was combined with a regular metre, *i.e.*, strict alternation of heavy and light syllables. But end-rime was not unknown to the native Germanic verse; *cf.* the "Riming Poem" in Anglo-Saxon of the Tenth Century. It was familiar to the oldest Latin poetry. In the Saturnian Verse we have such rimes as : —

> "Terra pestem teneto   salus hic maneto.
> Bicorpores Gigantes   magnique Atlantes.

End-rime occurs even in classic Latin verse. Wilhelm Grimm has collected (*Proceedings Berlin Acad.,* 1851) a host of examples, though the rime is often imperfect. Rime, therefore, is a natural quality of verse, not the invention of a particular race — *e.g.*, of the Arabs — as was once supposed.

The Latin hymn, which made systematic end-rime so popular, consisted of stanzas of four verses, mostly of four feet, these feet having each two syllables with accent on the second. It was popular, and opposed to the traditional quantitative verse. The rimes were often in pairs; but sometimes took in all four verses. Since each verse had but one rimed word, and that at the end, the accented and unaccented syllables alternated regularly; for the absence of rime within the verse made impossible the old Germanic freedom of dropping or adding light syllables.

Another model which influenced English verse was the rimed lyric poetry of the troubadours and Norman minstrels. In the time of Henry II. all the western part of France, Provençal and Norman, was under British rule. The troubadours and singers about the court of their countrywoman, Eleanor, invented new forms of lyric, and in every way spread the use of their rimed verse. English poets copied this foreign lyric. They took their old native verse, shorn of its beginning-rime, or else, dragging that with it, cut it in halves, joined the ends by rime, and so produced the rimed couplet — a bridge over which English verse passed to more complicated forms. An odd mixture of English and French, and of both kinds of rime, is a song to the Virgin (end of Thirteenth Century) : —

> "Mayden moder milde,
> Oiez cel oreysoun;
> From shome thou me shilde,
> E de ly malfeloun."

"Maiden mother mild, hear this prayer; shield me from shame and from the evil-one." — Finally, the two kinds of rime changed places in English verse. End-Rime became a principle — especially of lyric poetry; Beginning-Rime became an ornament.

End-Rime is *single* ("masculine") when it falls on the last syllable of the verse: *sing: ring*. It is *double* ("feminine") when accent and rime fall on the penult; *cunning: running*. Of course the unaccented syllables also rime; — mostly they rime *perfectly*, as in the last example. The accent and rime may fall on the *antepenult;* or there may be *two accents* rimed in each case. Example of first: *pitiful: city full;* example of second: —

"Heaven send it *happy dew*,
Earth lend it *sap anew*." — Scott.

Note, in this last, still another and third rime in the middle of the verse, — *send: lend*. These involved rimes are common enough. *Cf.* "And sweep thro' the deep" (Campbell); which is like the only modest end-rime on which the oldest Anglo-Saxon verse could venture, — as "frôd and gôd." Further, "Hark, hark, the lark at heaven's gate sings;" "And the heart that would part sic love." More complicated yet is Hood's —

"Here end as just a friend I must."

But rimes must not *clash* — as in "teach each." The ear must decide how far to employ rime. As a rule, rime must fall upon an accented syllable, though some poets have broken this rule, — Wyatt, for example. Guest quotes: —

"Right true it is, and said full yore ago,
Take heed of him that by the back thee *claweth*,

> For none is worse than is a friendly foe.
> Though thee seme good all thing that thee *deliteth*,
> Yet know it well that in thy bosome *crepeth*;
> For many a man such fire ofttimes he kindleth,
> That with the blase his beard himself he singeth."

Lines 2, 4, 5, are examples of rime on unaccented syllables. Lines 6 and 7 are examples of imperfect rime on accented syllables. This last is called *Assonance*. — 3. ASSONANCE is a principle of verse in some of the Romance languages, as in the *Chanson de Roland*, the famous French epic. It occurs in Spanish poetry. In her *Spanish Gypsy*, George Eliot imitated "the trochaic measure and assonance of the Spanish Ballad," — as in Juan's Song : —

> "Maiden crowned with glossy *blackness*,
> Lithe as panther forest-*roaming*,
> Long-armed naiad, when she *dances*,
> On a stream of ether *floating*."

As in the above, assonance generally deals with the vowels alone, and hence is not strictly end-rime: *cf. black-* and *danc-*. It characterized the earliest Latin poetry of the church, but soon gave place to regular end-rime. In Germanic literature it has never been more than an accident: "it appears only here and there, and really only in the form of imperfect full-rime." Marston, in one of his satires, makes *Œdipus* rime with *snufs* (verb), and *unrip* with *wit*. — To sum up: "Alliteration" deals with initial sounds; Assonance with the interior or middle sound (vowel) of a syllable; and End-Rime — rime proper — with the middle and final sounds. Perfect Rime — *i.e.*, of all these sounds, initial, middle, end — is not regarded as legitimate in modern English verse.

§ 6. BLANK VERSE.

We saw that the verse which depends for its existence solely upon accents must call in rime as a necessary element for unity of structure. This rime within the verse (alliteration, chiefly) yielded to the new metrical principles which informed poetry written in greater or less imitation of classical models. Regularity in alternation of accented and unaccented syllables gave new harmony; rime was needed simply to show the end of the verse. In lyric poetry, which is mostly in stanzas, rime is still a necessity. But for the flow of epic or dramatic verse, rime is less desirable. Hence, a total dispensing with rime, and the unincumbered gait of BLANK VERSE. While blank verse approaches the freedom of prose, and so appears very easy to manage, it is in reality the most difficult of ordinary metres. Its origin, growth, and perfection mark the modern period of English poetry. Imitated from the Italian poets, and first used, in any notable way, by the Earl of Surrey in his translation of the second and fourth books of Vergil's *Æneid*, the fortunes of English blank verse were soon assured. In the same century, the drama, just breaking from the bonds of petty Moralities and Mysteries, seized upon blank verse as the fittest instrument it could find. The crude efforts in *Gorboduc* soon yielded to the "mighty line" of Marlowe, the first poet to handle blank verse with that ease of stateliness familiar to us in his greater scholar, Shakspere. Then came Milton, and the epic was almost identified with blank verse. Milton's sweeping charges against rime as "the invention of a barbarous age to set off wretched matter and lame metre," and as "a thing of itself, to all judicious ears, trivial and of no musical delight"; his definition of true metre as consisting "in apt numbers, fit quantity of syllables, and the sense variously drawn out from one verse into another" (*cf.* § 4, on Rhythmical Pause), may, with certain allowances, hold good for stately epic and for dramatic verse; but they will not hold good for the lyric. Who would reduce Milton's own *Lycidas*, or his Sonnets, to blank verse? Indeed, he seems half to admit this by the saving phrase "in longer works especially." Marvell, *On Milton's Paradise Lost*, praises the poet for scorning to "allure with tinkling rhyme," and recognizes the fitness of his metre to his subject : —

> "Thy verse, created like thy theme sublime,
> In number, weight and measure, needs not rhyme."

There was later a slight reaction on dramatic ground. Dryden set the fashion of writing plays in rimed couplets, after the French custom. But in *All for Love* (the only play, he tells us, he wrote *to please himself*) he came back to blank verse, and "disencumbered himself of rime." Blank verse is to-day regarded as the proper measure for epic, dramatic, and longer reflective poems. Exceptions are the heroic couplets of lighter epic, like Keats' *Endymion* (but *cf.* his *Hyperion*, with its splendid Miltonic cadences), or, for these days, Swinburne's *Tristram of Lyonesse*, with its memories of Marlowe's *Hero and Leander;* the stanzaic narrative verse — as in *Childe Harold;* and the short rimed couplets of Scott and Byron.

In thus speaking of blank verse, we have supposed it to be the same thing as unrimed "heroic" or five-accent verse. But there are other forms of rimeless verse;— besides such cases as the four-accent blank verse of *Hiawatha*, there are imitations of classic metres, which, however, cannot be said to have obtained a very sure foothold in our poetry. True, Webbe and Puttenham looked with disfavor on rime, and Thomas Campion broke a lance in the defence of unrimed lyric measures. In his *Observations in the Art of English Poesie* (1602), he made war on rime, and urged poets to follow classical models. He gives examples of the new style. There is some melody in his

> "Rose-cheekt Lawra, come
> Sing thou smoothly with thy beawties
> Silent music, either other
> Sweetly gracing."

But we see that beginning-rime slips in repeatedly: *cf.* further his so-called "Anacreontic" verses:—

> "Could I catch that
> Nimble trayter,
> Skornful Lawra,
> Swift-foot Lawra,
> Soone then would I
> Seeke avengement."

In 1603, Samuel Daniel answered with his *Defence of Ryme*, "wherein is demonstratively proved that Ryme is the fittest harmonic of words that comports with our language." His views have prevailed.[1] There are

---

[1] The famous "Areopagus," a club for the extinction of the tyrant rime, of which Sidney and Spenser were members, could do nothing for their purpose; and Spenser most elaborately confuted his own theory. There

some fine rimeless lyrics in modern English poetry, but they are sporadic: Collins' *Ode to Evening* and Matthew Arnold's *Rugby Chapel* may be instanced as two different types.

The main thing to remember is that the success of blank verse is modern, and is due to the harmony and regularity brought to our poetry by the study of classic metres. So late as 1600, Thomas Heywood could say that

> " not long since —
> . . . there was a time
> Strong lines were not look'd after, but if rime,
> Oh, then 'twas excellent."

§ 7. THE QUALITIES AND COMBINATIONS OF SOUNDS.

Sounds of the human voice have an endless variety of shades and gradations. Think of the modulations of spoken words by which we express grief, joy, threats, entreaties, pain, and so on. The sharp, "explosive" consonants, the lingering effect of the liquids, the broad vowels, the thin vowels, — all these, with their combinations, make up a wonderful material for the skilful poet to work with. Such qualities of sound add to the mere rhythm of poetry what melody adds to the rhythm of music. The most evident use of these qualities lies in the imitation of natural sounds. This may be confined to words — like "hiss," "cuckoo," "murmur," "buzz," "susurrus," etc. Or the imitation may extend to more

---

are verses by Ben Jonson against rime, themselves rimed, in which he calls it "rack of finest wits"; praises Greek as "free from rime's infection"; and ends by cursing the inventor of rime. But we need not take the verses too seriously.

than one word, and so suggest some action or situation — *onomatopœia*. Homer has a line which resounds with the swell and surge of an ocean billow. Shakspere's verse —

"The multitudinous seas incarnadine" (*Macbeth*, II. 2) —

does not so much imitate as give a distant echo and hint of tossing and storm-swept waves; and the suggestion of a sea-beach, far below the speaker who describes it, is certainly audible in

". . . the murmuring surge
That on the unnumber'd idle pebbles chafes." . . .
—*Lear*, IV. 6.

More directly imitative is Milton's description of the opening doors of hell : —

". . . On a sudden open fly
With impetuous recoil and jarring sound
The infernal doors, and on their hinges grate
Harsh thunder" (*Par. Lost*, 2. 879);

or of heaven : —

". . . heaven open'd wide
Her ever during gates, harmonious sound
On golden hinges moving" (*Par. Lost*, 7. 206).

Chaucer's verse about the monk whose bridle men could hear "gynglen in a whistlyng wynd" as he rode, is itself full of the breezy morning. A comic effect and direct imitation are reached in that line of Ovid about the frogs : —

"Quamvis sint sub aqua, sub aqua maledicere tentant."

Metrical effect can produce onomatopœia, apart from the quality of the sounds, by the slow or fast march of the syllables : *cf.* the verse from Vergil, quoted in § 2, or the hackneyed lines, from Pope's *Essay on Criticism*, about Ajax and swift Camilla. In that same poem, we are told that "the sound should seem an echo to the sense." This is true in general terms. But a perpetual imitative jingle would reduce poetry to the functions and virtues of a parrot. The suggestion, the hint, must lurk in the background, as is the case with all the great poets. Shakspere rarely used direct imitation; an instance is the "Double, double," etc., of the witches as they stir their boiling caldron. But some writers go so far as to insist that every isolated sound has a special suggestion and meaning. Somebody has fancied that he hears a rubbing or boring in the sound *tr;* and so on, to the wildest nonsense. As Professor Whitney says, there is "no natural and inherent significance of articulate sounds." Of course, he would not deny direct imitations of natural sounds; nor would he exclude from certain combinations the quality of 'pleasant' or 'unpleasant,' 'sweet' or 'harsh.' It is the combinations of sounds that give the peculiar quality to a verse. Thus, combinations of liquids suggest harmony, beauty: —

"Morn, in the white wake of the morning star,
Came furrowing all the orient into gold." — Tennyson.

"stars . . .
May drop their golden tears upon the ground."
— George Peele.

Sounds difficult to utter give a harsh effect to verse: note the *combinations of consonants* in Milton's famous line from *Lycidas:* "Grate on their scrannel pipes of wretched straw." Even liquid consonants may be rough when combined, as in this verse, or in the "grate harsh thunder" quoted above, with sounds which are hard to utter. A *crowding of light syllables* may be combined with this harshness :—

> " So he with difficulty and labour hard
> Moved on, with difficulty and labour he."
> *—Par. Lost*, 2. 1021.

The *combination of sounds in a verse* is a matter for which no definite rule can be given. It is not even possible to say, as we can say of rime, that this is good or that bad. " Solvitur ambulando." Here lies the skill, the genius of the poet ; and no rules can take the place of a poetic ear. The poet combines sounds with forcible or melodious effect, just as the composer puts together his various notes. The " cadence " of poetry — such a quality as in Spenser Mr. Arnold calls " fluidity " of verse — is easier to feel than to explain. Let us take two stanzas, each in precisely the same metre, but differing in cadence as a jog-trot differs from the pace of an Arabian charger. Cristofer Tye, in his metrical version of the *Acts of the Apostles*, says :—

> " It chauncéd in Iconium,
> As they ofttimes did use,
> Together they into did come
> The sinagoge of Jewes."

Shelley, Chorus in *Hellas :* —

> " Another Athens shall arise,
> And to remoter time
> Bequeath, like sunset to the skies,
> The splendor of its prime."

Even after allowing for the difference in the subject, and in the associations called up by each, even after setting aside any advantage one may have over the other in style, there still remains a something whose presence in the versification of the second extract makes poetry, whose absence reduces the first to a dull jingle.

§ 8. SLURRING AND ELIDING.

Slurring is a term used by writers on metre to denote the rapid pronunciation of certain light syllables, and is commonly applied whenever we have two light syllables to the stress in a regular metre which has normally one light syllable to each stress-syllable. Thus Chaucer:—

> " Of Éngelónd, to Cáunterbúry *they* wénde ; "

or Milton : —

> " No ánger fínd in thée but píty *and* rúth."

Here we do not suppress the syllables, we simply hurry over them, pronounce them rapidly; and the poet is therefore careful to use for such a purpose those words alone which allow of a rapid pronunciation. Slurring is a common license in poetry, and must be distinguished from *contraction*, where a syllable is totally suppressed : *e.g.*, in our familiar *I'll* for *I will*, or in many Shaksperian words, to be noted below.

Elision is where the final (sounded) vowel of one word is so combined with the initial vowel of the following word that the effect is to make a single syllable of the two. We shall note this license more particularly in speaking of Chaucer's metres : it is common enough in such cases as Milton's "the infernal doors" = *th' infernal;* and in his

> "Hurl'd headlong flaming from the ethereal sky,"

when there is also a case of slurring in *ethereal*. It is, perhaps, possible to substitute in these cases for elision a very rapid slurring. Where elision does not take place, we have *Hiatus*.

CHAPTER VII.—METRES OF ENGLISH VERSE.

§ 1. GENERAL PRINCIPLES.

HAVING considered the elements which make up our versification, it remains to treat English Metres themselves. The task is not easy. There is an infinite amount of contradiction about the very foundations of our verse. Mr. Ruskin asserts that stress "may be considered as identical with quantity" (preface to his *Eng. Prosody*). Mr. Henry Sweet, while granting that accent tends to lengthen a short syllable, and lack of accent tends to shorten a long syllable, says emphatically that quantity can *not* "be identified with stress." The union of quantity and accent is only a *tendency;* and Schipper's statement (quoted on p. 138) may be accepted as true. In all cases, we should base a metrical rule on observed facts; not, as the late Mr. Lanier did in his *Science of English Verse*, force a theory on all possible facts, whether carefully analyzed and tested, or not. Thus, there is much justice in Mr. Ruskin's statement that "the measures of verse . . . have for second and more important function that of assisting and in part compelling clearness of utterance, thus enforcing with noble emphasis, noble words, and making them, by their audible symmetry, not only emphatic but memorable"; but it is only a statement, an observation, —nothing upon which we may found any rule. The only method that can lead to good in the study of English verse is to make the study historical and analytical. Every conclusion must be based on a careful study of facts.

Then we have this difficult matter of nomenclature. Certain names for "feet" in classical metres — iamb, trochee, anapest, dactyl — were long ago applied to English verse. But every one knows, or ought to know, that the classical iamb or dactyl is very different from the iamb or dactyl of modern poetry. Is it right, then, to apply to verse based on accents a term which properly applies only to verse based on quantity? The answers vary. Some say we may so apply the terms, bearing always in mind the difference of the two systems of verse. Others propose to drop the old terms, and substitute the "*rising*" foot of two or of three syllables (iamb, anapest), and the "*falling*" foot of two or of three syllables (trochee, dactyl). Still another class propose that we give up any distinction between iamb and trochee, or rising and falling, and in all cases *begin the first foot of the verse with the first stress-syllable.* The character of the verse will then be regulated (1) by the number of metrical stresses: as 3-accent verse, 5-accent, etc.; (2) by the presence or absence of a syllable or syllables before the first stress; and (3) by the number and distribution of unaccented syllables or of pauses. — In marking the feet of a verse, some writers use upright lines to denote the relative stress: thus, iamb ₋|, trochee |₋, anapest ₋₋|, dactyl |₋₋. The old system is, however, retained by many: ∪ —, — ∪, ∪ ∪ —, — ∪ ∪.

Of these three answers, the advantage would lie with the last, were it not that it lacks precision when we apply it to actual verse. If we retain the old names, we are able by a single word to give the general character of the verse. We may venture the decision that while it is productive of little good to insist on precise terms for the *separate feet*, we are justified in applying these old names to *the general movement of the whole verse*. We need not waste our time in establishing such results as Mr. Spedding's distinction of "*quantity*" as a dactyl, and "*quiddity*" as a tribrach. But we shall find it profitable and, in the present state of things, necessary, to speak of iambic or trochaic or anapestic or dactylic verse; — though in regard to the last Mr. Swinburne tells us (*Studies in Song*, p. 68) that "dactylic . . . forms of verse are unnatural and abhorrent" to the English language. Our chief concern, therefore, will be for the metrical scheme underlying the verse. No one can read Pope, or even Shakspere and Milton, without being conscious of such a definite metrical scheme. In the so-called "heroic" verse used by these poets, the reader feels that the general scheme is a regular alternation of light and heavy syllables, opening with light and ending with heavy, this last stress being the fifth from the beginning. Remembering that quantity has only a general and "regulative" office here, and that accent is "the grave governour of numbers," there is no harm in calling this scheme iambic. The use of such a metrical scheme depends on the regularity of the verse. For long poems, and for those which follow Pope's advice about "smooth numbers," terms like iambic or dactylic apply very well. But a great mass of lyric verse is difficult to bring under definite metrical systems; for these poems, our only test is to count the accents, and note the number and distribution of light syllables. In Milton's *L'Allegro*, out of 142 regular verses, 86 have the iambic, 56 the trochaic movement. But it is all practically the same metre. A trochaic movement, by the way, is not simply a verse which begins with an accented syllable. Such a verse is

"Scátter the reár of dárkness thín,"

but it is iambic. There is trochaic movement in

"Stóutly strúts his dámes befóre."

But all "trochaic" means here is that the light syllable of the first foot is dropped.

There is technically a change of movement from trochaic to iambic in the couplet, —

"Sometime walking, not unseen,
By hedge-row elms, on hillocks green; —

but it is a very slight change. *Cf.* for shorter lyric work, William Blake's *Tiger*. — We conclude that the use of such terms as iambic or trochaic is, for these short lyric verses, of doubtful advantage. The unit of a modern verse is a stress-syllable together with one or two (rarely three) unaccented syllables. From two to (say) eight of these units may be combined to form a verse. Verses of more than eight "groups," or "bars," or "feet," cannot easily be recognized by the ear; four and five are popular numbers. Now, when each of these feet contains the same number of *unaccented* syllables (it must have one, and only one, rhythmically *accented* syllable), the verse is regular. When the number varies, the verse is irregular. The poem (*L'Allegro*) just cited is regular; the movement is a regular alternation of light and heavy. So with blank verse, as a general rule. But there is a great mass of irregular verse: take, *e.g.*, Swinburne's Chorus from *Atalanta in Calydon:* —

> "When the hóunds of Spríng are on Wínter's tráces,
> The móther of mónths in méadow or pláin
> Fílls the shádows and wíndy pláces
> With lísp of léaves and rípple of ráin."

No one will deny that there are both melody and vigor in this. No exact foot is adopted as unit; the verse is irregular in the number of light syllables; but there is an undoubted anapestic movement. There are four accents to each verse, and in the third verse the first "foot" has no light syllable at all.

We may now go on to the consideration of our metres in detail. But first let us try to sum up, from what has been said, the substance of English metrical principles. A verse of our poetry must be looked at from three points of view. —

I. THE METRICAL SCHEME. — The poet decides — consciously or unconsciously matters not — that he will base his verse on a certain scheme, will give it a certain movement. It makes no difference whether or not other schemes now and then are suggested. He plans his verse as an architect plans a building, — with a general idea of the style and effect intended. The majority of his verses will convey the impression of a definite scheme. This scheme he may follow with great fidelity, or with great license; but he *cannot in any case follow it absolutely*. First, he will intentionally deviate from it, in order to give variety to his verse. If his scheme is iambic, he will now and then begin with a heavy syllable, or take a similar license, such as slipping in extra syllables. *Secondly*, he involuntarily deviates from the scheme by reason of the laws of language itself. So we come to

II. THE ACCENT AND QUALITY OF WORDS. — The poet's heavy syllables cannot be all equally heavy, the light cannot be all equally light. Mr. Sweet gives the proportion of stress for the different syllables of "impenetrability" thus: im-pe-ne-tra-bi-li-ty $\overset{2}{\text{im}}$-$\overset{3}{\text{pe}}$-$\overset{7}{\text{ne}}$-$\overset{5}{\text{tra}}$-$\overset{1}{\text{bi}}$-$\overset{6}{\text{li}}$-$\overset{4}{\text{ty}}$. We are not here concerned with the finer gradations of stress, but recognize only three: *primary*, *secondary*, and *unaccented* syllables, — or, as Ellis terms them, *strong*, *mean*, and *weak*. But verse is constantly forced to accept a mean accent, now as strong, now as weak; and so the strict metrical scheme is violated. Here we see how little reliance can be put upon "feet" in and for themselves. In the ballad "High upon Highlands and low upon Tay," *High upon* is a so-called dactyl; read "High upon a golden throne," and *on* is a metrically strong syllable equal to *High*.[1] Again, the *quality* (and also the quantity) of words can vary infinitely; the same metrical scheme may be filled with thin and short, or with full and long sounds. — We have already noted the occasional direct conflict of word-accent and verse-accent (*cf.* p. 142).

III. ACCENT AND QUALITY IN THE SENTENCE. — As with syllables of words, so with words of a sentence. "It is a mistake," says Mr. Ellis, "to suppose that there are commonly or regularly, five stresses, one to each measure" (he is speaking of Chaucer's verse of five

---

[1] In the first case: high$\overset{2}{\text{ up}}$-$\overset{0}{\text{on}}$; in the second case: high$\overset{2}{\text{ up}}$-$\overset{0}{\text{on}}$.

measures); and this is correct, if we take the point of view of the syntactical or rhetorical accent. In reading verse, we often run lightly over four or five syllables in order to accent a prominent word with special force. A great many of Pope's and Dryden's verses have, rhetorically speaking, only four accents, as: — "Which Jews might kiss, and Infidels adore." Often there are only two or three real stress-syllables. Mr. Ellis (*Early Eng. Pron.* i. p. 334) marks the stress on the syllables of the six opening lines of Byron's *Corsair*, as follows, the relative amount of stress being denoted by the figures 0, 1, 2: —

$$\overset{1}{\text{``O'er}} \overset{0}{\text{ the}} \overset{1}{\text{ glad}} \overset{2}{\text{ waters}} \overset{0}{\text{ of}} \overset{0}{\text{ the}} \overset{2}{\text{ dark}} \overset{1}{\text{ blue}} \overset{2}{\text{ sea,}}$$
$$\overset{1}{\text{Our}} \overset{1}{\text{ thoughts}} \overset{0}{\text{ as}} \overset{2}{\text{ boundless}} \overset{0}{\text{ and}} \overset{0}{\text{ our}} \overset{0}{\text{ souls}} \overset{2}{\text{ as}} \overset{0}{\text{ free,}} \overset{2}{}$$
$$\overset{2}{\text{Far}} \overset{0}{\text{ as}} \overset{0}{\text{ the}} \overset{1}{\text{ breeze}} \overset{0}{\text{ can}} \overset{2}{\text{ bear,}} \overset{0}{\text{ the}} \overset{1}{\text{ billows}} \overset{0}{\text{ foam,}} \overset{2}{}$$
$$\overset{0}{\text{Survey}} \overset{1}{\text{ our}} \overset{0}{\text{ empire,}} \overset{2}{\text{ and}} \overset{0}{\text{ behold}} \overset{0}{\text{ our}} \overset{2}{\text{ home!}} \overset{0}{} \overset{2}{}$$
$$\overset{2}{\text{These}} \overset{0}{\text{ are}} \overset{0}{\text{ our}} \overset{1}{\text{ realms,}} \overset{2}{\text{ no}} \overset{1}{\text{ limits}} \overset{0}{\text{ to}} \overset{0}{\text{ their}} \overset{2}{\text{ sway,}} -$$
$$\overset{1}{\text{Our}} \overset{2}{\text{ flag}} \overset{0}{\text{ the}} \overset{2}{\text{ sceptre}} \overset{0}{\text{ all}} \overset{1}{\text{ who}} \overset{2}{\text{ meet}} \overset{0}{\text{ obey.''}} \overset{2}{}$$

Different readers, as Ellis remarks, may vary in some details of stress; but the proportion here given will be preserved in the main by every one. The pause, as we easily feel, tends to divide the verse into two, sometimes three groups, each of which is dominated by a chief accent: note especially lines 2 and 4, which resemble the favorite "balance" of Pope and Dryden. Now, the strict metrical scheme calls for 02, 02, 02, 02, 02; to this the last line comes nearest. But the nature of spoken words is such that this scheme can never be exactly and perfectly realized. When we say that a verse has five accents, we mean that the metrical scheme calls for five stress-syllables; but we do not expect the concrete verse to show five strictly equal stresses. We do demand, however, that the concrete verse shall give us the *general effect* of five stress-syllables, shall make us feel the uniform metrical scheme underlying the rhythm.

Here, then, are three sets of claims. IT IS THE BUSINESS OF THE POET TO MAKE AN EQUATION OF THESE CLAIMS, THE METRICAL SCHEME HAVING THE PREFERENCE; and in proportion as this is done with such art that we feel no conflict, no clash, by so much does the poet's handicraft approach perfection.

§ 2. ANGLO-SAXON METRES.

English Metres fall into three groups or periods. The first period is the *Anglo-Saxon*. It embraces the interval from the Germanic conquest of Britain in the Fifth Century, to the Norman conquest in the Eleventh Century. This latter date is not exact. Not only did the old metres still flourish under the early Norman kings, but they were used as late as the Sixteenth Century. Still, the actual period when our poetry knew no other metrical rules than those of the old Germanic verse ended with the conquest. The high-water mark of this old poetry is seen in *Beowulf*, in certain of the "Cædmon" poems, and in the graceful verses of the poet Cynewulf. The second period is that of *Transition*, and ends with the New Learning and the Italian influences of the reign of Henry VIII. Chaucer is the one great name of this period. The third and *Modern* period begins with the Earl of Surrey and with Wyatt, and reaches its greatest height in Shakspere and Milton.

The characteristics of the metre of this our own period are regularity and harmony, a stricter ordering of light and heavy syllables, proportion, symmetry, ease. The main characteristic of the earliest period in our metre is strength, — a sort of breathless vigor: the accented syllables are the chief consideration, and they are emphasized not only by their weight, but also by the use of beginning-rime. For the period of transition, we have mingled characteristics of both the other periods, which must be described in detail. In naming Chaucer as its greatest poet, we must bear in mind that he stands much nearer to our own period than to the Anglo-Saxon. His versification is smooth and vigorous; it is the language, not the metre, which makes him seem so removed from modern verse. But the metres before Chaucer, and, to some extent, after him, were not of the modern kind. He is the greatest name in the English poetry of his period, but he is not its most faithful representative. He stands above it.

The Anglo-Saxon Verse, at its best — say, as in *Beowulf* — consists of two half-verses, which may be said to correspond to the forward-and-back of the old dance. These two half-verses are firmly bound together by *beginning-rime*. It is, therefore, a mistake to print them in separate lines, as was done by the first editors. In each half-verse there are *two strongly accented syllables:* that is, — a reduction from the old dance-steps, — four to each verse.[1] *The first accented syllable of the*

---

[1] So Rieger, in his excellent article: "Alt- und Angelsächsische Verskunst," Ztsft. für deutsche Philologie, VII. 1 ff., on which the above rules are based. It is fair to state that some prominent scholars — *e.g.*, Ten Brink — oppose this particular statement, and insist on *four* accents to each half-verse, — eight in all.

second half-verse is the rime-giver: with it MUST *rime one*, and MAY *rime both, of the accented syllables of the first half-verse: but the last accented syllable of the verse must not rime with the rime-giver.* Alternate rimes, however, were allowed. The following table gives the allowed rime-combinations: —

a : *a* ‖ *a* : *x*	*B*eowulf wæs *b*reme	*b*læd wide sprang.	18
a : *b* ‖ *a* : *b*	thær æt *h*ythe *st*od	*h*ringed *st*efna.	33
a : *b* ‖ *b* : *a*	tha *w*æron *m*onige	the his *m*æg *w*rithon.	2983
a : *x* ‖ *a* : *x*	*B*eowulf mathelode	*b*earn Ecgtheowes.	1474
x : *a* ‖ *a* : *x*	hi 'hine þa æt*b*æron	to *b*rimes farothe.	28

As to the quality of the rime: (1) all vowels rime with one another, on account of the smooth breathing (*spiritus lenis*); (2) a consonant rimes with itself alone; further, *sp,-sc,-st*,- are treated as single consonants: *sp*- does not rime with *st*- or *sc*-, etc. (3) Unaccented syllables do not count as rime-bearers; thus in

"*h*ean *h*uses   *hu him H*ring-Dene" (116),

hu him are unaccented, and their *h* has nothing to do with the rime of the accented syllables.

These unaccented syllables may (1) *be omitted between the accented syllables*, as in the line last quoted: *héan hús-* are each accented; so with *Hring-Den-*. But *no half-verse may be entirely without an unaccented syllable.* Further, unaccented syllables may (2) *be added to the verse*, within reasonable limits. The favorite place for adding unaccented syllables is the beginning of the second half-verse: in

"*m*anna ængum   thara the hit mid *m*undum bewand" (1462)

there are five such light syllables before the rime-giver.

The rules for the words on whose root-syllables the

verse-accent shall fall, are too detailed to be given here. In general it may be said that the accent falls on the important words — nouns, emphatic pronouns, and the like; and that an emphatic word cannot be unaccented.

The accented syllables were (in recitation) further marked by a stroke on some loud instrument. The importance of marking these four accents, the carelessness about unaccented syllables, are the chief characteristics of the Anglo-Saxon verse. The presence of such unaccented syllables and the consequent need to hurry over them so as to come to the strong ones, gave a sort of irregular but powerful leap to the rhythm. It is all weight, force, — no stately, even, measured pace, as in Greek epic verse. Our old metre inclines, like our ancestors themselves, to violence. It is at its best in describing the din of war, the uncertain swaying of warriors in battle;—a verse cadenced by the crashing blows of sword and axe. But we do not move forward. As was pointed out when we spoke of the parallelisms and repetitions of the Anglo-Saxon diction (p. 86), there is an eternal leaping back and forth, but there is little actual advance. As Scherer says, the Germanic nature was fond of raining its blows on the same spot. Often, however, the verse has an admirable effect, — as in the description of the launching of Beowulf's boat (211–218).

Our early verse was at its best in the Eighth and the Ninth Century. Then it began to decline. In *Byrhtnoth* (993) the verse is here and there corrupt, though still full of life and vigor. End-rime increases, whereas in the older verse it had been confined to short forms like "frôd and gôd." Now the two half-verses began to use end-rime as a new connecting-link. The *Rime*

Song, one of the poems preserved in the Exeter codex (Tenth Century), uses end-rime not only thus in the half-verses, but it also often binds whole verses together: —

"gold gearwade, gim hwearfade,
sinc searwade, sib nearwade."

Confusion sets in. Poems are written now in the old verse, now with end-rime alone, now with a mixture of both systems. Finally, two distinct tendencies emerge from the confusion.[1] One is conservative, and restores the old rules, which had fallen into neglect. A poem about *King Edward*, written in 1065, is correct in the old fashion, and has no trace of end-rime. The other tendency is progressive. Out of the old long-verse it makes two short verses connected by end-rime, — the short couplet. A *geographical difference* is now apparent. In the south, where Norman influences abound, there is a disposition to count the syllables and make the verse metrical as well as rhythmical — if we may so distinguish these terms. In the north, the old verse keeps upper hand. Although in this latter case the strict rules of rime and accent-position are somewhat relaxed, the poets are careful to avoid end-rime, and sometimes use beginning-rime to excess, thus breaking the old restrictions. But as late as Chaucer's time, the poet who wrote about *Piers the Plowman* is practically free from end-rime, and also correct in his use of beginning-rime: occasionally a line occurs (Skeat) like

"Tyle he had *s*ylver for his *s*awes and his *s*elynge,"

but the verse is fairly regular, and always vigorous. It is a sort of Indian Summer for the old Germanic metre.

[1] Schipper, p. 76.

The *Brut* of Layamon (about 1200) though earlier, is far less rigid in adherence to the old rules; it breaks away frequently into rimed short verses. But after it, and before or contemporary with *Piers Plowman*, come the so-called "alliterating romances" — *William of Palerne, Sir Gawayne and the Green Knight, The Destruction of Troy,* and others. These were of northern, the *Brut* of south-western, origin; and the latter betrays the Norman influence of its model.

A verse or two from *Piers Plowman* will show in more modern shape than Anglo-Saxon the swing of our old metre:—

"In a somer seson ·   whan soft was the sonne,
I shope me in shroudes ·   as I a shepe were,
In habite as an heremite ·   unholy of workes,
Went wyde in this world ·   wondres to here . .
. . . I was wery forwandred ·   and went me to reste
Under a brode banke ·   by a bornes side,
And as I lay and lened ·   and loked in the wateres,
I slombred in a slepyng ·   it sweyued so merye."

Prologue, 1–4, 7–10.

The first line breaks the old rime-rule of Anglo-Saxon metres; the others are in the main correct.

§ 3. THE TRANSITION PERIOD.

Even so late as the beginning of the Sixteenth Century we find the great Scotch poet, Dunbar, writing his longest piece — *The Twa Maryit Weman and the Wedo* — in the old "alliterating" verse. Although his longest poem, it is the only one known to us which he wrote in this metre. Still, he preserves substantially the old rules, barring a tendency to overdo his "alliteration."

End-rime is practically excluded. But on the other hand, we find elsewhere decided changes and corruptions overmastering the Germanic verse. In the *Brut*, these changes and corruptions do not succeed in removing the main features of Anglo-Saxon metre, although in many cases end-rime breaks a long-verse into a rimed couplet which has, or has not, beginning-rime. But this exceptional couplet of Layamon becomes regular and sole principle in *King Horn*, a popular romance dating from the second quarter of the Thirteenth Century, — say about 1240. The metre of *King Horn* seems, therefore, to be the old verse banishing beginning-rime as principle and assuming end-rime to bind together the half-verses into a couplet, and giving accent to syllables previously unaccented. This change was helped by the example of the popular French eight-syllable verse (also in rimed couplets) which was introduced about this time into our southern poetry; but the two systems were as yet not identical. The *King Horn* measure is, like its parent verse, free to drop unaccented syllables, while the French verse is more regular. Later, the two systems fall together (the French predominating) in the metre of such poems as Chaucer's *House of Fame* (about 1384). — For license of dropping light syllables, *cf.*

> " The sé bigán to flówe,
> And *Hórn Chíld* to rówe," etc.

But there are other corruptions of the old verse. Instead of splitting one long-verse into a short couplet, end-rime binds together two or more long-verses. Beginning-rime thus released from its old duties grows erratic, now flooding the verse to excess, now disappearing altogether, and becoming simply an ornament.[1] The accented syllables, too, sometimes increase to three in each half-verse, so that the whole verse is practically an "Alexandrine." Such corrupt (that is, corrupt as far as the old rules are concerned) verse became popular in the Fourteenth and the Fifteenth Century, particularly in the ballad poetry. *Cf.* one of Laurence Minot's political songs, written before 1350:—

> "Whare er ye, Skottes of Saint Johnes toune?
> The boste of yowre baner es betin all doune;
> When ye bosting will bede,[2] Sir Edward es boune[3]
> For to kindel[4] yow care and crak yowre croune."

We notice an increasing regularity in the use of unaccented syllables, as in the lyric poems of this period generally.

Most interesting and important, however, is the use of this old verse in our *early English Drama*. "The earliest popular productions of dramatic literature, like the lyric, gave a last refuge to the old national measure, although the latter was forced to share its privileges with more aristocratic guests" (Schipper). The old Moralities and Mysteries let their ordinary characters speak in this metre; while "Virginius, Appius, Conscience, Cambyses, Venus, Cupid, and such distinguished personages conversed in formal Septenary or Alexandrine (after classical models), or else in light, regular couplets"—(after the French). Among many other old plays, the already (Part I. p. 65) mentioned *Every Man* contains much of the old metre; so does our first English comedy, *Ralph Roister Doister*. But

---

[1] Schipper, p. 214.   [2] 'offer.'   [3] 'ready.'   [4] 'prepare.'

this brings us almost to the time of Blank Verse and
the modern period; and we note even in the metre of
these old plays, rough as it often is, a tendency to regu-
larity and precision. Unaccented syllables are omitted
only after the middle pause, or cæsura; and in every
way the influence of the now popular French and
Italian measures makes itself felt.

The last stage of the old Germanic rhythm, before it
is lost in the modern measures of the Elizabethan age,
is the so-called *Skeltonic Verse*. John Skelton (died
1529) employed it often and happily, but he did not
originate it; for we find it used here and there in the
old Mysteries. But it is justly associated with Skel-
ton's name. He wields it with much power in his light
humorous pieces, such as the *Boke of Phyllyp Sparowe*
or *Colin Clout* (a satire on the clergy), and in his
Morality *Magnyfycence;* indeed, the reckless priest was
a fitting guide and comrade for this spendthrift metre
which finally dissipated the last inheritance of ancestral
verse. We give a line or two from *Phyllyp Sparowe*
(description of Envy)[1]: —

> "He frowneth ever,
> He laugheth never,
> Even nor morowe;
> But other mennes sorowe
> Causeth him to grin
> And rejoice therein.
> No sleep can him catche,
> But ever doth watche," etc.

This restless movement is quite different from the
couplet in *King Horn*.

[1] *Cf.* Guest, p. 396.

Finally, we abandon all influences or reminiscences of the old Anglo-Saxon verse, and come to what must pass as its modern representative, — the common four-accent metre, variously treated in a host of ballads and lyrics, and in such tales as Scott's or Byron's, or in Coleridge's *Christabel*, in a preface to which the poet announced his system of counting accents rather than syllables, as a new kind of verse!

Foreign Influences. — Schipper names three foreign metrical systems which came into our literature during this period: the Latin *Septenary;* the French *Short Couplet;* and the French *Alexandrine.* — In late Latin poetry a metre had become common which consisted of a half-verse of four accents, the last accent falling on the last syllable, joined to a half-verse of three accents with double ("feminine") ending: on account of the seven accents of the whole verse, the metre was called *Septenarius.* It was furnished with end-rime. Both in the church hymns, and in the songs of wandering "clerks" who strolled from nation to nation secure in their common language, this metre was very popular. *Cf.* the following opening couplet of a convivial song (*cf.* p. 52) : —

" Méum ést propósitúm   ín tabérna móri
 Ét vinúm appósitúm   sítiénti óri," etc.

This measure was soon used for English verse. The *Poema Morale*, already mentioned as a sort of medieval Gray's *Elegy*, is a good example of the rimed Septenary, though the trochaic movement is dropped: —

" Ich ám nu élder thán ich wás | a wíntre ánd a lóre.
 Ich wéalde móre thán idúde | mi wít oh tó be móre.
 To lóng ich hábbe chíld ibén | a wórde ánd a dáde.
 Théih ibíe a wínter eáld | to júng ich ám on ráde."

"I am now older than I was in winters (years) and in lore (experience); I wield (control myself) more than I did, my wisdom ought to be greater. Too long I have been a child in words and deeds; old though I be in years, I am too young in counsel."— The alternation of accented and unaccented syllables is observed; there is occasional "slurring" of light syllables; the general movement is prevailingly iambic. This same metre *without rime* is used by the monk Orm in his *Ormulum*,— a sort of paraphrase and commentary for the gospels of the church year, written early in the Thirteenth Century. Orm is more regular; and is invariably iambic. This rimeless metre of Orm's "appears to have found little applause and still less imitation." The Septenary, split into two verses of four and three accents respectively, is very popular in later English in the "common metre," and in ballads; while its original form, with some modifications, is retained in the vigorous measure which Chapman chose for his translation of Homer's *Iliad*. The translators, Golding and Phaer, also employed it. We find it frequently in modern poetry, *e.g.*, in Byron's verses (which are not to be split into "common" measure) : —

"There's not a joy the world can give like that it takes away,
  When the glow of early thought declines in feeling's dull decay:
  'Tis not on youth's smooth cheek the blush alone, which fades so fast,
  But the tender bloom of heart is gone ere youth itself be past."

Here, however, as with Chapman, the rime is masculine.

Of indirect Latin origin, but taken directly from the French, is the *Short Riming Couplet of four accents*, noticed above as having much influence on the similar couplet that resulted from halving the old native verse. This *Riming Couplet* of eight and nine syllables (according as the rime was masculine or feminine), and iambic movement, was a favorite for French narrative poems. Thence it found its way into English poetry about the middle of the Twelfth Century. In the Thirteenth and the Fourteenth Century this verse was constructed almost as regularly as its French model, and was popular throughout England; although the northern poets always inclined somewhat to the freedom of dropping or adding light syllables. It is nowhere used with prettier effect than in *The Owl and the Nightingale* (south of England, about 1250):—

> "Ule," heo[1] sede, "seie[2] me soth;
> Wi dostu[3] that unwightes doth?
> Thu singest anight and noght adai,
> And al thi song is wailawai.[4]"

It is used in certain religious pieces in the north — with considerable license — and in poems like Barbour's *Bruce* and Wyntown's *Chronicle of Scotland*. Among southern poets who adopted this metre, we may mention particularly Gower (*Confessio Amantis*) and Chaucer (*House of Fame; Boke of the Duchesse*). The general tone of the verse is iambic; but the opening light syllable is often dropped, and "hovering accent" is freely used. The peculiarities of verse in the individual poems cannot be discussed here; they belong to the special study of middle-English metres.

Thirdly, we have the *Alexandrine*. This metre of six accents was early imitated from the French; but

[1] She. [2] Say. [3] Why dost thou. [4] Alack-a-day.

was at first used (as in the *Chronicle* of Robert of Gloucester, about 1300) in company with the Septenary. About the beginning of the Fourteenth Century, Robert Mannyng wrote a rimed chronicle of England in Alexandrines, which were copied from the verse of his model, Langtoft's French *Chronicle of England.* There are six accents, with a pause, commonly after the third accent; and often rimes are given to the half-verses so formed: —

"Toúrne we now óther wéys   untó our ówen géste
And spéke of thé Waléys   that liés in thé fóreste."

This metre was popular both as here printed and also in the lyric stanza of four verses with three accents to each. Regular Alexandrines are very common in the Moralities and Mysteries, and in other poems, even in Elizabeth's time: *e.g.,* Drayton's *Polyolbion.* The great rival of the Alexandrine was the Septenary: in Robert of Gloucester, as noted above, the two were used side by side. This combination became popular in the Sixteenth Century, and was called by Gascoigne "poulter's measure," because the poulterer "giveth XII for one dozen and XIIII for another": this, of course, refers to the number of syllables. *Cf.* Surrey: —

"Layd in my quiet bed, in study as I were,
 I saw within my troubled head, a heape of thoughtes appeare."

Gascoigne calls this "the commonest sort of verse which we use nowadayes" (*sc.* 1575).

This scanty description must suffice for the transition-period, except so far as Chaucer is concerned. Enough has been said, however, to show for this epoch a steady advance of *metrical* principle in the place of the purely *rhythmical* nature of the Anglo-Saxon verse. By this is meant the increased demand for *proportion* and *regularity;* the loss of beginning-rime as factor of the verse; curbing of the old license to drop or add light syllables; the exclusive use of end-rime. Chaucer is really a modern poet, even in his metre and cadences. But inasmuch as the Italian studies and imitations of Wyatt and Surrey, the change to a language practically modern, and the introduction of blank verse, all make the early and middle part of the Sixteenth Century the evident beginning of a new period of English Poetry, we must give Chaucer a place by himself, as to one who anticipates the future. The popular comparison which likens Chaucer to a lovely day of earliest spring, soon succeeded by the old frost and rain, will apply equally well to his metre.

§ 4. CHAUCER'S METRES.

Chaucer's metres may be referred to two systems: the short verse of four accents (*Short Riming Couplet*, mentioned above), and the so-called heroic verse of five accents. Both are "iambic" in movement; the heroic verse being more strict in this respect than the short verse, which in a number of cases begins with a heavy syllable. When the heroic verse seems so to begin, Ten Brink would assume always a "hovering accent," *i.e.*, an equal division between the claims of the metre and the claims of the word. This hovering accent of Chaucer we discuss below; but the constant practice of English poetry is to allow great freedom with the opening foot of an "iambic" verse, and after the pause, as in (Milton)

"Áthens, the éye of Gréece, *móther* of árts."

So Chaucer : —

"*Tróuthe and* honóur, *frèdòm* and cúrteisíe."

Here there is undoubtedly transposed accent, and we should call the first foot "trochaic" by license; *frēdom*, really a compound word, may have the hovering accent. Further, we must always bear in mind that not a single "foot," but the combination of accented and unaccented syllables in a whole verse, is what we chiefly regard. But regularity — *not* monotony — is a quality of good metre; hence we properly call Chaucer's verse "iambic." The short verse is in rimed couplets. The poet used it in his earlier work (*e.g., Boke of the Duchesse*); but after his Italian journey abandoned it for the heroic verse, returning, however, to the old metre in his *House of Fame*. Heroic verse was used sporadically before Chaucer; but practically it was he who introduced it into our poetry. In his hands it became so flexible and powerful that it has since steadily maintained its place as the most popular measure of our verse. He uses it in couplets (*Prologue* and many of the *Canterbury Tales; Legende of Goode Women*, etc.) and in the strophe (*Troilus; Monkes Tale*). Epic rimed verse tends to be more regular than dramatic verse, on account of the freedom of recitation in the latter; more regular than blank verse in general, because rime promotes uniformity. Chaucer's verse, therefore, if compared with Shakspere's or Milton's, is eminently smooth. Yet the person, who unprepared tries to read Chaucer, will not be disposed to agree with such a statement. By observing the following rules, however, one will find a music and breadth of harmony in Chaucer's verse not surpassed by any English poet except perhaps the two named above.

Difficulties in the scansion of Chaucerian metres are to be referred (*a*) to the words themselves or (*b*) to their connection. Then, too, we carry our silent letters and syllables into Fourteenth-Century English; whereas we should (as in modern German) carefully sound final *e* and final -*es*, -*ed*, etc. Exceptions are noted below.

The Anglo-Saxon and older inflexional syllables had become greatly weakened in Chaucer's time; but, with some exceptions, they were not yet lost or silent. Thus the infinitive ending -*an* had weakened to -*en*, then, in many cases, to -*e*. The full vowels (*a, o, u*) were likewise mostly weakened to -*e*. This weak -*e* was either *sounded*, *slurred*, or *silent*. It was (when *final*) *sounded* in the plural of attributive adjectives; in definite adjectives; in the infinitive mood; in adverbs; in the dative singular of nouns. It was *silent* in the pronouns *hire, oure, youre, here, myne, thyne; thise, some;* in strong past-participles where *n* is dropped: *write;* in *before, there, heere*. Note, further, that the above -*e* is unaccented and follows the primary word-accent. In other cases,—*i.e.*, not covered by the above words where it is silent, or by the kinds of word which always sound it,— weak *e* final following the primary word-accent is sometimes sounded, sometimes silent. It is not unreasonable to allow Chaucer the freedom in this respect which is so common in German poetry. While for *nouns* the general rule holds that final -*e* is more likely to be silent in words derived from the French than in native words, still we find Chaucer using a good English word like *love* now as one syllable, now as two. Exactly so with German: *Liebe* is normally of two syllables; but Scheffel can say, "O Lieb', wie bist du bitter!"

When weak *e* is *not final*, it is mostly pronounced in such cases as *floures, litel, comen,* etc. But it is also, in many cases, *slurred,—i.e.,* a syllable is so rapidly passed over and brought so close to its neighbor, that the two syllables have metrically the value of only one. So that in many cases we are free to sound separately, or to slur, as the verse demands. This holds good of plurals in *-es;* of verbs in *-en, -est, -eth;* of nouns ending in *-el, -en, -er,* etc. Thus *e* is slurred, *e* is silent, in

"And thinkęth ' Herė cometh my mortel enemy.'"
"And forth we ridęn a litel morė than paas,"

although in the first verse the slurring really amounts to *contraction: think'th, com'th.* — For *e sounded, cf.*

"In thilkë coldë frosty regioun."

This slurring is common where liquid consonants are concerned: *stoln, born, loveres,* etc.

When two syllables come together, each containing an unaccented *e*, one of these is slurred, or else may become silent. Slurred in *lovędė,* silent in *huntedė,* in

"To ryden out, he lovęde chyvalrye."
"How Atthalaunte [1] huntedė the wilde boor."

Also, when a syllable unaccented, but capable of bearing accent, is followed by an unaccented *e*, the latter is slurred or silent: *lóveres, pilgrimęs.* After a secondary word-accent, *e* is sometimes sounded, some-

[1] *Cf.* under *Elision.*

times slurred or silent: *émpèroùrès, mésùráble*. Unaccented *e* between primary and secondary accent is mostly sounded: thus *enemy*, — and *cf*.

"The *pikepurs* and eek the pale drede."

In *every*, on the contrary, the second *e* is always silent. Other vowels than *e* may be slurred. So *parisshe:* —

"Wyd was his *parisshe* and houses fer asonder."

So *charitable, naturally, amorously*. Contractions, however, occur; *benedicite* and *Jerusalem* have each only three syllables with Chaucer; *aventure* = *aunter; whether* = *wher*, etc.

Thus, with the general rule that all vowels are sounded, we have cases where, for grammatical reasons, a weak vowel is silent, or else is so situated that it may be sounded or slurred according as the metre demands. But there is another freedom of equal importance with slurring: *Elision*. This is when a final vowel is silent before the vowel which begins the following word: —

"*Thestaat, tharray*, the nombre and eek the cause."

Elision may often take place before *h*: in *he, his*, etc.; the verb *have; honour, humble*, etc.: —

"That in that grove he wolde him hyde al day."

But even this *h* may prevent elision: compare

"Wel cówde hé fortúnen the áscendént."

Where the two vowels do not coalesce, we have *Hiatus*, — mostly *after a pause*, or for *sake of emphasis* — as in

"Withouten doutë, it may stonde so."

"Purs is the ercedeknes helle, quod he."

Of course, when final *e* is accented, it is not liable to elision, — *e.g.*, *pitée*. — Finally, we have the contraction of two words into one — often indicated by the spelling: as *not* for *ne wot* (know not); *nadde = ne hadde; this = this is*.

Before leaving this subject it is well again to remind the reader of the importance attached to *slurring*. It is pedantic to refuse Chaucer a license claimed by every English poet, — even by so exact a versifier as Pope; and what may seem corrupt to mere syllable-counting will become harmonious verse by the use of this freedom. *Cf.* Shaks. *All's Well*, II. 2 : —

"To enter*tain it* so *merrily* with a fool."

Chaucer : —

"*I ne saugh* this yeer so *mery a* companye." — *Prol. C. T.* 764.

So Milton : —

"No anger find in thee, but *pity and* ruth."

THE RHYTHM. — To make verse-accent and word-accent fall on the same syllable is the general principle of Germanic metres. Chaucer observes this rule; but, like all great poets, he avoids any see-saw effect; he does not construct his poetry by the foot, but by the verse; and he aims at a wider harmony than the ticking of a clock. His *rhetorical* accent seldom clashes with the rhythm of his verse; while to prove every foot a perfect ($\smile\,-$) is impossible. Attentively consider the verse : —

"That if gold ruste, what schulde yren doo?" (*C. T.* 500),

and the force of the above statement will be evident. The rhetorical accent and the general rhythm of the verse agree; the strict metrical scheme of regularly alternating light and heavy syllables will not apply. But the line is still "iambic" in movement, just as Milton's "Universal reproach, far worse to bear" is "iambic," despite two so-called "trochees" at the start.

As to *word-accent*, we must here note the peculiarity of Chaucerian verse alluded to above, called "Hovering Accent" (*Schwebende Betonung*). Many words, mostly of Romance origin, were, it is true, pronounced with the stress (probably a slight one) now on one, now on another, syllable: *hónour, honóur; pítee, pitée;* etc. *Cf. goddesse* in : —

"I not whether (= wher) sche be womman or goddésse" (rimes with *gesse*) (*C. T.* 1101),

and : —

"I mene nought the góddesse Dyane." — *C. T.* 2063.

So, also, Romance words in *-age, -ance, -ence,* etc. This freedom of word-accent was probably not so great as it seems. The first two syllables of *goddesse* were pronounced with nearly equal accent. But still more emphatic was the license allowed in the Hovering Accent; here no help comes from the word itself. It demands one accent, the verse another. Compromise results in an equal stress on both syllables, — a sort of "spondee." Thus in a line quoted above: "How Átthalaúnte hùntèdè the wílde bóor," the word-accent is on *hunt*, the verse-accent on *ede*. Result is hovering accent. *Cf.* "The rude *forefathers* of the hamlet sleep." (Gray.)

RIME. — End-rime is the rule; considerable alliteration occurs. Owing to the inflexional syllables, there is an abundance of "feminine" or double rimes, thus adding variety and melody to the verse. A peculiarity of Chaucer's rime is that two words identical in form rime with each other, provided they differ in meaning (see § 5, Chap. VI., on Perfect Rime); *seeke* (to seek): *seeke* (sick). The rimes are useful in proving grammatical points: thus from the rimes *Rome: to me; allow the: youthe*, we know that final *e* must have been sounded.

VERSE.—We have yet to note the variety introduced in Chaucer's verse by his skilful use of *pauses*. His verse is regular: technical licenses are rare, as, when the light syllables disappear from a "foot" leaving but one (heavy) syllable (*e.g.*, Al | bysmótered wíth his hábergeóun), or when the said foot has two light syllables instead of one (*e.g.*, Of Eng'clónd, to Cánterbúry *they* wénde). Most cases of the latter kind may be rectified by "slurring" (*e.g.*, For mány *a* mán so hárd is óf his hérte; and the last example). But his pauses show variety and skill. Ten Brink notes four principal varieties of the Chaucerian "*cæsura*": (1) after the fourth accented syllable (masculine; *i.e.*, the accent falls on the syllable immediately preceding the pause); (2) after the fifth syllable, the accent falling on fourth (feminine); (3) after the sixth accented syllable (masculine); (4) after the seventh, accent falling on sixth (feminine). Examples:—

(1) "Benign*e* he was | and wonder diligent."
(2) "Ful worthi was he | in his lordes werre."
(3) "With him ther was his son*e* | a yong Squyer."
(4) "The holy blisful martir | for to seeke."

Double cæsura often occurs:—

"With grys | and that the fynest*e* | of a lond."

Chaucer is very careful about the variety of his metre; he does not employ so many "end-stopt" lines as to be monotonous, nor does he entirely break up the integrity of his verse-system by constant "run-on" lines; note the skilful mingling of pauses with both "end-stopt" and "run-on" lines in the following: —

> "A kníght theré wás, | and thát a wórthy mán,
> Thát fròm the týme | thát he fírst begán
> To rýden oút, | he lóvede chývalríe,
> Tróuthe and honoúr, | frèdòm and cúrteisíe.
> Ful wórthi wás he | in his lórdes wérre,
> And thérto hádde he ríden, | nóman férre,[1]
> As wél in Crístendom | ás in héthenésse,
> And évere honóured | fór his wórthinésse."

Chaucer uses the end-stopt lines far more in his short couplets than in his heroic verse; for the latter, by its length, gives opportunity for variety by means of groups within the verse limits.

Further particulars about Chaucer's verse should be sought in Ten Brink's *Chaucer's Sprache und Verskunst*, and in Ellis' *Early English Pronunciation*; while, for his language, every student of Chaucer should become familiar with Professor Child's admirable essay, — on which all Chaucer work in this field is now based, — perhaps most accessible in Part I. of Ellis' above-quoted work. — After Chaucer, the five-accent verse was used by his scholars, Occleve and Lydgate; by Stephen Hawes, Barclay, Henrysoun ("Chaucer's brightest scholar"), Dunbar, Douglas, and Lyndesay. With the Earl of Surrey and the rise of Blank Verse, we come to our modern epoch.

[1] "Farther."

§ 5. MODERN METRES.

The first part of *Tottel's Miscellany* (1557) gives a number of shorter poems by Surrey and Wyatt; and a few more of them are added towards the end of the book. Of the 40 poems attributed to the Earl of Surrey, *all are iambic in movement*, and 21 are five-accent (the so-called "heroic pentameter"); 9 are in the Poulter's Measure (Septenary alternating with Alexandrine); 6 are regular four-accent; 3 are regular three-accent; and 1 has a stanza made up of a quatrain in ballad-measure, — *i.e.*, the Septenary split into a four-accent and a three-accent verse, by the riming of the pauses in successive verses, — with a couplet in four-accent, and a single concluding five-accent verse: *e.g.:* —

> "O happy dames that may embrace
> The frute of your delight,
> Help to bewail the wofull case,
> And eke the heavy plight
> Of me that wonted to rejoyce
> The fortune of my pleasant choyce:
> Good Ladies, help to fill my moorning voyce."

As far as metre is concerned, this is quite the modern lyrical manner. — Of the 96 assigned to Wyatt, practically *all are iambic;* 70 are *five-accent;* 16 are in *four;* 5 are in *three;* 2 are in *Poulter's;* 1 is in *four and three;* 1 is in *five and three;* and one is quite irregular (p. 223).[1]

This shows what is meant by naming Surrey and Wyatt as the earliest poets of our modern period. We see how great a favorite the five-accent verse with iambic movement is growing in English lyric poetry.

[1] Arber's Reprint.

As to iambic movement, George Gascoigne, nearly twenty years later, in his *Certayne Notes of Instruction in English Verse*, laments that "wee are fallen into suche a playne and simple manner of wryting, that there is none other foote used but one." Of course, however, lyric poetry knew other movements — as, for example, the trochaic measures of Greene, Barnefield, Constable, Sir P. Sidney, and others: thus, the latter's *Serenade* (*cf.* p. 81) from his *Astrophel and Stella*: —

> "Who is it that this dark night
> Underneath my window plaineth?
> *It is one who from thy sight,*
> *Being, ah! exiled, disdaineth*
> *Every other vulgar light.*" [1]

This four-accent verse, in couplets, with prevailing trochaic movement, became popular, and is familiar to us in Greene, *e.g.*, *Philomela's Ode;* in such songs as that from the *Passionate Pilgrim* ("*As it fell upon a day In the merry month of May*"); in *The Phœnix and the Turtle;* and in Shakspere, *e.g.*, the song in *Love's Lab. Lost*, IV. 3 (also printed in *Passion. Pil.*): "*On a day, alack the day,*" etc.

But the iambic movement was overwhelmingly the prevailing measure. The verse varied in its number of accents. As we saw in Surrey's case, the Septenary was split into four-and-three; when the ending of the original was feminine, and the rhythmic pause masculine, we have alternate single and double rimes, — *e.g.*, in Puttenham's example (*Arte Eng. Poes.* p. 85): —

> "The smoakie sighes, the bitter teares,
> That I in vaine have wasted,

[1] *English Garner*, I. 578.

"The broken sleepes, the woe and feares,
That long in me have lasted," etc.

That this new verse is not simply the older metre differently printed, is evident if we compare a couplet or two from Chapman's *Iliad:* —

" As when about the silver moon, when air is free from wind,
And stars shine clear, to whose sweet beams, high prospects, and the brows
Of all steep hills and pinnacles thrust up themselves for shows,
And even the lowly valleys joy to glitter in their sight,
When the unmeasured firmament bursts to disclose her light,
And all the signs in heaven are seen that glad the shepherd's heart;
So many fires disclosed their beams, made by the Trojan part," etc.[1]

Similarly, the Alexandrine was split into two verses of three accents each : *cf.* Surrey : —

"The fire it cannot freze :
For it is not his kinde,
Nor true love cannot lese
The constance of the minde."

The chief mark of this new period is the rise of Blank Verse. Surrey, so far as we know, was the first to use it. In his translation of Vergil's *Æneid*, Books II. and IV., he employed the five-accent measure, which was also the metre of his predecessor, Gawin Douglas ; the difference lay in the fact that Douglas made his translation of the *Æneid* in heroic rimed couplets, while Surrey, after the model of the Italian, rejected rime. His example was soon followed. Gascoigne (*e.g.*, in his *Steele Glas*, "a first experiment in English satire"), Lyly, Peele, Greene, and others, all improved, as was

[1] *Iliad.* VIII. See Epic Simile, p. 109.

natural, on Surrey's somewhat stiff verses. These poets clung to the rigid system of *counting syllables*, after the Italian fashion;[1] but they were less guilty than Surrey in regard to the *wrenched accent* (*cf.* p. 142): thus in Surrey's verse —

"Whoso gladly halseth the golden meane,"

only the last two feet have the iambic movement. But Peele and Greene wrote very pretty blank verse; and the poets soon learned to make their rhythm fit more closely to the word-accent. *Hovering Accent*, however, abounds, and is frequent enough in Shakspere and Fletcher.

In *Tamburlaine the Great* by Christopher Marlowe, published 1590, the drama at last found the metre best suited to its purposes, and used it with conscious ease. Marlowe's somewhat boastful prologue to *Tamburlaine* is famous: —

"From *jigging veins of riming mother wits*,
And such conceits as clownage keeps in pay,
We'll lead you to the stately tent of war,
Where you shall hear the Scythian Tamburlaine
Threatening the world with high astounding terms
And scourging kingdoms with his conquering sword.
View but his picture," etc.

In Shakspere's hands this weapon of blank verse almost became a bow of Odysseus; although Milton rivals Shakspere as far as majesty and vigor are concerned. Since Milton's time, the quantity of blank verse has much surpassed its quality, though Keats in his *Hyperion*, and Tennyson in certain parts of the *Idylls of the*

[1] *Cf.* Schröer, *Ueber die Anfänge des Blankverses in England*, "Anglia," IV. 1.

King, have done excellent work, — Keats in mingled sweetness and strength, and Tennyson in delicacy of construction.

Meanwhile, popular as blank verse became, rime really lost no ground. For epic purposes the *couplet* (iambic), though rejected by certain critics and poets, was polished into beauty — *cf.* the exquisite cadences of Marlowe's part of *Hero and Leander;* while the *stanza* came again into favor — *cf.* Shakspere's narrative poems, or Spenser's *Faery Queene.* Then, too, lyric poetry multiplied its forms of verse and combinations of rime, so as to keep pace with that profusion of melody which made Elizabeth's England "a nest of singing birds." In short, the variety of verse becomes so marked that we must abandon any attempt at historical statement, and, taking the broad field of modern metres, shall briefly consider them according to their number of accents, the general features of their movement, and their combination in stanzas. The characteristics of our ordinary metres we have already noted, — stricter reckoning of light syllables and more regular alternation with the stress; an added ease of rhythm; disappearance of beginning-rime as a metrical factor; more attention paid to the regulative force of quantity; the rise of blank verse. There is a smoothness, a finish, in modern work, which results from a higher standard of general culture and a closer study of classic and foreign models. The variations of stress, pitch, quantity, and tone fall over the rigid scheme of the metre like clinging drapery about the limbs of a statue, at once revealing and softening the outlines.

The simplest way to classify metres is by the number

of stress-syllables in the individual verse. By "verse" we here mean the simple plan of the rhythm, uninfluenced by the actual words with their separate and collective emphasis; we deal simply with the metrical scheme, before we have made that equation of claims which was mentioned above, p. 173. A second and subordinate factor of classification is the regularity or irregularity of the metrical scheme : — whether it has a constant alternation of light and heavy syllables, and thus can be classed as "iambic," etc., — or whether it approaches the old freedom, and appeals simply to the poetic ear.

(*a*) VERSE OF ONE STRESS.

Such verses occur at the end of a stanza, or within the stanza, but can hardly be used continuously. To be sure, we might so print a line of Hood's (already quoted) : —

> " Here énd
> As júst
> A friénd
> I múst,"

but we should soon have to divide words, and otherwise fall into an intolerable jolting; only for a comic or like effect can such verse be thought of. *Cf.* parts of Southey's *Lodore*. In the stanza, however, it is often used — as in Herrick's *Daffodils :* —

> " We have short time to stay, as you ;
> We have as short a spring ;
> As quick a growth to meet decay,
> As you or any thing.
> We die
> As your hours do, and dry
> Away,

> Like to the summer rain;
> Or as the pearls of morning's dew,
> Ne'er to be found again."

See, also, the same poet's *White Island*. Used at the end of a stanza, such a verse is sometimes called the "bob" or "bob-wheel."

(*b*) VERSE OF TWO STRESSES.

Regular, with *iambic* movement, are Herrick's verses (*To the Lark*):—

> " Because I do
> Begin to woo,
> Sweet singing Lark,
> Be thou the clerk," etc.

Regular *trochaic*, with feminine rimes, in Swinburne's *Song in Season*:—

> " Dust that covers
> Long dead lovers
> Song blows off with | breath that brightens;
> At its flashes,
> Their white ashes
> Burst in bloom that | lives and lightens."

There is *anapestic* movement in Scott's *Coronach;* *dactylic* in parts of Hood's *Bridge of Sighs*. Irregular but harmonious is the movement of Shelley's *Arethusa*, of Baroness Nairn's *Land o' the Leal* (with the old license of dropping light syllables), of parts of Shakspere's song in *Mid. Night's Dream*, III. 2:—

> " On the gróund
> Sléep soúnd:
> Í'll applý
> Tó your éye,

> Géntle lóver,
> Rémedý.
> Whén thou wákest
> Thóu tákest
> Trúe delíght," etc.

It would be perilous for any one but Puck and his fairies to try this metre. See, however, the song at the end of *Twelfth Night*, Act IV. — and we remember (*cf.* p. 181) Skelton's fondness for irregular two-accent verse.

(*c*) VERSE OF THREE STRESSES.

The old Alexandrine, when halved, allowed four different combinations in a regular stanza, according as the old pauses and endings were masculine or feminine: thus, all the new verse-endings could be masculine; all could be feminine; 1 and 3 could be masculine, and 3 and 4 feminine; or *vice versa*. Further, we have the presence or absence of initial light syllables (iambic or trochaic). Thus there is a difference in metrical effect between Surrey's verses on p. 197, and Moore's

> " Fill the bumper fair!
> Every drop we sprinkle
> O'er the brow of care,
> Smooths away a wrinkle."

The extra (light) syllable at the end is more important than at the beginning: thus it would make little difference if we put an "O" before the word "Fill"; it would make considerable difference if we said "fairly" instead of "fair"; — not, of course, counting the loss of rime. Another alternation of endings is found in Shelley's *Skylark* (also with trochaic effect). — It is very common to combine the anapestic with the iambic movement, the dactylic with the trochaic; but there is also much verse where all these distinctions, flimsy at best and only adopted for ease in classification, disappear, — and we must rely simply on the natural sense of harmony, the sympathy of an appreciative ear for the beat of free rhythm. This appreciation for rhythm is almost universal with children, but is often spoiled by too much analysis and bewildering theories; nobody but a pedant could go wrong on the verses about Till and Tweed quoted on p. 146, but they refuse to fit into the metrical scheme of the schools. — Example of general anapestic movement : —

> " My héart is a bréaking, dear Títtie,
> Some counsel unto me come len',
> To anger them a' is a pity, —
> But what will I do wi' Tam Glen?"— Burns.

For dactylic movement, *cf.* R. Browning's " *This is a spray the bird clung to.*" Irregular are parts of Shakspere's song in *Twelfth Night*, II. 4 : —

> " Come away, come away, death,
> And in sad cypress let me be laid;
> Fly away, fly away, breath;
> I am slain by a fair cruel maid," etc.

See, also, Shelley's beautiful lines " *When the lamp is shattered.*"

(*d*) VERSE OF FOUR STRESSES.

This is a measure long enough for continuous work, and admits of a decided rhythmic pause. Verse of four accents is popular in light epic (*cf.* Chaucer, Scott, etc.) as well as in lyric poetry. Coleridge (in *Christabel*), and after him, Scott and Byron, varied with anapestic feet the regular alternation of heavy and light syllables. But this freedom which Coleridge claimed as a "new principle" is old enough, though Coleridge certainly gave it popularity. In its regular forms the four-stress verse leans toward its French prototype, the "old eight-syllable" metre; while in its freer guise it reminds us of the earliest popular English measures, and has decided echoes of Anglo-Saxon rhythm. This four-accent verse embraces such extremes as the regular "iambics" of *In Memoriam:* —

> " This truth came home with bier and pall,
> I feel it when I sorrow most, —

and the triple measure of Burns' *My Nanie's Awa:* —

> " Now in her green mantle blythe nature arrays,
> And listens the lambkins that bleat o'er the braes," etc.,

in which we note the beginning-rime, as well as the rhythmic beat, of our old verse, and think of Laurence Minot's line (p. 180) : —

> " The boste of yowre baner es betin all downe."

That wide-spread ballad, *Lord Donald*, or as Scott called it, *Lord Randal*, has the four-accent verse, and uses it with freedom : —

> " O whére hae ye béen, Lord Rándal, my són?
> O whére hae ye béen, my hándsome young mán?"
> " I hae béen to the wíldwood: mother máke my bèd sòon,
> For I'm wéary wi' húnting, and faín wald lie doún."

The third verse is very bold in the beginning of its second half: "mother" is slurred somewhat after the Anglo-Saxon fashion (*cf.* p. 175).

Regular measures other than iambic are common: for trochaic, compare Cowper's *Boadicea*, Ben Jonson's *Queen and huntress, chaste and fair*, Burns' *Farewell to Nancy* (feminine rimes), and the rimeless verse of *Hiawatha*. For anapestic, *cf.* Swinburne's chorus *When the hounds of spring*, on p. 170. Dactylic are Byron's lines, quoted by Guest: —

> "Warriors and chiefs, should the shaft or the sword
> Pierce me in leading the host of the Lord," etc.

But even if we accept such grouping (only brevity, convenience, and custom can warrant the use of "dactylic," "trochaic," etc.) in regular measures, there remains an immense amount of four-accent verse — *e.g.*, in *L'Allegro*, as noted on p. 169 — which cannot be so classed, notwithstanding the fact that there is regular alternation of heavy and light syllables. The above measures were constant in beginning with a light or with a heavy syllable, and in carrying this through the whole poem. But variety is given to measures like the four-stress couplet by (1) the presence or absence of a light syllable before the first stress; (2) the presence or absence of a light syllable after the last stress (double or single ending); (3) occasional license in the distribution of light syllables within the verse; (4) use of the rhythmic pause. Dr. Guest has teased these light variations into the fetters of a useless system, and gives a table of definite combinations of "sections." Thus the couplet (*L'Allegro*): —

> "And to the stack or the barn-door
> Stoutly struts his dames before"

is analyzed as   A b b A : A b b A
　　　　　　　　A b A : b A b A ;

but this sort of labor amounts to little, and is like a classification of the successive waves that break on an ocean beach. The verses are alike, but yet different. Their art lies in giving, amid all this variety of distribution, a constant sense of four rhythmic "beats" or stresses, which does not exclude frequent transfer of weight among the syllables. Of course, nobody will read : —

"And to' the stack' or the' barn door';"

but Dr. Guest's "section" does not remove the difficulty, for he lays the stress on "*And*," "*or*," and makes "*barn*" light, whereas the real accents are "*stack*," — which is further emphasized by the following pause, — "*barn*," and "*door*"; the first accent is divided between "*And*" and "*to*"; "*the*," "*or*" and "*the*" have no accent at all. Or perhaps it is better to call "*stack*," "*barn*" and "*door*" the three main stresses, and let the fourth stress divide itself among the five small words. The next verse is much nearer to the metrical scheme of alternating light and heavy syllables, and has a pronounced trochaic movement. Hovering accent (*a*), and the well-known license of changing the distribution of accents after a pause (*b*), are both very common in such verse : —

(*a*) "Róbes lòosely flówing, háir as frée."
(*b*) "Stíll to be néat, stíll to be drést."
(*b*) "Thére to méet with Macbéth."

Perhaps we should here read with the old license of dropping light syllables (*cf.* p. 175), and so emphasize the name : —

"Thére to méet with *Mácbéth*."

Transposed accent is very prominent in Byron's line: —

> "Wélcome, wélcome, ye dárk blue wavés,
> And when ye fail my sight," etc.

Reference has already (p. 196) been made to the popularity of this measure in Shakspere's day; and it is used constantly in modern lyric. — The triple measure — two light syllables to each stress — was also a favorite with Byron and with Moore, — as in the opening stanzas of the *Bride of Abydos*, and in certain poems of *Lalla Rookh;* in our time, Swinburne combines double and triple measures with good result: —

> "There lived a singer in France of old
> By the tideless, dolorous, midland sea;
> In a land of sand and ruin and gold
> There shone one woman and none but she."

Browning's measure is more dactylic: —

> "Where I find her not, beauties vanish;
> Whither I follow her, beauties flee;
> Is there no method to tell her in Spanish,
> June's twice June since she breathed it with me?"
>
> — *Garden Fancies.*

The combination of four-stress and three-stress verse in lyric poetry is extremely popular, and has already been noticed in the description of the Septenary and its later forms. Examples lie on every hand. There is a stately march to this measure in the iambic movement: *cf.* Shelley's chorus from *Hellas:* —

> "The world's great age begins anew,
> The golden years return."

(e) Verse of Five Stresses.

This commonest of English metres is met in the couplet, in the stanza, and in blank verse. The movement is prevailingly iambic; that is, the metrical scheme calls for an opening light syllable and a closing stress-syllable; in all, five stresses alternating regularly with five light syllables. But the laws of word-accent, the rhetorical emphasis, and the license of double endings, etc., so modify this scheme that we seldom find a perfect example of the measure (*cf.* p. 172); but, on the other hand, there is no good poetry in this measure where the ear does not easily recognize the underlying rhythm of five beats, so distributed as to produce a general iambic movement.

The popularity of this metre is easy to account for. It hits the golden mean, avoiding the too short and tripping effect of four-stress verse, which suits lyric poetry and light narrative, but is unfitted for the purposes of the epic and the drama; and yet it does not fall into the monotonous pace of the Alexandrine with an invariable middle cæsura. The odd number of measures or feet allows five-stress verse exquisite variety in the position of its pause (*cf.* Chap. VI. § 4).

Compared with iambic, other movements of this verse are rare. For rimed trochaic, *cf.* Mr. Arnold's *Tristram and Iseult*, II.: —

> "Fear me not, I will be always with thee;
> I will watch thee, tend thee, soothe thy pain;
> Sing thee tales of true, long-parted lovers
> Join'd at evening of their days again."

Trochaic blank verse of five stresses we find in Browning's *One Word More:* —

> "Oh, their Rafael of the dear Madonnas,
> Oh, their Dante of the dread Inferno,
> Wrote one song — and in my brain I sing it,
> Drew one angel — borne, see, on my bosom!"

The same poet has written anapestic five-stress verse : —

> "And the sleep in the dried river-channel where bulrushes tell
> That the water was wont to go warbling so softly and well."
> — *Saul.*

Irregular is the metre of Moore's song — *At the mid hour of night:* —

> "Then I sing the wild song 'twas once such pleasure to hear,
> When our voices commingling breathed like one on the ear."

A constant feminine or double ending gives a new character to iambic verse : as in Fletcher's part of *Henry VIII.* (Wolsey's famous speech, for example); and when combined with a less regular arrangement of accents, it becomes a quite different measure, — as in Lamb's *Old Familiar Faces:* —

> "I have had playmates, I have had companions,
> In my days of childhood, in my joyful schooldays;
> All, all are gone, the old familiar faces."

Turning to the more popular measure, we first make the broad distinction between rimed and rimeless verse. Rimed five-stress verse is common in many forms of the stanza — *e.g.*, the metre of Spenser's *Faery Queene*, the sonnet, the simple quatrain of Gray's *Elegy*, etc. What calls for most comment in these cases is the stanzaic form; the rules for the individual verse present no difficulties. But when we come to the simplest rimed form of this measure, the "heroic" *couplet*, we must distinguish between the rhetorical and clear-cut verse of Dryden or Pope, and the verse of those poets who, according to the modest claim of Keats, "stammer where old Chaucer used to sing." The latter verse strives for variety and a "fluid" movement. Let us take Pope in his best vein, his brilliant, rhetorical vein, in that climax at the end of the *Dunciad* which Dr. Johnson and Thackeray have both praised so strongly:—

> " See skulking truth to her old cavern fled,
> Mountains of casuistry heap'd o'er her head!
> Philosophy that lean'd on heaven before,
> Shrinks to her second cause, and is no more.
> Physic of Metaphysic begs defence,
> And Metaphysic calls for aid on Sense!
> See Mystery to Mathematics fly!
> In vain! they gaze, turn giddy, rave, and die.
> Religion blushing, veils her sacred fires,
> And unawares Morality expires.
> Nor public flame, nor private, dares to shine;
> Nor human spark is left, nor glimpse divine!
> Lo! thy dread empire, CHAOS! is restored;
> Light dies before thy uncreating word;
> Thy hand, great Anarch! lets the curtain fall,
> And universal darkness buries all."

Pope does not belong to our greatest poets; but for brilliant workmanship, for mingled ease and vigor in handling verse, he is without a superior; and the above extract merits careful study and a consequent insight into the grace and strength of its construction. For technical points, we note in Pope a careful observance of word-accent; insistance on the rhetorical emphasis; a verse mostly, and a couplet always, "end-stopt." The verse is protected from monotony by the matchless ease with which it is handled, and by the variety of tone and rime. Like Dryden's, Pope's verse tends to split into half-verses with two stresses in each; see the antithetical lines quoted on p. 126.

But much as we admire this brilliant verse, our tribute ceases with admiration. It is the other verse, the verse of Marlowe and Keats, that claims our sympathy and touches the heart. We will take no particularly beautiful or famous passage, but simply quote a few lines from Keat's *Endymion:* —

> "Now while the silent workings of the dawn
> Were busiest, into that self-same lawn
> All suddenly, with joyful cries, there sped
> A troop of little children garlanded;
> Who, gathering round the altar, seemed to pry
> Earnestly round, as wishing to espy
> Some folk of holiday: nor had they waited
> For many moments, ere their ears were sated
> With a faint breath of music, which even then
> Fill'd out its voice, and died away again."

This is not faultless, like Pope's work; there is a repetition, and we note some awkwardness; but we forgive all that to the verse, *quia multum amavit.* It has its "eye on the object," not on the public to see whether applause is coming. Technically, we mark the run-on lines, and a tendency to irregularity in the weight of accented syllables (*spéd: garlandéd*). Highly finished modern work in this metre will be found in the Prelude to Swinburne's *Tristram of Lyonesse*, especially in the list of love-signs of the different months; as for older verse, the exquisite music of Marlowe's *Hero and Leander* (first two Sestiads: the rest are Chapman's) has never been surpassed by any couplets in our literature.

With regard to rimed "heroic" verse in general, it is to be noted that the very fact of rime tends to make the metre regular. Licenses are far more frequent in blank verse,— for example, *light endings*, which are thrown into unpleasant prominence by rime, but slip by smoothly enough in rimeless poetry. At the beginning of a stanza, they are not so rare: *cf. Don Juan*, IV. : —

> "Their faces were not made for wrinkles, *their*
> Pure blood to stagnate, their great hearts to fail;
> The blank grey was not made to blast their hair," etc.

Other licenses are of the ordinary kind. Thus, after or with a pause, either of an entire verse, or of a rhythmic section of a verse, English poetry favors (*a*) a trochaic license, and (*b*) extra syllables. A modern ear hardly allows Surrey's

> "Whóso gládly hálseth the gólden méane,"

or even

> "Bríttle béautie, that náture máde so fráile;"

but any verse may begin with a stress-syllable; and the same is true of the verse-section after a pause: —

> "O géntle chíld, *beáutiful* as thou wert!" — Shelley, *Adonais*,

or with very faint cæsura: —

> "What sófter vóice is húshed *óver* the déad?"
> — Shelley, *Adonais*.

For extra syllables: —

> "I sée befóre *me the* gládiátor lié." — Byron.
>
> "I héard thee ín the gárd*en, and* óf thy vóice." — Milton.

Slurring is common: especially with "of the," "in the," etc. In Tennyson's blank verse we have a not unpleasant cadence:—

> "Elaine the fair, Elaine the lovable,
> Elaine, the lily maid of Astolat,
> *High in her chamber up a tower to the east,*" etc.,

or in the verse:—

> "*Myriads of rivulets hurrying* through the lawns."

BLANK VERSE. — SHAKSPERE AND MILTON.

We shall take Shakspere as representative of dramatic blank verse, and Milton for the epic. Shakspere uses five-stress verse to the almost total exclusion of other kinds. Exceptions are made by Sonnet 145, by the songs referred to above, and by some occasional six-stress and seven-stress verse (*e.g.*, in *Love's Labour's Lost*). His dramas are written mainly in rimeless verse; the narrative poems (*Lucrece, Venus and Adonis*), and sonnets, in rimed stanzas. The early plays show the most rime. In the *Winter's Tale* there is no rimed verse at all; in the *Tempest* there is *one* riming couplet: these are both late plays. But in *Love's Labour's Lost*, one of the earliest plays, there are more than *one thousand* riming verses; in *Mid. Night's Dream*, over 850. Taking a play of the middle period, say *Julius Cæsar*, which represents neither extreme of the poet's development, we find 2,241 lines of blank verse to 34 rimed lines.[1] It follows that our main concern will be with the laws of Shakspere's blank verse.

[1] All these figures are taken from Fleay's table, *Trans. New Shaks. Soc.* I. p. 16.

The chief thing to remember in reading Shakspere's verses is that they were made for the ear, not for the eye. The poet who

> "For gain, not glory, wing'd his roving flight,
> And grew immortal in his own despite,"

had, when he wrote, little regard for his future commentators' rule-of-thumb scansion, but a great regard for the pleasure his rhythm would give to the hearers at the theatre. It is the general effect of the lines, their musical flow, which we take into account; though we must pay some attention to the individual elements of the verse.

Rhythm is natural, and appeals to an inborn instinct for harmony; therefore, if we can know how Shakspere sounded his words, that is, if we become thoroughly acquainted with the material in which he worked, it will not be difficult to make his verses melodious to our ears. Hence, *contracted* or *expanded* words must be understood, as well as the Elizabethan *word-accent*, which in some cases differed from modern usage. For the rest, we must allow Shakspere, as we allowed Chaucer, freedom to *slur;* and what Gascoigne said in his day about Chaucer, we, who stand much in the same relation to Shakspere, may apply to the latter poet: "Who so euer do peruse and well consider his [Chaucer's] workes, he shall finde that although his lines are not alwayes of one selfe same number of Syllables, yet beyng redde by one that hath understanding, the longest verse and that which hath most Syllables in it, will fall (to the eare) correspondent unto that whiche hath fewest sillables in it: and like wise that whiche hath in it fewest syllables, shal be founde yet to consist of woordes that have such naturall sounde, as may seeme equall in length to a verse which hath many moe sillables of lighter accentes." (Arber's Reprint, *Certayne Notes*, etc., p. 34.) In other words, a skilful poet can vary the distribution of his accents and add (light) syllables to his verse, yet preserve intact the rhythm which his chosen scheme demands. He can also drop a light syllable and let pause or emphasis make up for the loss, as we shall see below. In the verse, —

"The sénate hath sént aboút thrèe sèveral quésts"
(*Oth.* I. II. 46),

it is not necessary to contract "senate" to "sen't," and so make an unpleasant repetition in the next foot. The word is slurred, or rapidly pronounced, and the verse satisfies our ear. Ellis gives examples of this slurring in all parts of the verse. From his list of "Trisyllabic Measures" (*Early Eng. Pron.*, p. 941) and from Abbott, we select a few cases; the first is Guest's "slovenly" rhythm : —

"*I beséech* your gráces bóth to párdon hér."—*Rich. III.* I. I.

"*Let me sée, let me sée*; is nót the léaf turn'd dówn?"
—*J. C.* IV. 3.

"At ány time *have recóurse* untó the princes."
—*Rich. III.* III. 5.

"Delíver thís with *módesty* tó the quéen."
—*Hen. VIII.* II. 2.

"Excépt immórtal Cǽsar *spéaking of Brútus*."—*J. C.* I. I.

There is no need to do violence to these words, and read *b'seech, let m' see* (say, *lem' sée!*), *'course* (Abbott), etc. It is rapid pronunciation, not suppression of the sounds in question, which satisfies the metre. Indeed, in the fourth example we may pronounce *modesty* with distinctness, for the third syllable borrows a part of the stress and importance of the next rhythmic accent, which is the weak word *to*. A slight rhythmic pause after *modesty* also countenances the added syllable. We shall find that Milton uses this license very often. Contractions, of course, are common enough in Shakspere: *this is* to *this'* ; *I will* to *I'll*, as now, — and the like (see below); but trisyllabic measures, at least with slurred syllables, are also frequent in Shakspere, and cannot be explained away. As regards *double* and *triple endings*, the former are often found, but Shakspere is not half so fond of them as Fletcher is, who uses them in continuous verse, and the latter poet's share in *Hen. VIII.* can be marked off by the use of this simple test. In *Hamlet*, out of 3,924 verses, 508 have double endings; in *Hen. VIII.* there are 1,195 out of 2,754 (Fleay). Triple endings are rare and mostly can be contracted or slurred: —

"I dare avouch it, sir; what, fifty *followers?*" — *Lear*, II. 4.

Fletcher, *Pilgrim* (Ward): —

"The wind blows thro' the leaves and *plays with 'em*."

Fleay cites Middleton: —

"As wild and merry as the heart of *innocence*."

It is not easy to say just where slurring ends and full contraction takes place. In

"To entertain it so merrily with a fool" (*All's Well*, II. 2),

the *it* is perhaps to be contracted (*entertain't*), while *merrily* is slurred. Cf. *Hamlet*, I. 1: —

"That hath a stomach in't: which is no other."

We may distinguish between the contraction of two words into one, and the contraction of a single word into fewer syllables. Contracted to one word are *in his* (= *in's*), *of his* (= *o's*), *they have* (= *they've*, as now), and the like: *e.g.*:—

"The morning comes *upon us;* we'll leave you, Brutus,"

where, however, an extra syllable could easily be sounded before the pause. So *God b' wi' you*, as in *Hamlet*, II. 1 (Browne):—

"*R.* My lord, I have.
P. God be with you, fare you well."

So *by our* and *by your*, to *by'r*.— Lastly, final *r* easily runs into a following initial vowel or *h*,—thus, *Cym.* III. 4:—

"Report should *render him* hourly to your ear."

But contraction often takes place within the word. Thus *prefixes* are dropped. *Cf.* '*count* for *account* in *Ham.* IV. 4:—

"Why to a public count I could not go."

Many other cases are given by Abbott, *Shaks. Gram.* § 460. Other bold contractions are *ignomy* for *ignominy*, *caustick* for *candlestick*, etc. Many modern English proper names are similarly contracted: *cf. Cholmondeley*. Again, a "liquid" consonant followed by a vowel is easily contracted; *spirit* is mostly one syllable in Shakspere: *cf.* the metathesis *sprite*. So also *parlous* (= *perilous*); *punishment* (slurring is more probable here); *barbarous; promising:* indeed, any light syllable which comes between primary and secondary accent (*cf.* in Chaucer's metres, p. 190), or the weakest syllable among several, can either be slurred or drop out altogether: *specŭlative* (*speclative*); *medĭcine*; *sanctuăry*, etc. In such cases as these, almost any one with a good ear will "scan" the verse correctly enough without instruction. It is not proposed to give here a list of Shakspere's slurred and contracted words;— for details, *cf.* Abbott, and also *Notes on Shakspere's Versification*, by G. H. Browne, A.M.[1] We add a few common cases: *whether* to *whe'r*: —

"And see whether Brutus be alive or dead." — *J. C.* v. 5.

So *devil, marvel* (to *marle* in Ben Jonson), *needle* (*neele*); also contracted is final *-ed* after *t* or *d: executed* to *execute'*; *exceeded* to *exceed'*; *mistrusted* to *mistrust'*; *fitted* to *fitt'*, etc. Similarly, the possessive or the plural *-s* is dropped after *-se*, *-ce*, etc.: —

"I'll to him; he is hid at *Laurence'* cell." — *R. & J.* III. 2.

On the other hand, many words which are monosyllables to us could be so *expanded* in Shakspere's time that they either were actually dissyllabic, or else were so prolonged as to have the same effect: this is independent of the pause, which may itself take the place of a syllable. Then, too, an emphatic monosyllable, without any pause or any expansion at all, may fill out a "foot"; thus, in *As You Like It*, III. 4, —

"Bríng | us tó this síght, and yóu shall sáy,"

Bring seems to be sufficient through its rhetorical and syntactical emphasis; and the emendations of Pope, Malone, and others are needless. Still more certain is

[1] Boston: Ginn, Heath, & Co. 1884.

the case where an emphatic pause follows the monosyllable, as in the often quoted verse (*R. II.* I. 3) : —

"Stáy! the kíng hath thrówn his wárder dówn."

There is not the slightest need to pronounce "sta-ay," or even "stay-*y*" (Browne); for the sharp exclamation is spoiled by dwelling on the diphthong. On the contrary, "O!" *is* so prolonged, and takes the place of two syllables : —

"O the différence of mán and mán."—*Lear*, III. 7.

It does not become two syllables (O-o), but is simply prolonged, as in the natural cry of wonder or protest. So we would read *Macb.* I. 2 : —

"'Gaínst my captívity. *Háil!* bràve friènd."

The liquids, *r*, *l*, etc., lend themselves readily to expansions, being used now as consonants, now as vowels : —

"That croaks the fatal *ent(e)rance* of Duncan."—*Macb.* I. 5.

"Look how he makes to Cæsar! *mar-k* him.—*J. C.* III. 1.

"I knów a bánk *where* the wíld thýme blòws."[1]
—*M. N. D.* II. 1.

"And mean to make her queen of Eng(e)land."
—*R. III.* IV. 4.

The termination *-ion* in Shakspere counts either as one syllable or as two; so also *-ier* (*sold-i-er*), *-iant*, *-ean*, etc., *e.g.* : —

"By the o'ergrowth of some *complexion*."—*Haml.* I. 4.

"Your mind is tossing on the *ocean*."—*M. of V.* I. 1.

---

[1] Note in this verse, as in *Macb.* I. 2 above, how the single syllable in question is helped by the hovering accents and heavy stresses that follow.

Cf. Milton : —

"Whispering new joys to the mild oc-e-an."—*Nativ. Hymn.*

Then, too, the old inflexional endings still asserted themselves here and there ; *e.g.*, the noun *ach-es: Temp.* I. 2 : —

"Fill all thy bones with achës, make thee roar."

Accent. — In reading Shakspere, we often have to throw the accent of a word either forward or back of its modern place. Lists of such words, and lines where they occur, are given by Ellis (verses are simply referred to, not quoted) *E. E. P.* p. 930, and by Abbott, *Gram.* §§ 490 ff. Many cases show undoubted difference from modern usage : thus *Aliéna* (proper name), *revénue, arch'bishop, con'fessor, perséver*, etc.

"Ay dó perséver, coúnterféit sàd loòks."—*M. N. D.* III. 2.

This is quite natural if we consider what a shifting thing "pronunciation" is when it deals with words derived from foreign sources, and if we recall the fact that the foreign accent at once enters into strife with the Germanic impulse to accent the root-syllable, or when that is not evident, the first syllable. But we find Shakspere, as we found Chaucer, accenting a word now one way, now another, as the metre demands (*cf.* p. 192) ; and we conclude that in many cases use may be made of the *hovering accent* previously mentioned. Thus in *W. T.* IV. 4, —

"Mark our *contract* ; mark your divorce, young sir,"

we need not throw the entire weight of accent on *-tract*. The stress may be divided ; though in this case, the second syllable has a slight preponderance. Take other verses :—

"That thóu, deàd còrse, agaín in cómplíte stéel."
— *Haml.* I. 4.

"His means of death, his óbscúre funeral." — *Haml.* IV. 5.

"Now for the honour of the fórlòrn French."
— 1 *Hen. VI.* I. 2.

"*I myself* fight not once in forty years."— 1 *Hen. VI.* I. 3.

In these we have undoubted hovering accent. While the difference is stronger in (*Haml.*, I. 4)

"Why thy *canónízed* bones, hearsëd in death";

nevertheless, in cases like

"O Harry's wife, *triumph* not in my woes"(*R. III.* IV. 4),

"That comes in *triumph* over Cæsar's blood" (*J. C.* I. 1),

we have practically the same word-accent, though the metre makes a slight counter-claim in the first example; — in other words, it is not necessary to shift the entire stress from the first to the second syllable.

We have already noted the license given to English blank verse by the *pause*, — whether it be the end of the verse or the so-called "cæsura." Thus two stress-syllables may come together, provided the pause intervenes; as in

"Bè in their flówing cúps | *fré'shly* remémber'd "
(*H. V.* IV. 3);

and with a slight rhythmic pause in

"Seé how my swórd | *weéps* for the poòr king's deáth."
— 3 *H. VI.* v. 6.

Again, an *extra syllable* is frequent before a pause. An excellent example, giving this license both within the line and at the end ("feminine" or double ending) is —

"Obéy and bé attént*ive:* cànst thòu remém*ber?*"
— *Temp.* I. 2.

Shakspere does not allow this extra syllable at the end to be a monosyllable: Fletcher, however, is fond of such endings, and we find many in his part of *Hen. VIII.*, *e.g.* : —

"Féll by our sérvants, bý those mén we lóv'd *most.*"

Occasionally Shakspere slips into an *Alexandrine;* and while many of these can be explained away by contraction or slurring, there still remain a few undoubted cases, — small wonder, considering the popularity of the measure in the Sixteenth Century, and the freedom with which Shakspere handles his dramatic material.

It is the mutual relations of the metrical scheme and the word-groups which give character to rhythm. We have already noticed this strife between type and individual, between unity and variety, and the beauty which results when a true poet is in the question. Now we can see a decided growth in Shakspere's art of verse-making, a steady progress from the fetters of slavish obedience to his metrical scheme, towards the strong and chainless music of his later verse. From *Love's Labour's Lost* with "unstopt" to "end-stopt" in the proportion of 1 : 18.14, to *The Winter's Tale* with 1 : 2.12, is a long stride; it means that our highest dramatic art found its best instrument in a metre which allowed all possible variety of word-groups. Mr. Spedding (*Trans. New Shaks. Soc.* 1874, I. p. 30) gives the same subject ("the face of a beautiful woman just dead") as treated by Shakspere at different periods; thus *Rom. & Jul.* (say 1597) :—

> "Her blood is settled and her joints are stiff.
> Life and those lips have long been separated.
> Death lies on her like an untimely frost
> Upon the fairest flower of all the field."

Cf. Antony & Cleop. (say 1607) :—

> "If they had swallowed poison, 'twould appear
> By external swelling: but she looks like sleep,
> As she would catch another Antony
> In her strong toil of grace."

Aside from the gain in vigor of style shown by the second extract, note the freedom of movement and the strength and variety imparted by the shifting pause. Note, too, the trisyllabic opening of the second verse of the same extract.

Another feature of Shakspere's later work is his use of *light* and *weak* endings: *light* being such words as *am, are, be, can, could,—do, does, has, had* (as auxiliaries),—*I, they, thou; weak* are words like *and, for, from, if, in, of, or* (Dowden).[1] "In *Macbeth* light endings appear for the first time in considerable numbers; weak endings in considerable numbers for the first time in *Antony and Cleopatra*." The same progress is seen in the poet's increasing use of *double endings*.

So much for a very meagre outline of Shakspere's versification. We have assumed throughout (1) that the regular metrical scheme of five accented syllables, alternating regularly with five unaccented syllables, is valid only so far as it makes the foundation and ground-

[1] See also *Trans. N. Shaks. Soc.* 1874, II. p. 448.

plan of the rhythm, and is so modified by word-accent, rhetorical accent, quantity, and tone, that it can rarely, if ever, be applied with literal exactness to the concrete verse; but that (2) it is certainly present as the skeleton of the verse, can always be detected by the ear, and is our one test of correct rhythm.

Milton's Verse.

The sonorous roll of Miltonic rhythm is unique in our poetry, although it has enticed countless bardlings to a superficial imitation whose inversion and verbosity resemble Milton's work as tinsel resembles silver. But in Milton's hands epic blank verse becomes worthy of such praise as this from Mr. Arnold:[1] "To this metre, as used in the *Paradise Lost*, our country owes the glory of having produced one of the only two poetical works in the grand style which are to be found in the modern languages; the *Divine Comedy* of Dante is the other." The verse thus highly praised can present no difficulties to a sympathetic ear which allows the freedom of *slurring*, the variety of the pause, and the use of hovering accent. Occasionally there is transposed accent, but mostly in its usual place after the pause. The "inversions" are matters of style.

Often Milton's hovering accent is very subtle, and Mr. Arnold has somewhere made it a test of one's ear for metre whether or not one finds good rhythm in the last verse of the passage:—

"Those other two equal'd with me in fate,
So were I equal'd with them in renown,

[1] *On Translating Homer*, III.

> Blind Thamyris and blind Mæonides,
> And Tiresias and Phineus, prophets old."

In this last verse, which the ear of Bentley rejected as bad metre, the rhythm accents Tí-resiás (slurring of *i*), the word accents Tiré-sias; but the first syllable is a diphthong and is helped by its quantity, so that with hovering accent the verse "scans" admirably. *Cf.* Shelley's verse: —

> " The blue *Mediter*ranean, where he lay."— *West Wind.*

A case of accent changed after a pause is

> " *Floats* as they páss, *fann'd* with unnúmber'd plúmes."
> — *Par. Lost*, 7.

Slurring is frequently used: —

> " How qúick they whéel'd, and fly*ing* behínd them shót."
> — *Par. Reg.*
>
> " Your milit*ary* obed*ience*, to dissolve."
>
> " Thy condescens*ion and* shall be honor'd ever."
>
> " A pill*ar* of state: deep on his front engraven."

As *Romeo and Juliet*, with its soft cadences, is to the vigorous stride of Shakspere's last plays, so is the *Comus* of Milton to his *Paradise Lost.* In *Comus* the versification is exquisite, full of such movement as —

> " What need a vermeil-tinctur'd lip for that,
> Love-darting eyes, or tresses like the morn?"

or

> " O welcome, pure-ey'd Faith, white-handed Hope,
> Thou hovering angel girt with golden wings!"

This verse is full of the beauty of Elizabethan rhythm; but there is a splendor, a majesty, in the later epic, for which we have no adjective but " Miltonic." *Cf.* with the above extracts this from *Paradise Lost* (Book VI.): —

(1) "Sérvant of Gód, wèll dòne, wéll hast thou fóught
(2) The bétter fíght, who síngle hást maintáin'd
(3) Agáinst revólted múltitúdes the cáuse
(4) Of trúth, in wórd míghtiẹr than théy in árms;
(5) Ànd fòr the téstimóny of trúth hast bórne
(6) Univérsal reproách, far wórse to béar
(7) Than víolence."

Note the distribution of the pauses; the "run-on" lines, which, according to Dr. Johnson, "change the measures of a poet to the periods of a declaimer," but, for our ears, give vigor as well as variety to the verse; the shifting of accents, — as in (4) where the real rhythmical pause is after *word*, and so allows transposed accent in the next foot; the hovering accent (1) *wèll dòne;* the slurring of (4) (5) *-iẹr* and *-ny of;* and the light accent in (5) on *And for*, which allows extra emphasis for the following phrase. Other examples of a very weak initial accent are (Guest, p. 239) : —

"Bý the wàtèrs of lífe, wheré'er they sát."
"Tó the gàrdèn of blíss thy séat prepár'd."

Here, with hovering accent for *waters* or *garden*, thus dwelling on the chief word, we can help the metre, which to Guest's ear was "far from pleasing." The most famous license, however, is (6) : —

"*Universal* reproach, far worse to bear."

Read with proper emphasis, this verse is not at all unpleasing; indeed, the metre helps the sense (= "reproach on all sides, — absolute"). The very pronounced pause after *reproach* throws the emphatic words into prominence; and altogether we may call this admirable metrical workmanship. "Trochaic," entirely, is a well-known line in Keats' *Hyperion:* —

"Thea, Thea, Thea, where is Saturn?"

Again, Guest objects to the verse, —

"Beyond the polar circle: to them, day,"

because it lays too much stress on a weak word *to;* but by applying the principle of hovering accent, the verse is harmonious enough: —

"Beyónd the pólar cíṙcle: tò theṁ dáy," etc.

Finally, there can be lines when it is almost impossible to talk of light or heavy syllables: —

"Rocks, caves, lakes, fens, bogs, dens, and shades of death."

With this, we leave English Blank Verse; but no account of it can afford to forget the splendid promise and melody of Keats' fragment, *Hyperion:*

"Cut is the branch that might have grown full straight,
And burned is Apollo's laurel bough."

(*f*) Verse of Six Stresses.

The *Alexandrine* has already been noticed. Popular at the beginning of Queen Elizabeth's reign, it was gradually thrust aside by heroic verse; though Drayton's *Polyolbion* (1612) employs it consistently. When we read a little of this poem, we understand why the metre lost ground in spite of the efforts of so able a poet.

"Of Albion's glorious isle the wonders whilst I write,
The sundry varying soils, the pleasures infinite,

> Where heat kills not the cold, nor cold expels the heat,
> The calms too mildly small, nor winds too roughly great,
> Nor night doth hinder day, nor day the night doth wrong;
> The summer not too short, the winter not too long."

But combined with heroic verse at the end of a stanza, as in Spenser, or incidental to the regular couplet, as in Dryden, the Alexandrine has a pleasant effect:—

> " So pale grows Reason in Religion's sight,
> *So dies and so dissolves in supernatural light.*"

The Alexandrine is iambic; a trochaic movement in six-stress verse gives a stately or mournful effect,—as in Swinburne's lines:—

> " Dárk the shríne and dúmb the foúnt of sóng thence wélling,
> Save for words more sad than tears of blood, that said:
> Tell the king, on earth has fallen the glorious dwelling,
> And the watersprings that spake are quenched and dead."

Irregular six-stress verse is met in couplet and stanza:

> "Oút of the gólden remòte wild wést where the séa without shóre is,
> Fúll of the súnset, and sád, if at áll, with the fúlness of jóy,
> As a wínd sèts ìn with the aútumn that blóws from the région of stóries,
> Blóws with a perfume of sóngs and of mémories belóved from a bóy."

Cf. the metre of the opening stanzas of Tennyson's *Maud*, and the strong verse of Morris' *Sigurd the Volsung*.

Here, finally, belongs the so-called *Hexameter*. It is, of course, quite clear that the actual classic hexameter cannot be imitated in English verse; that is plain to any one who can distinguish quantity from accent. Nor can we reproduce the full effect of the classic hexameter by the simple substitution of accented for long syllables, and unaccented for short. But there is no reason why we cannot, by such a substitution, imitate the general *movement* of the old metre. The English verse thus obtained becomes a measure which may please some and displease others, and is to be judged precisely as we judge the Alexandrine or any given verse-system. For surely, if we, with our English sounds and English accents and dull ear for exact proportions of quantity, can read aloud with pleasure (the test of an agreeable metre) the verse of Homer or Vergil, it follows that a verse of similar effect in movement can be obtained in our own language; the difference between the two metres will be the difference between the structure of English and the structure of Greek or of Latin, together with the loss of delicate quantity-relations, which, indeed, are with classical scholars rather thought than felt. This is a loss; but it is absurd to maintain that we cannot transfer to English verse the general movement (*i.e.*, the distribution of verse-accents) of classic hexameter. The trouble lies in the lack of any good English substitute for the classic *spondee* ($-\ -$); whereas the purely dactylic hexameter, without relief through spondaic effects, is, in the long run, monotonous. Perhaps this is what made Platen, the German poet, declare the hexameter "fit only for short poems." Mr. Arnold, however, says "*Solvitur ambulando*"; and wants us to practise hexameters till we can make perfect ones. Certainly, if we look at early attempts in this metre, we can gather comfort for our own condition and hope for the future. Nash said of certain hexameter verse of his day: "that drunken, staggering kind of verse, which is all up hill and down hill . . . and goes like a horse plunging through the mire in the deep of winter, now soused up to the saddle, and straight aloft on his tip-toes." Campion more gravely says that such verse is not successful because "the concurse of monosillables make (*sic*) our verses unapt to slide." Now Nash, when he made his comparison, was thinking of one Richard Stanyhurst's translation (Leyden, 1582: now reprinted by Arber) of four books of the *Æneid* into what he called hexameters, — of which Nash further remarked that it was "a foule, lumbring, boystrous, wallowing measure." Take the opening of Book II., which will make the reader quite agree with Nash : —

> "Wyth tentiue lystning eeche wight was setled in harckning,
> Thus father Æneas chronicled from lofty bed hautye.
> You me bid, O Princesse, too scarrify a festered old soare."

But there were far better specimens even at that time; thus Greene : —

> "Oft have I heárd my lièf Còridón repórt on a lóve-day
> Whèn bònny máids do méet with the swáins in the válley by Témpe."

Klopstock (to come to more modern times) chose the hexameter for the metre of his German *Paradise Lost*, the *Messias;* Goethe often used it, — *e.g.*, in *Hermann und Dorothea;* and, for English, Longfellow's *Evangeline*, Clough's *Bothie of Tober-na-Vuolich*, and (perhaps best of all) Kingsley's *Andromeda*, at least should make us recognize this measure as a belligerent, though some writers speak of the English hexameter as a proved failure. To these practical examples, add Mr. Arnold's critical remarks in his *Essay on Translating Homer*. We have no space to enter into the discussion.

But we may point out that besides the lack of spondaic effect, there is often a *false accent* in hexameter verse which ought to be carefully avoided: thus

"*In* that delíghtful lánd which is wáshed by the Délaware's wáters,"

if read metrically, has an almost ludicrous effect. Better is

"*Bént* like a láboring oár which toíls in the súrf of the ócean."

Then, too, the *pause* should be varied; occasionally two pauses in a verse have a pleasant effect:—

"Níght after níght, when the wórld was asleép, as the wátchman repéated."

(*g*) Verse of Seven Stresses.

This has already been noticed in the ballad measure (*cf.* Chapman's translation), both in its original form, and in the popular arrangement of four-and-three, whether with or without rimed pause-accents.

A verse of more than *eight* stresses can in nearly all cases be separated into two verses of four stresses each. Tennyson's *Locksley Hall*, however, is best printed as eight-stress verse: thus

"Full of sad experience, moving toward the stillness of his rest"

is better than

"Full of sad experience, moving
 Toward the stillness of his rest."

Cf. also Poe's *Raven*, which has interior rime.

(*h*) MISCELLANEOUS.

Imitations of classic metres are not confined to hexameter verse. The "elegiac" verse, in which "pentameter" alternated with "hexameter," has been occasionally tried by English poets, but not so much as in Germany; Coleridge's translation from Schiller is well known:—

"In the hexameter rises the fountain's silvery column,
In the pentameter aye falling in melody back."

Tennyson has some "Alcaics" to Milton:—

"O míghty-móuth'd invéntor of hármonies,
O skíll'd to síng of tíme or etérnity,
Gòd-gífted órgan vóice of Éngland,
Mílton, a náme to resóund for áges!"

Milton himself has very gracefully Englished one of Horace's Odes (1. 5):—

"What slender youth bedew'd with liquid odours
Courts thee on roses in some pleasant cave,
Pyrrha? For whom bind'st thou
In wreaths thy golden hair?"

Compare with this the exquisite *Ode to Evening* of Collins.

The difficult "Hendecasyllabic" verse, as used by the Roman Catullus, has been imitated by Coleridge, Tennyson, and Swinburne. The latter poet has even essayed the "Choriambic" verse:—

"Lòve, whàt | áiled thee to leáve | lífe that was máde | lóvely, we thóught | with lóve?
Whàt swèet | vísions of sleép | lúred thee awáy | dowń from the líght | abóve?"

Bulwer wrote a collection of stories, *The Lost Tales of Miletus*, all in classical metres; nor must we forget the rimeless rhythm of Southey, as in *Thalaba*, or of Matthew Arnold, as in *The Strayed Reveller*, and the highly successful choruses (with sporadic rime) of the *Samson Agonistes*.

But it may be said, notwithstanding these cases, that with the possible exception of the hexameter, the movement of classical metres does not harmonize with the fundamental conditions of Germanic rhythm.

CHAPTER VIII.

§ 1. THE STANZA, OR STROPHE.

This is a subject which presents few difficulties; for the construction of a stanza appeals to the eye, and cannot be mistaken. A verse is the unit of every poem. Verses are combined in two ways,—either continuously, as in blank verse, the classic hexameter, and our Anglo-Saxon metre; or they may be bound together in a stanza, which in its turn goes with other stanzas to make up a poem or a division of a poem. The simplest of these combinations is the *couplet*, which, however, in practice is not looked on as a stanza; for the heroic couplet often has a continuous, epic effect. Next comes the *triplet*, which is decidedly stanzaic in effect: *cf.* Tennyson's *Two Voices*.

Strophe means literally "a turning": *cf. verse*. At the end of the strophe we turn, and repeat the same conditions: it is "the return of the song to the melody with which it begins." *Stanza*, under another symbol, means the same thing. We demand for the stanza identity of structure and a close connection of statement and subject-matter. The two factors of the stanza are the *Refrain* and *Rime*. Thus Lamb's *Old Familiar Faces* has no rime; but the recurrence of these three words marks the end of a strophe. The Refrain, according to Wolff (*Lais, Sequenzen*, etc.), "probably arose from the participation of the people or congregation in songs which were sung by one or more persons on festal occasions,—at church, play, or dance. The whole people repeated in chorus single words, or verses, or whole stanzas ... or in the pauses of the chief singer, they answered him with some repeated cry.... This became finally a regular form." Through the Provençal poetry these refrains came into England. They are common in the old folk-song, and the reader is familiar with them in many modern ballads; *cf.* also the *Epithalamion*. The refrain may be in another tongue: *cf.* Byron's *Maid of Athens*.

But the prevailing method of combining verses is by end-rime; and here we distinguish between stanzas where the verses are homogeneous, and stanzas made up of verses with a varying number of accents, though rarely with varying movement. It would require a volume to catalogue all the combinations in our poetry; any one can easily determine the form of a stanza for himself by noting the order of rimes. A decidedly different effect is made by two stanzas which may be alike in movement and number of verses, but unlike in rime-order. Thus the common four-stress quatrain with alternate rime (the number *four* being very popular in lyric poetry):

> "How happy is he born and taught
> That serveth not another's will;
> Whose armour is his honest thought,
> And simple truth his highest skill,"

has a quite different effect from the arrangement of the *In Memoriam* stanza, — a combination found in Ben Jonson, Prior, Lord Herbert of Cherbury, and others: —

> "Now rings the woodland loud and long,
> The distance takes a lovelier hue,
> And drown'd in yonder living blue
> The lark becomes a sightless song."

The first we denote by the letters *a b a b;* the second by *a b b a.* Still another variation is *a a b a,* the stanza made popular in Fitzgerald's translation of the quatrains of Omar Khayyam.

But of these the simplest and by all odds the most popular is the first, — *a b a b;* or with only two rimes, *a b c b.* Here, too, we may note another division of the simple stanza (*cf.* Schipper, p. 84). The rimes *b b* mark each the end of a "Period," — *i.e.,* they denote the *necessary* rime of the quatrain, and hence divide it into equal parts. Two verses make a period, two periods make a quatrain (if of this form), because one period exactly repeats the conditions of the other. To mark the end of this period, a *different ending* is often employed: thus, if *a a* (or *a c*) are masculine, *b b* will be feminine, and *vice versa.* Thus *a b c b* (Burns) : —

> "Go fetch to me a pint o' wine,
>   And fill it in a silver tassie;
> That I may drink before I go
>   A service to my bonnie lassie;"

or *a b a b* (Prior) : —

> "The merchant, to secure his treasure,
>   Conveys it in a borrowed name;
> Euphelia serves to grace my measure,
>   But Chloe is my real flame."

Still more marked is the period when *b b* are verses with fewer or more stresses than *a a* (*a c*), as was the case with the divided Septenary (common measure) already noted, in which *b b* have fewer accents than *a a* (*c*); a case where *b b* have more is

> "Art thou pale for weariness
>   Of climbing heaven and gazing on the earth,
> Wandering companionless
>   Among the stars that have a different birth?" — Shelley.

The quatrain, most popular of stanzas and the simplest, is also common in five-stress verse. The rime-order *a b a b* is that of our most read poem, the *Elegy*. Dryden used it in *Annus Mirabilis*, in imitation of Davenant's *Gondibert;* and we have seen even six-stress verse so combined. But there are more complicated forms. Thus to a quatrain we add a couplet, and so have the *three-part stanza*, consisting of two periods and the couplet; or we can combine differently — say *a a b c c b*, — the form of Shakspere's song in Hen. VIII. — *Orpheus with his lute;* or, with *varying verse-lengths*, of Wordsworth's *Three years she grew in sun and shower*. Thence we pass to the far more intricate combinations of lyric stanzas, — combinations which we shall not here attempt to analyze. The study of these forms is of more importance for our early poetry than for modern, and is of too special a nature for our attention. Many treatises, from Dante's *De vulgari Eloquentia* down to the dissertations of to-day, have been written on this subject: they are well summed up by Schipper in his *Metrik*, §§ 134–145.

It will be enough for our purposes if we simply name a few prominent English stanzaic forms. Thus the favorite stanza of Chaucer, the *Rime Royal* of his *Troilus* and some of the *Canterbury Tales*, has for its scheme *a b a b b c c*, — *e.g.* (*Prioresses Tale*) : —

> "My conning is so wayk, O blisful quene,
> For to declare thy grete worthinesse,
> That I ne may the weighte nat sustene,
> But as a child of twelf monthe old, or lesse,
> That can unnethes any word expresse,
> Right so fare I, and therfor I you preye,
> Gydeth my song that I shal of you seye."

Somewhat different is the stanza of his *Monk's Tale:* *a b a b b c b c*. Now if we add *c* to this, we have the famous *Spenserian Stanza*, — *a b a b b c b c c*, — the last line being an Alexandrine, the rest, like Chaucer's entire stanza, five-stress "iambic" verse. *Cf. Faery Queene:* —

> " And, more to lulle him in his slumber soft,
> A trickling streame from high rock tumbling downe,
> And ever-drizling raine upon the loft,
> Mixt with a murmuring winde, much like the sowne
> Of swarming bees, did cast him in a swowne.
> No other noise, nor people's troublous cries,
> As still are wont t' annoy the walled towne,
> Might there be heard: but carelesse Quiet lyes
> Wrapt in eternall silence far from enimies."

Mr. Arnold has justly praised the "fluidity" of the Spenserian stanza. Thomson (*Castle of Indolence*) and Byron (*Childe Harold*) have added to its popularity. Simpler than the above is the easy pace of the stanza (*Ottava Rima*), used by Spenser in some minor poems, and chosen by Byron for his *Don Juan*, and by Keats for his *Isabella: a b a b a b c c*.

It remains to mention two other kinds of stanza — what we may call the *run-on stanza*, and the irregular (and also regular) combinations of verses in the *Ode*. The *Terza Rima* of Dante's great poem was copied by Surrey (*cf.* the first poem in Tottel's Misc., ed. Arber), but without making it popular. Byron used it in his *Prophecy of Dante*, and Shelley in his *Ode to the West Wind*, though often the manner of printing conceals the metre. The stanzas of three lines are interlaced thus: *a b a — b c b — c d c — d e d*, etc.

"O wild West Wind, thou breath of Autumn's being,
Thou from whose unseen presence the leaves dead
Are driven like ghosts from an enchanter fleeing,

Yellow and black and pale and hectic red,
Pestilence-stricken multitudes ! O thou
Who chariotest to their dark wintry bed

The wingèd seeds, where they lie cold and low
Each like a corpse within its grave, until
Thine azure sister of the Spring shall blow," etc.

Cf. also some of the French forms of verse mentioned below.

The *Ode* is mostly written in arbitrary stanzas of varying verse-lengths : *cf* Wordsworth's *Immortality Ode*. But there is also a regular arrangement : *cf.* the elaborate "Pindaric" Odes of Gray, — *The Progress of Poetry* and *The Bard*.[1] For classical exactness, see the Choruses of Swinburne's *Erechtheus*, where the elaborate structure of Strophe, Antistrope and Epode is managed with great ability ; the same is true of other Odes by Swinburne.

§ 2. THE SONNET.

There are certain combinations of verse in which a single element of rime-arrangement dominates the entire poem. Most practised and best known of these is the Sonnet. This word, as Mr. T. H. Caine (*Sonnets of Three Centuries*) has pointed out, meant originally "a little strain," and was used by Italian poets "to denote

---

[1] There are nine stanzas so arranged that the *first, fourth,* and *seventh* are alike in construction; likewise the *second, fifth,* and *eighth ;* and the *third, sixth,* and *ninth.*

simply a short poem limited to the exposition of a single idea, sentiment, or emotion." The next step was to confine its *form; fourteen lines* became the fixed length of the sonnet. Lastly, these lines were required to be combined according to certain definite rules.

Our English sonnets, therefore, are of different kinds. Mr. Caine ranges under the first class sonnets like those of Shakspere. This form is by no means that of the strict Italian Sonnets; "it does not . . . as in the Italian form, fall asunder like the acorn into unequal parts of a perfect organism, but is sustained without break until it reaches a point at which a personal appropriation needs to be made." That is, we have the symbol and then — mostly in the concluding couplet — the application. The Shaksperian form is thus: —

$$a\,b\,a\,b\,c\,d\,c\,d\,e\,f\,e\,f\,g\,g,$$

that is, three quatrains with alternate rime, followed by a couplet.

Different is the form in the noble sonnets of Milton. The rimes follow Petrarch's rule of four different vowel-sounds, and the whole is divided into two unequal parts, the *octave* and *sestette*. The scheme is thus: —

$$a\,b\,b\,a\,a\,b\,b\,a \parallel c\,d\,c\,d\,c\,d,$$

though the sestette can be differently arranged. Still, even here it is merely the form that is Italian. The progress of the idea is English. The sense flows on without break from the octave into the sestette; whereas the Italian sonnet was required at the end of the octave to have a complete change in the idea.

Much closer to the Italian model is the sonnet as written by more recent poets. The excellence of

Shakspere's sonnet as critics esteem it, is the *climax* to which it rises by means of the closing couplet. Milton's sonnet has been compared to a rocket rapidly thrown off, then "breaking into light and falling in a soft shower of brightness." The later school, however, aim to write sonnets that shall reproduce the rise and fall of a billow, or its flowing and ebbing. The idea and the verse rise together in the octave, and in the sestette fall back again. The rime-order is Italian. For these three kinds of sonnet, let the reader study a good specimen of each, and compare the relative advantages, — say Shakspere's *When to the sessions of sweet silent thought* (Sonnet 30); Milton *On the Late Massacre in Piedmont* (*Avenge, O Lord*); and Keats *On first looking into Chapman's Homer*. Wordsworth's sonnets sway between the two last kinds: *cf.* his *Westminster Bridge* with the sonnet beginning *The world is too much with us*.

§ 3. FRENCH FORMS.

Of late, considerable effort has been put forth to introduce into our English verse-system the forms known to French poetry (*cf.* p. 55) as *Rondel, Rondeau, Triolet, Villanelle, Ballade,* and *Chant Royal*. "The first three," says Mr. Gosse, "are habitually used for joyous or gay thought, and lie most within the province of *jeu d'esprit* and epigram; the last three are usually wedded to serious or stately expression, and almost demand a vein of pathos." So far, these forms are not naturalized as English measures; but they are practised to a considerable extent. It requires an immense talent to write them with that ease and grace which they always demand; the slightest trace of effort ruins them. We have space for but one example, — a *Triolet* by Austin Dobson : —

> " I intended an ode
> And it turned into triolets,
> It began *à la mode:*
> I intended an ode,
> But Rose crossed the road
> With a bunch of fresh violets;
> I intended an ode,
> And it turned into triolets."

The *Rondel* and *Rondeau* are also light measures. The latter has thirteen verses and only two rimes. The *Villanelle* has also only two rimes, and is written in stanzas continued at pleasure (or as one's rimes last), and made up of three verses each, with a couplet at the end. The *Ballade* and the *Chant Royal* are much more complicated. The details of construction of all these forms, with examples, can be found in Mr. Gosse's article on *Foreign Forms of Verse* in the Cornhill Magazine for July, 1877. There are also examples in Adams' collection of *Latter-Day Lyrics;* and Mr. Swinburne has recently published *A Century of Roundels*. The ingenuity, however, which is required for the construction of these stanzas makes it doubtful that they will ever voice the higher moods of poetry. The great lyric poets, like Goethe, do their best work in simple forms of verse, in that "popular tone" nearest to the heart of singer as well as hearer.

INDEX.

INDEX.

ABBOTT, on Shaksp., 123, 215, 217, 220. Abstract, 84; for concrete, 93; personif. of, 101. Abraham and Isaac, 61. Academy, The, 134. Accent, 133 ff. 139 ff. 144, 166; of word, 139, 192, 211, 220; of verse, 141, 145, 220; of sentence, 140, 171 f. 191, 211, 214, 220 f.; see also Stress, Hovering Accent, etc. Action, in drama, 61, 72 f.; in mysteries, 63; unity of, 70; surroundings of, 74. Acts (drama), 72. Adjectives, 85, 106. Æneas, 21. Æschylus, 75, 116. Albert, Paul, 40. Alexander, 21. Alexandrine, 180, 182, 184 f. 197, 202, 208, 222, 227 f. 238. Allegory, 23 ff.; in style, 102 ff. Alliteration, see Rime. Alliterating Romances, 178. Allusion, 110. Anacreon, 52 f. Anapestic, 170, etc. Anglo-Saxon poetry, 11, 86, 108, 112 f. 120; metres, 174 ff. 204. Anticlimax, 131. Antithesis, 55, 119, 126 ff. Apostrophe, 121. Apposition, 105. Arabs, 154. Areopagus (club), 159. Ariosto, 34. Aristotle, 1, 42, 72, 74. Armstrong, 28. Arnold, Matthew, 4, 46, 51, 224, 229 f.; 29, 49, 160, 208, 233. Arsis, 136. Arthur, King, 25. Assonance, 156. Avesta, 142.

BACON, 84. Balance, 127, 172. Ballad, 34 ff. 38 f. 56; measure, 183, 197, 231. Ballade, 55, 241 f. Barbour, 184. Barclay, Alex., 194. Barnefield, R., 196. Batteux, Abbé, 41. Beaumont, 50; and Fletcher, 47, 52. Beast-Epic, 26. Bentley, 225. Beowa, 13. Beowulf, 11 ff. 86, 97 f. 112, 152, 173, 174 ff. Bestiary, 26. Blair, 115. Blake, W., 46 f. 169. Blank Verse, 41, 151, 157 ff. 197 ff. 213 ff. etc. "Bob," The, 201. Boccaccio, 33. Boileau, 32. Boniface, 24. Bowring, 43. Broadside, 38. Broken Construction, 125. Browne, G. H., 218. Browne, William, 30. Browning, E. B. 129. Browning, R., 38; 43, 47, 50, 82, 106, 108, 203, 207, 209. Brunanburh, 19. Bulwer, 233. Burns, R., 47, 57; 30, 32, 33, 38, 43, 44, 46, 52, 113, 122, 203, 204, 205, 236. Butler, 32. Byrhtnoth, 19, 36, 38, 176. Byron, 33, 43, 44, 57; 122, 124, 158, 172, 182, 183, 204, 205, 207, 212, 235, 238.

CADENCE, 163. Cædmon, 20, 94, 173. Cæsura, 135, 148, 193; see Pause. Caine, T. H., 239 f. Campbell, 38, 43, 155. Campion, 159, 230. Carew, 53, 96. Carey, H., 82. Carriere, M., 42, 57, 80. Catachresis, 94, 107. Catechisms, 28. Catullus, 232. Cenotaph, 56. Chanson de Roland, 156. Chant Royal, 55, 241 f. Chapman, 95; 34, 183, 197, 231. Characters (drama), 61, 64. Charade, 33. Charlemagne, 21. Charms, 56. Chatterton, 37. CHAUCER, 22, 24, 32, 76, 173; Canterbury Tales, 20 ff. 26, 33; 116, 128 f. 152, 161, 164, 187, 189 ff. Boke Duchesse, 184, 187; House Fame, 24, 46, 179, 184, 187; Troilus, 21, 104, 110; Legende G. W., 187; his verse, 172, 174, 186 ff. 203, 237. Child, 35, 36, 194. Children in the Wood, The, 39. Choriambic Verse, 232. Chorus, 9, 69, 74, 76, 82, 233. Chronicle, 22. Church, 7, 20, 59. Cicero, 121. Classic Simile, 107 f.

110, 144. Clerkes, 45, 52, 182. Climax, 72 f. 130 f. Clough, A. H., 33, 53, 104, 230. Clown, The, 60. Coleridge, 23, 38, 43, 130, 153, 182, 203, 232. Collins, 43, 47, 102, 117, 160, 232. Combination, Figures of, 125 ff. Comedy, 22, 61, 68, 73 f. 76 ff. Comic Histories, 32. Comparative Philology, 83. Conceits, 95 f. Concrete (for abstract), 84, 93. Congreve, 77. Consonants, 162. Constable, 196. Contractions, 164, 190 f. 214 f. Connexion, Tropes of, 111 ff. Contrast, Tropes of, 90, 114 f.; figures, 121 ff. Convivial Lyric, 52. Costumes, 62 f. Couplet (short), 154, 179, 182, 184, 186; heroic, 31, 41, 187 f. 199, 210 f. 228, 234. Cowper, 53; 27 f. 39, 49, 50, 103, 147, 205. Crashaw, 95. Crowley, 152. Cuckoo-Song, 46, 56. Cynewulf, 18, 20, 33, 152, 173.

DACTYL, 138, 167 f. etc. Dancing, 1 f. 9, 134 ff. Daniel, S., 54, 106, 144, 159. Dante, 24, 34, 76, 89, 94, 110, 224, 237 f. Davenant, 237. David, 39. Death (lyric), 49 f. 116. Deborah, Song of, 119. Dekker, 40. Derzhavin, 43. Description, 28 f. 48. Dialogues, 16, 60, 78, 82. Didactic, 22, 24, 51. Dionysian Feasts, 59, 75 f. Dirge, 49. Distribution, 112. Dithyramb, 42. Dobson, A., 242. Don Quixote, 21. Donne, 32; 119. Double Ending, 209, 216, 223; see Rime. Douglas, Gawin, 194, 197. Dowden, E., 77, 147. Drama, 58 ff. 70, 74 f. 80 ff.; rules for, 69 ff.; parts of, 72; metre of, 63, 157 f. 180, 187. Drayton, M., 38, 45, 148, 185, 227 f. Dream, see Vision. Dryden, 4, 79, 95, 126, 128, 145, 148, 158, 210; 25, 32, 51, 110, 237. Dumb-Show, 69, 72. Dunbar, 24, 178, 194.

E (final), 188 ff. Ebert, 24, 38. Eclogue, 80. Edward, 60. Elegy, 49 f. Elegiac, 50, 232. Eliot, Geo., 51, 156. Elizabethan (lyric), 45 f. 199; see also Drama. Elision, 164, 190 f. Ellis, 194; 134, 171 f. 215, 220. Emerson, 73. Emotion, 42. End-stopt, 147, 149, 194, 211, 222 f. Enthusiasm, 41 f. Epic, 10 ff. 19 ff. 33, 41; style, 109 etc.; verse, 187, 203, etc. Epigram, 55, 110, 127. Epilogue, 72. Episodes, 16. Epithets, 85, 87. Epitaph, 55, 103. Equation of Claims, 173. Eumenides, 116. Euphemism, 116. Euphuism, 126, 152. Every Man, 65 f. 180. Exodus, 20, 94. Expanded Words, 214, 218 f. Exposition (drama), 72.

FABLE, 25 f. Fair Helen, 36, 46. Falling Feet, 167. Farce, 77. Feelings, 42. Feminine (pause), 149; (rime), 155, 193; (ending), 209, 236. Fielding, H., 82. Figures, 85, 118 ff. Fitzgerald (Omar Khayyam), 236. Five-Stress Verse, 195 f. 208 ff. Fleay, 213, 216. Fletcher, 81, 146, 216. Fluidity (verse), 163, 238. Folk-Song, see Ballad. Fool (drama), 60. Foot, 135, 167, etc. Formula (epic), 16. Four (lyric), 235. Four-Stress Verse, 182, 186 f. 196, 203 ff. French Forms, 55, 241.

GAMMER GURTON'S NEEDLE, 52. Gascoigne, Geo., 142, 152, 185, 196 f. 214. Gawayne and Green Knight, 25, 178. Gawayne, Marriage of, 37. Gay, 26. Genesis, 101 f. 114. Genitive (style), 105 f. Germanic, 7 f. 86 f. 135, 153, 233; metre, rule of, 144, 191. Gervinus, 60. Gesture, 106. Ghosts, 73. Gnomic Dialogue, 26. Goethe, 41, 57, 242; 30, 50, 72, 80, 230. Golding, 183. Goldsmith, 77, 95, 107; 28, 39, 123. Gorboduc, 68, 72, 82, 157. Gosse, E., 43, 55, 241 f. Gower, 184. Grail, 20. Gray (Elegy), 50, 91, 112, 139, 192, 209, 237;

INDEX.   247

(misc.) 51, 93, 122, 239. Greek, 67, 140 f. 144 f. 176. Greene, R., 196 f. 230. Gregory, Pope, 24. Grimm, J., 3. Grimm, W., 14, 153. Guarini, 81. Guest, Dr., 146, 205 f. 226.

HARMONY, 1. Harrowing Hell, 63. Havelok, 19. Hawes, S., 194. Hebrew Poetry, 88. Hegel, 40, 108. Heinzel, 86. Heliand, 102. Hendecasyllabic, 232. Henrysoun, 30, 194. Herbert, George, 43, 51. Herbert, Lord, 235. Heroic Verse, 168, 186 ff. 209 ff. Herrick, 47, 53, 84, 200 f. Hexameter, 31, 41, 138, 228 ff. Heywood, J., 67. Heywood, Thos. 160. Hiatus, 165, 190. History, 20, 32; historical present, 122. Homer, 40, 107, 109, 229. Hood, T., 50, 120, 155, 200 f. Horace, 31, 72. Hovering Accent, 142, 186, 192, 206, 220, 224, 226 f. Human Interest, 29, 48, 60. Hunt, L., 26. Hymn, 9, 42, 153. Hyperbole, 115.

IAMBIC, 167 ff. 187, 192, 195 f. 213 f. etc. Ictus, 138, 143; see Stress. Idyll, 30, 80. Iliad, 18, 96, etc. Imagination, 2, 48, 90. Individual Author, 15, 57. Inflexional Endings, 188, 220. Instance, 110. Interlude, 67. International Literature, 18. Invention, 1, 4, 15, 23. Inversion, 84, 123 f. Irony, 117. Italian Influences, 54, 67, 173, 239. Iteration, 118 f.

JOHNSON, DR., 32, 127, 131. Jones, Sir W., 43, 127. Jonson, Ben, 5, 72, 160, 235; 51, 68, 81, 205 f. Judith, 20. Juvenal, 31.

KAIMS, LORD, 116. Katharsis, 42, 74. Keats, 22, 34, 37, 47 f. 54, 91, 99, 101, 105, 108, 119, 124, 126, 128, 145, 158, 198, 211, 227, 238. Kenning, 16, 87. King Edward, 177. King Horn, 19, 179. King John (Morality), 66. Kingsley, C., 230. Klopstock, 230.

LADY ISABEL, 37. La Fontaine, 26, 33. Lamb, 51, 209, 234. Landor, 55. Lanier, 166. Latin, 59, 67, 140, 145, 153 ff. Layamon, 19, 152, 178 f. Lee, 115. Legend, 9. Lessing, 5, 48, 70, 79, 107. Light Ending, 212, 223. Liquid (conson.), 162, 217. Litotes, 116. Locker, 53. Logical (style), 90, 113 f.; (verse), 148. Longfellow, 22, 138, 159, 205, 230 f. Lord Randal (Donald), 60, 204. Lovelace, 46, 115, 129. Lowell, 75. Lucretius, 28, 100. Lusty Juventus, 66. Lydgate, 194. Lyly, 126, 152. Lyndesay, 194. Lyric, 39 ff. 199; (Norman), 154.

MACAULAY, 3, 38. Madrigal, 45. Maker, 17 f. Malherbe, 49. Mannyng, R., 185. Mapes, 52, 182. Marie de France, 26. Marlowe, 69, 85, 157; 22, 45, 158, 198 f. 212. Marseillaise, 43. Marston, 32, 156. Marvell, 48, 51, 158. Masculine (pause), 149; (rime), 155, 236, etc. Mask, 68, 81. Mass, The, 59. Mathematical (style), 90, 111. Melody, 136. Messenger, 69, 71. Metaphor, 85, 90 ff. 94, 96, 104. Metonomy, 94, 113 f. Metre, 1, 133 ff. 137, 170 ff. 63; (Germanic), 144, 191; (modern), 173 f. 186, 195 ff. 199; (dist'd from *rhythm*), 185 f. Metrical Scheme, 170 f. 200, 208, 222 ff. Middleton, 216. MILTON, 54, 84, 123, 149; (on rime), 157 f. 173, 198; (his verse), 224 ff. Comus, 25, 68, 81, 98, 101, 111, 115, 225. Horace, 232. Il Pens. 48. L'All. 48, 98, 129, 148, 169 f.

205 f. Lycidas, 39, 43, 49, 54, 118, 125, 162. Nat. Hymn, 104, 123, 220. Paradise Lost, 34; (quoted), 91, 94, 100, 109, 112 ff. 116, 118 f. 120, 123 ff. 129 f. 149 f. 161, 163, 212, 224 ff. Par. Reg. 187. Samson, 76, 233. Sonnets, 54, 164, 191, 240 f. Minot, L., 180, 204. Minnesänger, 41, 45. Minstrels, 10, 13 f. 41. Miracle Plays, 59 f. 62. Monologue, 82. Mnemonic, 28. Mock-Tragedy, 82. Monte-Mayor, 30. Moore, T., 53; 202, 207, 209. Moral Plays, 59, 62, 64 ff. 157. Morris, W., 22, 228. Murder of Abel, 61, 63. Music, 1, 41, 134, 136 f. 143. Myrroure for Magistrates, 22 f. Mysteries, 59, 62 ff. 157, 180. Mythology, 9, 96 f. 101.

NAIRN, LADY, 201. Nash, T., 50, 229 f. National (heroes), 13, 19; (legends), 19. Nature (see Lyric), 49. New Learning, The, 173. Nichol, J., 105, 130. Nomenclature (verse), 167. Noah's Flood, 61. Norman Influences, 152, 154, 177. Number, Change of, 122. Nurture, Book of, 28.

OBJECTIVITY (drama), 58. Occleve, 194. Octave, 54, 241. Odyssey, 15 ff. 32. Ode, 42 f. 239. Omar Khayyam, 236. One-Stress (verse), 200. Onomatopœia, 139, 161 f. Opera, 41, 81. Ormulum, 183. Ottava Rima, 238. Ovid, 161. Owl and Nightingale, 32, 184. Oxymoron, 128 f.

PAGEANT, 62. Parable, 26. Paradox, 128. Parallel Constr. 126 f. 128. Parallelism, 120. Parfre, 64. Parody, 32. Passionate Pilgrim, 196. Pastoral, 29, 81. Pathetic, 51. Pause, 139, 145 ff. 224; compensating, 146, 218 f.; rhythmical, 147, 203, 216, 226, 231; logical, 148; in Chaucer, 193 f.; in Five-Stress Verse, 208, 221, 224; dramatic, 147. Pearl, The, 25. Peele, Geo., 162, 197. Period (stanza), 236. Periods of Eng. Verse, 173. Periphrase, 112 f. Personality, 41. Personification, 9, 93, 96 ff. 104. Petrarch, 240. Phaer, 183. Phonetic, 134. Physiologus, 26, 104. Pictures (words), 83. Piers the Plowman, Vision concerning, 25, 152, 177 f. Pindar, 41. Pitch, 134, 136, 143. Place (drama), 71. Platen, Count, 229. Plautus, 67 ff. 76. Poe, 231. Poema Morale, 27, 182. Poetics, Writers on, 5. Poetry, 1 ff. 90; compared with Prose, 2, 84, 134; style of, 83 ff. Pope, 101, 116, 126, 128, 145, 191, 210; 27, 30, 32, 34, 43, 99, 119, 122, 126, 129, 131, 148, 162. Poulter's Meas., 185, 195. Praed, 33, 53. Prefixes, 217. Prior, 26, 32, 53, 127, 235. Prolepsis, 124. Prologue, 72. Prose, 2, 84, 157. Provençal, 154, 235. Prudentius, 23, 38. Psalms, 42, 104, 120. Pun, 55, 120. Puttenham, 44 f. 119, 142, 159, 196.

QUALITY, 136, 171. Quantity, 137, 143, 151, 166. Quatrain, 235, 237. Question, 124 f. Quintilian, 121.

RALPH ROISTER DOISTER, 69, 180. Rant, 115. Reason, 17. Reconciling Drama, 61, 79. Reflective Poetry, 27, 42, 47 f. 51. Refrain, 234. Religion, 7, 56, 58 f. 97. Repetition, 1, 86, 118 ff. Resemblance (tropes), 90 ff. Resurrection, La, 59. Rhythm, 133 ff. 134, 136, 157; 135, 203, 214; 191 f. Richard (Lion-heart), 45. Riddle, 33. Riddle-Ballads, 27. Rieger, 174. Rime, 135, 145, 150 ff. 234; Beginning-Rime, 151 f. 174 f.; End-Rime, 152 ff. 176, 179, etc.; Perfect, 153, 156, 193; Clashing, 155; in Chaucer, 192 f.; in Shakspere, 213; Involved, 155; War on Rime, 159; Effect on Verse, 212. Rimed Phrases, 152; Rimeless Verse, 160, 233. Riming Poem, 153, 177. Rising Foot, 167. Robin Hood, 36. Rochester, 55. Robt. Gloucester, 22, 185. Rogers (drama), 62. Rogers (lyric), 40. Romance, 21; (words), 192. Romaunt Rose, 24. Rondeau, Rondel, 55, 241. Roxburghe Ballads, 38. Runes, 8. Run-on (Verse), 147, 149, 194, 211, 222, 226; (Stanza), 238 f. Ruskin, 4, 146, 166.

SACHSENSPIEGEL, 98. Sanskrit, 140. Sarcasm, 131. Satire, 31 f. Saturnian (Verse), 145, 153. Scenery, 29, 62. Scheffel, 189. Scherer, 136, 143, 176. Schiller, 70, 232. Schipper, 138 f. 150, 166, 180, 182, 237. Scott, 158, 204; 23, 130, 155, 201. Seneca, 67 ff. 82. Sense-group, 150. Sentimental, 51. Septenary, 182 f. 196, 207, 236. Serenade, 81. Sestette, 54, 241. Seward, 150. SHAKSPERE, 61, 70 ff. 78 f. 85, 95, 157, 173, 198; Verse, 213 ff. Narrative Poems, 199, 213; All's W. 110, 124, 191, 216; A. and C. 52, 106, 223; A. Y. L. I. 77 f. 83, 142, 218; Cor. 98, 105; Cym. 47, 49, 80, 114, 155, 217; Ham. 52, 58, 69, 71, 75, 79, 82, 94 f. 100, 102 f. 106, 111 ff. 121 ff. 131, 216, 219, 221; H. IV., I. 102; II. 106, 114; H. V. 44, 79, 82, 221; H. VI., I. 99, 221; III. 98, 117, 128, 221; H. VIII. 111, 113 f. 209, 215 f. 222, 237; Interludes, 68; John, 92, 98, 103, 109, 113; J. C. 74, 103, 112, 120, 128, 130, 213, 215, 217, 219, 221; Lear, 29, 70, 74, 78, 86, 92 f. 98, 102, 109, 161, 216, 219; L. L. L. 149, 213, 222; 152, 196; Macb. 74 f. 92 f. 99, 115, 117, 121, 124, 146, 161, 206, 219; M. for M. 44 f. 80, 105, 147; M. of V. 45, 80, 91, 106, 110, 114, 125, 219; M. N. D. 201, 213, 219; Oth. 52, 73 f. 93, 109, 131, 215; R. II. 44, 105 f. 109, 114, 126, 219; R. III. 75, 215, 219, 221; R. & J. 225; 58, 75, 81, 99 f. 114, 129, 218, 223; Sonnets, 240 f. 54, 92 f. 100, 119, 124, 126, 213; Temp. 130, 149, 213, 220, 222; T. N. 77, 202 f.; Two Nob. Kins. 77; W. T. 71; 213, 222. Shelley, 47 ff. 92, 163, 201 ff. 207, 212, 225, 236, 239. Sheridan, 77. Shirley, 50, 129. Sidney, 4, 30, 54, 71, 82, 101, 196. Simile, 86, 104 ff. Sincerity, 34, 40, 57. Sir Patrick Spens, 39, 60. Skelton, 181, 202. Slurring, 164, 189, 191, 213, 215, 224 f. Solomon and Saturn, 27. Songs (drama), 69. Sonnet, 54, 110, 239 ff. Sophocles, 75. Sounds, 160 ff. Southey, 200, 233. Spanish Poetry, 156. Spedding, J., 168, 222. Spencer, H., 86, 129. Spenser, 25, 30, 44, 80, 91, 99, 146, 199, 209, 235; (stanza), 238. Spondee, 229. Stanyhurst, 230. Stanza (Strophe), 9, 157, 187, 199 ff. 210, 228, 234 ff. Sterne, 117. Still, Bishop, 52. Street-Song, 38. Stress, 133 f. 137, 166 f. 171 f.; verse of one, 200 f.; of two stresses, 201; of three, 202; of four, 203 ff.; of five, 208 ff.; of six, 227 ff.; of seven, 231. Strife between Summer and Winter, 60. Style, 2, 83 ff.; factors of poetical, 93, 96. Subjective Drama, 80. Subject-Matter, 2, 7 ff. Sublime, 42. Suckling, 45, 53, 108. Supernatural, 23. Surrey, 54, 157, 173, 185, 194, 212, 238. Sweet, H., 166, 171. Sweet, The (lyric), 42. Swift, 53, 117, 127. Swinburne, 4, 168; 37, 47, 76, 91, 102, 142, 152, 158, 170, 201, 205, 207, 211, 228, 232, 239, 242. Syllable, 133, 137; light and heavy, 150, 154, 157, 175, 221, 227; crowding of, 161, 163; proportion of, 171 f.; silent, 188; counting of, 198; extra, 212, 221 f.; dropping of light, 146, 174 f. 186, 221, etc.; inflexional, 188, 220. Synecdoche, 111.

TACITUS, 7 f. 14. Tagelieder, 58, 81. Tasso, 34, 81. Ten Brink, 186 ff. 194. Tennyson, 30, 44, 49, 56, 89, 93, 106 f. 113, 124 f. 139, 146, 162, 198, 204, 213, 228, 231 f. 234 f. Tense, Change of, 122. Terence, 67, 76. Terza Rima, 238 f. Thackeray, 53. Theocritus, 80. Thesis, 136. Thomas of Ercildoune, 37. Thomson, 28, 114, 238. Three-Part Stanza, 237. Three-Stress, 202. Threnody, 39. Time, 1, 134, 139, 145; (unity), 70. Tone-color, 136. Tottel's Misc., 45, 195. Tragedy, 22, 61 f. 68, 73 ff. 78. Tragi-Comedy, 77, 79. Transition Period, 173, 178 ff. Translations, 34. Transposed Accent, 187, 206, 212, 224, 226. Travesty, 32. Tribrach, 168. Triolet, 55, 241 f. Triple (ending), 216; (Measure), 169 f. 207, 215, 223. Triplet, 234. Trochaic, 168, 192, 196, etc. Trochee, 167, etc. Troilus, 21. Trope, 84, 87, 88 ff. 118. Troubadours, 45, 154. Tusser, 28. Two-Stress, 201. Tye, C., 163.

UDALL, 69. Unities, 70 ff.

VARIATION, 87, 92, 120. Vedas, 86. Vergil, 229; 28, 30, 33, 110, 125, 137. Verner, 141. Vers de Société, 53 ff. Verse, 136, 141 f. 166, 169, 200. Verse-Group, 150, 169. Vice, The, 60. Villanelle, 55, 241 f. Vision, 24 f. 96; (figure), 122 f. Voice, The, 160 f.

WAGNER, 81. Waller, 110. Ward, A. W., 58 f. 72. Weak Ending, 149, 223. Weapons, 88, 97 f. Webbe, 159. Wesley, 42. Westphal, 135 f. Whetstone, G., 71. Whitney, W. D., 162. Whittier, 38, 43, 50, 89. Williams, Sir C. H., 117. Wither, 45. Wolfe, 39. Wolff, 234 f. Wolfram, 25, 81. Wordsworth, 27 ff. 43 f. 46 ff. 51, 54, 57, 92, 97, 237, 239. Word-play, 120. Wotton, 51, 235. Wrenched Accent, 142, 198, 211. Wright, T., 35. Wyatt, 54, 155, 173, 195 f. Wyntown, 184. Wyrd, 96, 102.

HIGHER ENGLISH.

(See also Classics for Children, pages 2 to 6.)

Minto's Manual of English Prose Literature.

Designed mainly to show characteristics of style. By WILLIAM MINTO, M.A., Professor of Logic and English Literature in the University of Aberdeen, Scotland. 12mo. Cloth. 566 pages. Mailing Price, $1.65; Introduction, $1.50.

THE main design is to assist in directing students in English composition to the merits and defects of our principal writers of prose, enabling them, in some degree at least, to acquire the one and avoid the other. The Introduction analyzes style: elements of style, qualities of style, kinds of composition. Part First gives exhaustive analyses of De Quincey, Macaulay, and Carlyle. These serve as a key to all the other authors treated. Part Second takes up the prose authors in historical order, from the fourteenth century up to the early part of the nineteenth.

H. C. De Motte, *Pres. of Chaddock College, Quincy, Ill.:* We are delighted with it. It is one of the most serviceable books I have seen on the subject. I shall recommend it for our work here. (*Sept. 23, 1886.*)

Hiram Corson, *Prof. of English Literature, Cornell Univ., Ithaca, N.Y.:* Without going outside of this book, an earnest student could get a knowledge of English prose styles, based on the soundest principles of criticism, such as he could not get in any twenty volumes which I know of. (*May 14, 1886.*)

Minto's Characteristics of the English Poets,
from Chaucer to Shirley.

By WILLIAM MINTO, M.A., Professor of Logic and English Literature in the University of Aberdeen, Scotland. 12mo. Cloth. xi + 483 pages. Mailing Price, $2.15; for Introduction, $2.00.

THE chief objects of the author are: (1) To bring into clear light the characteristics of the several poets; and (2) to trace how far each was influenced by his literary predecessors and his contemporaries.

The Practical Elements of Rhetoric.

By JOHN F. GENUNG, Ph.D., Professor of Rhetoric in Amherst College. 12mo. Cloth. xiv + 483 pages. Mailing Price, $1.40; for introduction, $1.25; allowance for an old book in exchange 40 cents.

THE treatment is characterized by:—

1. **Good Sense.** The author, while suitably magnifying his art, recognizes that expression is not a substitute for ideas, that the *how* of speech is secondary to the *what*, that Rhetoric is only means to an end, and that its rules and principles and devices must be employed with caution and good sense.

2. **Simplicity.** Great care has been taken to free the treatment from artificialities. The subjects are most logically ordered, but not too minutely subdivided. So far as possible, terms are used in their popular and usual sense.

3. **Originality.** In a subject so old and so thoroughly studied each new treatment must take large account of what has been done before. This the author has not failed to do. But principally he has made his book from the study of literature at first hand. Traditional principles and rules have been discarded unless found to rest on a basis of truth and practical value.

4. **Availability.** The treatment is throughout *constructive*. The student is regarded at every step as endeavoring to make literature, and is given just what is indispensable to this end. On every point the main problems of construction are stated and solved. Again, the work has been prepared not more in the study than in the classroom, and the adaptation kept constantly in mind of every usage and principle to the actual needs of the actual student.

5. **Completeness.** All of the literary forms have been given something of the fulness hitherto accorded only to argument and oratory. This method is clearly in line with modern requirements. Part I. deals with style; Part II. with invention. All questions arising under both these divisions are fully considered.

6. **Ample Illustration.** Mere precept cannot help seeming arbitrary. In the concrete it bears a different, a more intelligible, and a more convincing look. Accordingly the author has presented no important principle without illustrations drawn from actual usage. It is usage, too, of the best, the most standard writers.

BOOKS ON ENGLISH LITERATURE.

Allen	Reader's Guide to English History	$ .25
Arnold . . .	English Literature	1.50
Bancroft . .	A Method of English Composition	.50
Browne . .	Shakespere Versification	.25
Fulton & Trueblood:	Choice Readings	1.50
	Chart Illustrating Principles of Vocal Expression,	2.00
Genung . .	Practical Elements of Rhetoric	1.25
Gilmore . .	Outlines of the Art of Expression	.60
Ginn	Scott's Lady of the Lake . . . *Bds.*, .35; *Cloth*,	.50
	Scott's Tales of a Grandfather . *Bds.*, .40; *Cloth*,	.50
Gummere .	Handbook of Poetics	1.00
Hudson . .	Harvard Edition of Shakespeare : —	
	20 Vol. Edition. *Cloth, retail*	25.00
	10 Vol. Edition. *Cloth, retail*	20.00
	Life, Art, and Character of Shakespeare. 2 vols.	
	Cloth, retail	4.00
	New School Shakespeare. *Cloth.* Each Play .	.45
	Old School Shakespeare, per play	.20
	Expurgated Family Shakespeare	10.00
	Essays on Education, English Studies, etc. . .	.25
	Three Volume Shakespeare, per vol.	1.25
	Text-Book of Poetry	1.25
	Text-Book of Prose	1.25
	Pamphlet Selections, Prose and Poetry . . .	.15
	Classical English Reader	1.00
Johnson . .	Rasselas . . . . *Bds.*, .30; *Cloth*,	.40
Lee	Graphic Chart of English Literature	.25
Martineau .	The Peasant and the Prince . *Bds.*, .35; *Cloth*,	.50
Minto . . .	Manual of English Prose Literature	1.50
	Characteristics of English Poets	2.00
Rolfe	Craik's English of Shakespeare	.90
Scott	Guy Mannering . . . . . . *Bds.*, .60; *Cloth*,	.75
	Ivanhoe . . . . *Bds.*, .60; *Cloth*,	.75
	Talisman . . . . *Bds.*, .50; *Cloth*,	.60
	Rob Roy . . . . *Bds.*, .60; *Cloth*,	.75
Sprague . .	Milton's Paradise Lost, and Lycidas	.45
	Six Selections from Irving's Sketch-Book	
	Bds., .25; *Cloth*,	.35
Swift	Gulliver's Travels . . . . . *Bds.*, .30; *Cloth*,	.40
Thom	Shakespeare and Chaucer Examinations . . .	.00

Copies sent to Teachers for Examination, with a view to Introduction,
on receipt of the Introduction Price given above.

GINN & COMPANY, Publishers,
Boston, New York, and Chicago.

MODERN LANGUAGES, Etc

MODERN LANGUAGES.

		INTROD. PRICE
Becker:	Spanish Idioms	$1.80
Collar:	Eysenbach's German Lessons	1.20
Cook:	Table of German Prefixes and Suffixes	.05
Doriot:	Illustrated Beginners' Book in French	.80
Knapp:	Modern French Readings	.80
	Modern Spanish Readings	1.50
	Modern Spanish Grammar	1.50
Spiers:	French-English General Dictionary	4.50
	English-French General Dictionary	4.50
Stein:	German Exercises	.40

MISCELLANEOUS.

Ariel:	Those Dreadful Mouse Boys	.75
Arrowsmith:	Kaegi's Rigveda	1.50
Burgess:	The American University	.15
Channing:	Delbrück's Introduction to the Study of Language	.94
Culver:	Epitome of Anatomy	.20
Davidson:	The Place of Art in Education	.20
	The Parthenon Frieze and other Essays	1.50
	A Dante Handbook	1.12
Dippold:	Emanuel Geibel's Brunhild	.45
Fisk:	Teachers' Improved Class Books	
Flagg:	Pedantic Versicles	.75
Halsey:	Genealogical and Chronological Chart	.25
Harrington:	Helps to the Intelligent Study of College Preparatory Latin	
Hitchcock:	Manual for the Gymnasium	.25
Hofmann:	Inaugural Address	.25
Hudson:	Daniel Webster	.25
J. B. G.:	Queen of Hearts	.20
	Lectures on School Hygiene	.80
Leighton:	Harvard Examination Papers	1.00
Prince:	Courses of Studies and Methods of Teaching	.75
Monoyer:	Sight Test	.12
Packard:	Studies in Greek Thought	.80
Seelye:	Growth through Obedience	.25
Smith & Blackwell:	Parallel Syntax Chart	1.00
Stevens:	Yale Examination Papers	.75
Straight:	True Aim of Industrial Education	.10
Super:	Weil's Order of Words in the Ancient Languages compared with the Modern	1.12
Warren:	True Key to Ancient Cosmology	.20

Copies sent to Teachers for Examination, with a view to Introduction, on receipt of Introduction Price.

GINN & COMPANY, Publishers.

BOSTON. NEW YORK. CHICAGO.

www.ingramcontent.com/pod-product-compliance
Lightning Source LLC
Chambersburg PA
CBHW032141230426
43672CB00011B/2416